If Found, PLEASE RETURN TO:

~~Room 308~~

~~Hotel New Orleans~~

~~Eureka Springs~~

~~ARKAS~~

~~Ed la Crок~~
~~Crs Del.~~

~~Busch Ark.~~
Rt.
Box 342
Rogers, Ark. 72756

long walks won't do any good
horses fuck inside me and a river makes a bend in my shoulder
this is all I have up on death
I have wild dreams I live a wild life
I've seen things better not to tell
I am the son of the river

BOOKS BY FRANK STANFORD

The Light the Dead See: Selected Poems of Frank Stanford

Conditions Uncertain and Likely to Pass Away

You

Crib Death

The Battlefield Where the Moon Says I Love You: A Poem

Constant Stranger

Arkansas Bench Stone

Field Talk

Ladies from Hell

Shade

The Singing Knives

ALSO EDITED BY MICHAEL WIEGERS

This Art: Poems about Poetry

The Poet's Child

Reversible Monuments: Contemporary Mexican Poetry
(with Mónica de la Torre)

WHAT ABOUT THIS

Collected Poems
of Frank Stanford

EDITED BY MICHAEL WIEGERS

COPPER CANYON PRESS

PORT TOWNSEND, WASHINGTON

Printed in the United States of America

Cover art: Photograph of Frank Stanford by Ginny Crouch Stanford

Copper Canyon Press is in residence at Fort Worden State Park in Port
Townsend, Washington, under the auspices of Centrum. Centrum is a gathering
place for artists and creative thinkers from around the world, students of all ages
and backgrounds, and audiences seeking extraordinary cultural enrichment.

LIBRARY OF CONGRESS CATALOGING-IN-PUBLICATION DATA

Stanford, Frank, 1949–1978
 [Works]
 What about this : collected poems of Frank Stanford / Frank Stanford ; edited
by Michael Wiegers ; introduction by Dean Young.
    pages ; cm
 ISBN 978-1-55659-468-7 (hardcover)
 I. Wiegers, Michael. II. Title.

PS3569.T3316 2015
811'.54—dc23

                              2014045989

98765432 FIRST PRINTING

COPPER CANYON PRESS

Post Office Box 271
Port Townsend, Washington 98368
www.coppercanyonpress.org

ACKNOWLEDGMENTS

The editor wishes to thank the editors of the
following books for their work and their advocacy
of Frank Stanford:

Fifty Contemporary Poets: The Creative Process,
edited by Alberta T. Turner (New York: David
McKay Company, 1977)

Interview by Irving Broughton with Frank Stanford
originally published in *The Writer's Mind,* edited
by Irving Broughton (Fayetteville, University of
Arkansas Press, 1989–90)

*The Light the Dead See: Selected Poems of Frank
Stanford,* edited by Leon Stokesbury (Fayetteville:
University of Arkansas Press, 1991)

CONTENTS

(SEE INDEX ON PAGE 736 FOR INDIVIDUAL TITLES)

THE NINTH DISTRICT

TENNESSEE FEDERATION OF WOMEN'S CLUBS

presents this

Certificate of Award

to

Frankie Stanford

whose outstanding poem was awarded

THE *Fourth* PRIZE

in the

POETRY CONTEST

sponsored by the Ninth District

for school students in the Memphis and Shelby County Schools.

Mrs. John L. Dean
President, Ninth District

April 14, 1958

Mrs. R. B. Dubberley
Poetry Contest Chairman

Introduction by Dean Young

"I will let this go as technique. Mean and sing."

When I was in college in the 1970s and '80s, the poems of Frank Stanford were passed hand to hand like contraband: small editions from small presses, hard to get, guarded with secrecy, coming from far outside any known curriculum, and profoundly intoxicating. Even now, as I sit down with the immense treasure of this book, the poems are still surrounded by the aura of the forbidden. They are still able to deliver a shock akin to what the first viewers of Picasso's *Les Demoiselles d'Avignon* must have felt. Here's something authentically raw, even brutal, which seems both very old and utterly new, its vitality coming from roots that sink deep into the primitive wellsprings of art and the mud of the human heart and mind.

Many of these poems seem as if they were written with a burned stick. With blood, in river mud. There is something thankfully unexamined in their execution. I say "thankfully" because we have been through a long century of self-consciousness and irony, and while their brand of rigor and suspicion have brought intelligence to American poetry they have also brought rigor mortis, they have deadened the nerves and made poets fear the irrational. The side effect of demystification is the withering of the soul, if not of the very impulse to write in the first place. I'm sure someone will come along and show how these poems are just another collection of literary devices and tics, but so is a birth announcement, so is a suicide note. Frank Stanford, demonically prolific, approaches the poem not as an exercise of rhetoric or a puzzle of signifiers but as a way of "looking for his tongue," of knife-fighting with a ghost.

> When the rest of you
> Were being children
> I became a monk

To my own listing
Imagination.

Propulsive with an uncanny loquaciousness, these are poems by a poet with eyes in the back of his head and ears spackled all over his body: a poet, as Lorca recommends, aware that at any moment he could be devoured by ants. This voice comes from a mythology beneath us, one that is so metamorphic that it needs to be written again and again. Here is a true American surrealism, up from the silt and effluvia, spilled with blood. Imagine Vallejo growing up in a tent on the Mississippi. This isn't surrealism that percolates down to us from the starfish brains of Breton and Aragon but surrealism having far more in common with that of Latin America, the surrealism of the praying mantis, of blood sport. At the center of Stanford's oeuvre is a volcanic iteration that defies the rational so as to better reach passionate, often excruciating, truths and that sees the world in the red light of the predator's eye and hears the yelps of its prey.

> I think of a pyramid and an hourglass a voice
>   that gives off its own light
> my life I love it
> in the dark
> under the water of my shadow music

With the long-awaited publication of *What About This,* many claims will be made for Frank Stanford's work—gigantic claims, I hope—and it's likely I've missed some of this book's most important discoveries and contributions to poetry. I'm certain that with the wide readership this collection at last guarantees we will see a profound and tonic effect on contemporary poetry. You are holding in your hands lightning that comes up from the ground.

Editor's Note

"Finally there is the work."

So ends the short biography of Frank Stanford, as it appears in the second edition of *The Battlefield Where the Moon Says I Love You* (Lost Roads 2000). The amount of "the work" is staggering: eleven published volumes—ten poetry books and one prose collection—complemented by hundreds of pages of unpublished poems and short stories—all from an artist who died in his twenty-ninth year. A portion of this uncollected work Stanford organized into fluid manuscripts of varying sizes; some of it was assembled postmortem by his literary estate; and untold numbers of pages—fragments as well as entire poems and stories—never gained the structure of a book or chapbook. Until now the work has remained largely scattered and unavailable—limited to archives, out-of-print Mill Mountain Press volumes, and four collections from the press founded by Stanford, Lost Roads Publishers, as well as a small "selected" from the University of Arkansas Press.

In poring through his writing, one quickly understands that Stanford reused lines, dialogues, and images; he circled back on ideas, so that fragments one encounters might appear in poems later on—suggesting that the poet mined his own self-generated hoard from which he would eventually glean fully realized poems. Stanford reportedly claimed that even *Battlefield,* his massive opus, was drawn and distilled from a much larger book manuscript (whose working title is "Saint Francis and the Wolf"), from which come some of the fragments I've included. I did not try to make a *complete* gathering, and decided to leave materials out of this volume so as to avoid repetitions that might make the book less propulsive. To amass everything not only would be a fool's errand but also would require a book twice the size, which lies beyond the scope of bringing this work to an audience larger than the dedicated Stanford readers and scholars who have long lamented his anonymity. As a poetry editor and publisher, I naturally decided to focus primarily on Stanford's poems, and so one will find in *What About This* only a few previously unpublished examples of his prose.

This book is nearly split between Stanford's decades-old volumes and his unpublished writing. Further, of *The Battlefield Where the Moon Says I Love You*, Stanford's incredibly ambitious, ungovernable 15,000-line poem, I contrived a small yet piquant taste by scattering excerpts throughout the roughly chronological sections of *What About This*.

I imposed, lightly, standardization of usage and spelling. But as regards vernacular speech and the nuances of lineation, Stanford's eccentricities obtain, producing alternate spellings and grammatical errors as the poem requires. Frank Stanford appears here consistent with himself in his inconsistencies.

This book is the effort of very many hands. I am particularly thankful to Ginny Stanford and C.D. Wright for their courage and trust in working with me to see this book realized. Many thanks are due as well to Stanford's first publisher, Irving Broughton, who introduced him to readers nearly fifty years ago. I am also immensely indebted to Tonaya Craft, Phil Kovacevich, David Caligiuri, John Pierce, Matthew Brailas, Jake Schacker, Ata Moharreri, Alison Lockhart, and Michael McGriff for their selfless assistance in helping me pull the manuscript together; special thanks also to Nancy Kuhl and her colleagues at Yale's Beinecke Rare Book and Manuscript Library, and to Lannan Foundation, Ella Wiegers, Carol Bershad, and my incredible colleagues at Copper Canyon Press, who supported me with time, space, and patience as I wrestled with Frank's glorious ungovernability.

MICHAEL WIEGERS, COPPER CANYON PRESS

the warrior

I was born
I ride tomorrow

I live on when I sleep
I tell you what I will and don't ask me why
death means nothing to me
I think life is a dream
and what you dream I live
because none of you know what you want follow me
because I'm not going anywhere
I'll just bleed so the stars can have something dark
to shine in
look at my legs I am the Nijinsky of dreams

WHAT ABOUT THIS

A guy comes walking out of the garden
Playing Dark Eyes on the accordian.
We're sitting on the porch,
Drinking and spitting, lying.
We shut our eyes, snap our fingers.
Dewhurst goes out to his truck
Like he doesn't believe what he's seeing
And brings back three half-pints.
A little whirlwind occurs in the road,
Carrying dust away like a pail of water.
We're drinking serious now, and O.Z.
Wants to break in the store for some head cheese,
But the others won't let him.
Everybody laughs, dances.
The crossroads are all quiet
Except for the little man on the accordian.
Things are dying down, the moon spills its water.
Dewhurst says he smells rain.
O.Z. says if it rains he'll still make a crop.
We wait there all night, looking for rain.
We haven't been to sleep, so the blue lizards
On the side of the white porch
Lose their tails when we try to dream.
The man playing the music looks at us,
Noticing what we're up to. He backs off,
Holding up his hands in front, smiling,
Shaking his head, but before he gets half way
Down the road that O.Z. shoots him in the belly.
All summer his accordian rotted in the ditch,
Like an armadillo turning into a house payment.

PUBLISHED WORK

THE SINGING KNIVES

1971

The Blood Brothers

There was Born In The Camp With Six Toes
He popped the cottonmouth's head off

There was Baby Gauge
He tied the line to his wrist
He tied it to the alligator gar
He rode the fish

There was Ray Baby
He stole the white man's gold tooth
He knocked it out with a two-by-four
He rode the moon-blind horse

There was Charlie B. Lemon
He had four wives and a pair
Of long-toed shoes

There was Mose Jackson
He threw snake eyes in his sleep

There was BoBo Washington
A rat crawled in the bed
And sucked the blood
Out of his baby's head

There was Jimmy
He had the knife like night
He was white

I had the hands like dragonflies
I killed one white man
He was a midget
I did it with a frog gig

It was the summer of the Chinese daughter
I danced on the levee

The Singing Knives

The dogs woke me up
I looked out the window

Jimmy ran down the road
With the knife in his mouth
He was naked
And the moon
Was a dead man floating down the river

He jumped on the gypsy's pony
He rode through camp
I could see the dust

There was the saddlebag full of knives
He was crazy

When Jimmy cut a throat
The eyes rolled back in the head
Like they was baptized
I tell you
When he cut a throat
It was like Abednego's guitar
And the blood
Flew out like a quail

He had the red hand
He poked the eyes out

I dreamed I stepped over a log
And there was fire in my foot
I dreamed I saw a turkey and two wildcats
Jumped on me at the same time
I dreamed Jimmy was pouring ice water

Over my head at noon
I dreamed I heard somebody
Singing in the outhouse

I dreamed the mad dog bit the gypsy
And they tied him to a tree
I dreamed I was buried in the Indian mound
And Moon Lake rose up
I dreamed my father was wading the river of death
With his heart in his hand
I dreamed Jimmy rowed out the front door
With a hawk on his shoulder
And I was in the bow kneeling down
I dreamed the blacksnake rode the guitar
Down the river
I dreamed the clouds went by
The moon like dead fish
I dreamed I was dragging
A cotton sack with a dead man in it
I dreamed the fish bandits stole the hogs
Off my lines
And one of them was a hunchback
I dreamed the night was a horse
With its eyes shut
I dreamed I had to fight the good man with the bad arm
And he had the dynamite
I dreamed I trailed a buck from Panther Brake to Panther Burn
I dreamed the Chickasaw slit his throat in the pawpaw
I dreamed that rising sun was smoking blood
You could pick up and throw
I dreamed the Chinaman's peg leg
I dreamed I was fishing in heaven with Sho Nuff
And Jesus cleaned the fish
I dreamed a man flies wouldn't bite

I dreamed I was riding through Leland in a dragline bucket
And the cotton making everyday
I dreamed we got the bootlegger's truck out of the mud
I dreamed the levee broke
I dreamed the gypsy was laughing under the water
And the minnows were swimming through his eyes
I dreamed I reached down in Moon Lake
And untied his arms and one hand
Floated up the way it did
When he threw those knives
I dreamed the pony that fights in the water
And the boat that towed the dead man
I dreamed I felt the knife singing in Abednego's back
I dreamed I pulled the ring out of his ear
And Jimmy put it on his finger
And swam through the water
I dreamed he was looking for Abednego's boot
And when he came up
He had the jackknife between his teeth
I dreamed he was so beautiful
He had to die someday
I dreamed a knife like a song you can't whistle

"Let's go, I got to throw tonight" he says

He had the bandanna around his neck
And the pilot's cap on
He played the harp in the moonlight

I led the horse out back
I tied him to the chinaberry tree

"What you want" I says
But I knew he wanted me

Standing at the back of that outhouse
"Shut up" he says "don't move"

The dirt daubers flew around my head

He threw Boo Kay Jack at me
He threw Django at me

The mosquitoes drew blood
I looked on the ground
I saw the shadows coming like gars
Swimming under me at night
I saw the red moon too
I wished I was running a trot line
I wished I was in a fight
I wished I was fanning myself in church
But there was a heart on the fan
With a switchblade through it

And the knives came by

The bone handled one
The hawk handled one
The one with a blade like a skiff
Out of his boot
Behind his back
Mexican style
The way Abednego showed him

Singing in the outhouse
Like a horse breaking wind

He took the knife and ran it
Across his arm
Then he ran it across mine

Blood came out like hot soda

He tied our arms together
With the blue bandanna
And we laid down in the cotton
I wished I was riding a mule somewhere
Blowing a jug
With a string full of crappie
And the cotton making everyday

Living

I had my quiet time early in the morning
Eating Almond Joys with Mother.
We'd sit on the back porch and talk to God.
We really had a good time.

Later on,
I'd sort baseball cards
Or look for bottles.
In the afternoon I'd shoot blackbirds.

Jimmy would go by the house for ice water
And make the truck backfire.
Oh, I really liked that.
That was the reason he did it.

In the evening the cottontails ran across the groves.
I shot one and put him in the backseat.
He went to the bathroom.
Jimmy said I knocked the shit out of him.

At night we would listen to the ballgame.
Then to the Hoss Man.
Jimmy liked "Take Out Some Insurance On Me Baby" by Jimmy Reed.

The Pump

There was always a lizard
Or a frog around the pump,
Waiting for a little extra water
Or a butterfly to light.

Jimmy said the pump gave him the worms.
I got the worms under the slick boards.
The pump would bite you in the winter.
It got hold of Jimmy and wouldn't let go.

The blades of Johnson grass were tall
And sharp around the pump stand.
I had to hoe them all the time.
Nobody filled the prime jar, though.

One time, I cut the tongue
Out of a Buster Brown shoe
And gave it to the pump.
It made a good sucker washer.

Sometimes, the pump seemed like Jesus.
I liked bathing buck naked
Under the pump,
Not in a goddamn washtub.

The Gospel Bird

I   SUPERMAN

Dressed in a superman suit
On the front porch of Chitum's store
I told all the Negroes "I can fly"
And jumped off the high end.

A German crop duster crashed.
A chicken ran out of the hole
And shit on a rusty threepenny nail,
Then ducked back under the stoop.

Blood and chickenshit
Dripping out of the hole
Into the good hand,
Jimmy says, "What you saving it for?"

He went to the fire
And nobody was studying me
But toad frogs and a dog.
"Whoa somebody! I done cut my hand off."

Nobody came but the Rollie Pollie man,
Skipping chuckholes and swinging coal oil
In a copper-wired Co-Cola bottle.
He says, "I'll tend to you boy, I'll tend to you."

II   FIRE

Chitum's cripple nigger carpenter
Ate porch bugs and did magic.

He had a police dog that brought him
Dead chickens in the night.

"Put hog lard on an oak tree,
Steal me whiskey and coal oil,
And this dog will bring your chicken back."
I wanted that bird.

"Lockjaw and penicillin all the same,
Kill the chicken to kill the pain."
I got the nigger a fifth of gin
And he sent his dog after the bird.

The Rollie Pollie man told me how it was:
"The blood spurt out when that son-of-a-bitch
Chitum blew my crooked-necked
Chicken-killing dog in half.

"Black gnats was dying in the blood,
Some already drowned, I took coat wire
And drug him deep into the Diamond Woods."
My hand and Chitum's store burned that night.

III   FLY AWAY, FLY AWAY

My father talked like he was singing
When he bought the burnt-out land and store,
But all I cared about was
The one thousand chickens in the deal.

He said to kill all the birds
And sell the meat to the levee camps
Up and down the river.
The Rollie Pollie man was on the run.

Jimmy was wringing their necks
And making a clean kill,
But I was knocking
Their heads off with a tomato stick.

Everytime I connected
I'd go check the bird out.
They'd bat their wings and squirt blood,
Winking at me.

I was busting green heads off ducks, too.
Jimmy had to hold me back.
"What's wrong with you, Superman?"
"Fly away, fly away, Gospel Bird," I cried.

The Albino

"I am afraid of you, MacCulduff,"
I told my father's foreman.
He rubbed pomade on his face
And put the headdress of an Arab on.
"Get in the boat," he said and smiled.

The albino was a strange man
Who spoke like an Indian
And looked like a real angel
Until he opened his mouth.
"You only have two teeth," I said.

MacCulduff handed me his pole
And told me to put it together.
The only light we had was lightning.
"Don't stick a hook in your finger."
He yawned like a hawk spreading its beak.

"In an hour there will be a sun."
He took a tiger moth from the tholepin
And threw it in the river.
"I don't know about other things,
But fishing will be good today."
The low water and the fog in the swamps
Made the cypress knees look like tombstones.
The old lines of other fishermen
Were snagged around them.
"What have the old men made you do?"
"Rip off my shirt and dip it in deer blood,
Chew the red wattle of a tom gobbler,
And swallow a fish eye, MacCulduff."
"I was made to cut the throat of a fawn
And wear its blood for a week," he said.

MacCulduff worked the paddle like a spoon
Stirring some brew. He feathered it so well,
Turkeys above us shit in the boat.
"Tell me, my boy, what strange things have you seen?"
"I saw three things, yesterday, MacCulduff:
A blind rabbit, a cow peeing on its calf,
And a snake on a power line."
"I have seen all that," the albino said.
Switchwillows dropped a heavy dew
Down my neck and whipped back into his face.
Sometimes, they got so thick, I couldn't see
The boat, MacCulduff, or the water.
"You hear a boat back there? You hear?"
He shook his head and said, "Mosquitoes."
"Shoot man, it's getting dark out here, not light.
When are we going to get to the hole?"
With a willow resting on his neck,
MacCulduff lifted the scull from the swamp
And struck three matches for his limpsy roll,
Then looked at the dark east and rubbed his joints.

                        "Listen out there," he said.
Buono! Buono! The Italians yelled *Buono!*
As they hauled in their nets from the river.
I listened to the Dago fishermen
Sing to the fish in the lightning
And saw the place close up for the first time.
The hole was like a lake in a forest,
With fog way up in the cypress tops,
And the fish after gadflies sounded
Like someone shooting a Twenty-Two.
"This morning it smells like a lady," he said.
And hung from thunder, a moccasin
With four fangs fell into the boat.

MacCulduff grinned at the snake,
Then broke its neck with the scull
When it crawled towards the gunnel.

Tornadoes hit the country that afternoon;
And while MacCulduff was scaling a fish,
The point of a knife, twenty years old,
Began working its way out of his knee.

Elegy for My Father

1883–1963

When Alfalfa was afraid,
Spanky and Buckwheat
Put a gar in his sock
And said it was his leg.
Everyone thought he was sick;
He sang in the bed all night long.

The devil was beating his wife
In the Bear Creek Woods
And I was alone
In the roots of a cypress tree.

I had one finger in my ear
And one in my toes looking for jam,
Waiting for the Negro
To set off the dynamite.

There were coons in the mussels
And sticks of powder
Under every stump.
Toadspit was washing off the weeds.

A fish head was nailed to each tree.
And the gar bladders going down
Sounded like a thousand slow leaks.
A kingfisher dived for the river;
Fish bladders and dynamite began to blow up.

I saw half a bullfrog
Fly under the rainbow
And land on the bank.
It hopped for the rest of itself.
It hopped for the rest of its life.

The devil is beating his wife
In the Bear Creek Woods;
Alfalfa sings in the bed
With his gar leg on;
My father's socks sit in the drawer
Like old bullfrogs.

Tapsticks

In hornbeam woods only jug men would see
I would climb sixty feet in the sycamores
And skin the gray branches like rabbits
Then throw them down to the Negroes below
White and slick as a catfish belly
The limbs were light and untrue
Unless we drove a nail through a washer
At the end   nails   were the hard part
The woods were all over

               Baby Gauge   Jimmy
Born In The Camp With Six Toes   and I
Walked the bank for run-up barges
The cypress barges put together   way back
With spikes and pitch   before we were born
Trapped when the cutoff changed the river's course
When we found one   the sink mud around it
We took turns letting each other down
Through the rotting bow with the tapsticks
Saying to each other "Quick! Let me down quick!"
Sometimes seeing a moccasin move
In the bilge   by the light
That broke   through the holes in the deck
Sucking blue gook to our navels and necks
We smelled bellies in the dead river's mud
And pulled   ourselves up   to the sun   to dry
Back on the bank   snake doctors tending to us
We beat the sticks in the old boat's pitch
And watched the bulrush wave   on the other side
So once out of trees and river wind
The jugs   pulling against the current
And the earth cracking

On our backs for protection
We'd leave cudweed and cottonwood   behind
With the new tapsticks
Held up   high   and balanced   well
To look for rabbits on the levee
Butterflies   lighting on our butts and on
The sticks too   hands over our mouths   squealing
Listening for cottontails' stop and start
Within the same circle of flight
Crossing the bar pit   canebrake   and tangles
Of honeysuckle   their white tails weaving
Through the joe-pye and jimson weed
We'd break into deer jumps   tapsticks high
Leaving our blood and wind in the buckthorns
"Hello! Brother Rabbit!"   someone would yell
And we all let loose with the long white sticks
Blood   new mud   and broken breath   we
Ran to the spot to see what we had

They stood behind me as I bent over
In their shadows   smelling its breath like oatmeal
The tapsticks' shadows   rising   I turned
Towards the sun and saw Jimmy's gold tooth
And the blood on the washer   shine
Smiling   he pointed towards the cottontail
Pumping the buckshot dirt with its lucky foot
Working around like Harpo Marx

The Bass

He jumps up high
against the night,
rattling his gills
and the hooks
in his back.
The Indian says
he is like a goose
passing in front
of the moon.

The Nocturnal Ships of the Past

There was always a great darkness

moving out
like a forest of arrows

So many ships in the past

their bows bearing women
as stalks bear eyes

The burning ships

that drove their bowsprits
between the thighs of dreams

With my ear to the ground
I hear the black prows coming

plowing the night
into water

and the wind comes up
and I smell the sour wood

leaving a wake I want to be
left alone with

Night after night

like a sleeping knife that runs deep
through the belly

the tomb ships come

The Minnow

If I press
on its head,
the eyes
will come out
like stars.
The ripples
it makes
can move
the moon.

The Picture Show Next Door to the Stamp Store in Downtown Memphis

The movie has not begun.
Girls from a private school
are forming their lines.
They have long socks on,
tweed skirts, blue weskits,
berets. The colors
of God and their school
are sewn in their scarfs.

My money and my hand
are in a machine.
The cup does not come down,
but the ice and cola do.
I make a cup with my hands.

They stand there, moving
in one direction
like does in clover.
The nun tells them to form.

Why are they afraid of me?

I am holding my hands together
like a gloveless hunter
drinking water in the morning
or calling up owls in the forest;
I am holding my hands together
like a hunter in winter
with his hands in the water
washing away the blood.

Outside, a man with a lunch box
walks past the marquee.
His new stamps
fly out of his hands;
orange triangles from San Salvador
fly into the traffic.

I am holding my hands
like the nun.

Then fly over Front Street.
He is looking up;
other people are looking up.
The stamps tremble
like the butterflies
from the Yazoo Basin
stuck to the radiator
of my father's car.

The girls are in the seventh grade.
The backs of their thighs
and their foreheads are damp.

What are they learning?
Ballet? French?

The nun is on her toes.

Their booties dance
in the leotards,
rounding out like the moon.
They are making a debut.

The girls are following the nun
into the dark.

The movie is beginning.
The lid on the machine
comes down like a guillotine.

Poem

When the rain hits the snake in the head,
he closes his eyes and wishes he were
asleep in a tire on the side of the road,
so young boys could roll him over, forever.

Transcendence of Janus

I am not asleep, but I see
a limb, the fingers of death, the ghost
of an anonymous painter
leaving the prints of death
on the wall; the bright feathers
of soft birds blowing
away in the forest;
the bones of fish and
the white backs of strange women;
your breathing
like the slow thunder
on the other side of some river
as you sleep beside me; old
dancing teachers weeping in their offices;
toads with bellies as quiet
as girls asleep in mansions, dreaming
of saddles and pulling the sheets
between their legs; fireflies
going to sleep on moonseed flowers
around a plantation gazebo at dawn;
a girl sweating in bed; hawks drifting
through the moon; a woman's hair,
the flavor of death, floating
in the fog like a flag
on a ship full of ghosts,
the ghosts of soldiers
searching for the graves of their mothers; june bugs
listening to Leoncavallo;
christ weeping on Coney Island,
inevitable, like a fissure
in a faggot's ass; a widower

with no sons, a lonesome janitor,
a worm in the sun, the dusty sockets
of poets, who have lost their eyes, their

Strappado

I was thinking about back then
before I thought I
heard chords on a flute
when there was no young bird
beating its wings inside my belly
no light in my eyes
This was long ago
before the wise shadows
of the fantoccini
commanded the land
when the moon
was the blind eye of a fish
in the back of a cave

If I Should Wake

Sleeping on a willow raft
in a quiet inlet—
the feathergrass
carries the shapes
of wolves, as though there were
a stillness in the night,
wet and heavy,
like the tongue of a buck
or a root. It glows
in the incomplete
skeletons of crayfish,
and in their claws
detached in battle, left
behind like footprints.
It is also present
in the nocturnal eyes
of snails.

If I should wake,
I would see the blue bones
of crayfish rise up
and return
to their osseous claws,
walk into the shadows
of themselves,
reared on the shore,
turned red to brush
the clean whiskers
of the beast, forever.

There are wagons
passing in the night,
crushing the wands of snails.
A Choctaw dreaming in his tent.

Wishing My Wife Had One Leg

Caryatid with eyes of nails
    always being driven
with thighs of a canoe
    and of horses fighting
with the back of nine maidens drowning
Caryatid with the hair of a flag
    raised in battle
with the thoughts of a severed member
    and of orphans sleeping
with nipples of amethyst on lifted chalices
Caryatid with the neck of a bow
    drawn towards the forest
with the sex of a ship coming about
    and of a wing in a bamboo cage
with the voice of a silent chisel
Caryatid with the heart of a feather

Narcissus to Achilles

Yesterday, I passed over a bridge
and saw a boot underwater.
Such thoughts I had,
I cannot tell you.

Bergman the Burning Ship

I swim
through the cold and open blood of bandits
one-armed with a ghost sword
and a boy with a wounded hand
his curls in my teeth
his neck in my mouth
we make for the burning deck
this child
part bear like myself
who calls me "Bee Wolfe"
I who have towed my tomb ship
out of the earth
to set us both afire
again
with my song
so the boy can
bite down on the rope
so I can say "Swim my son
tow me through the poison waters
with my spirit
standing at the prow
see me asleep a bending fire
and I will unlock my hoard of dreams
and give them all to you
I will bestow them like rings
but keep an eye
out for those who would wield
their glory behind your back
and loot your heart O
I know the prows
that crossed mine

Hrunting
the bloodsucker
who double-crossed me with that blade
I don't remember
there was the often sung sword of the gods
that melted
down to the hilt
there was one called Ing
and when it failed
I knew I was meant to drain the blood cup
alone
but I used my own sword Naegling once more
my beloved blade
it betrayed me too
it broke into firewood
a kindling I'll always recall
by god the hug of my arm
was stronger than any weapon
it is not meant for men
to wield glory"
I sing of my wake a burning masthead
and a son like a swan
I with the tributaries of night
on my lips and the silent
she-wolves of a river in my heart
I know
no man can forge a sword to grip
my hand

Planning the Disappearance of Those Who Have Gone

Soon I will make my appearance
But first I must take off my rings
And swords and lay them out all
Along the lupine banks of the forbidden river
In reckoning the days I have
Left on this earth I will use
No fingers

The Intruder

after Jean Follain

In the evenings they listen to the same
tunes nobody could call happy
somebody turns up at the edge of town
the roses bloom
and an old dinner bell rings once more
under the thunder clouds
In front of the porch posts of the store
a man seated on a soda water case
turns around and spits and says
to everybody
in his new set of clothes
holding up his hands
as long as I live nobody
touches my dogs my friends

The Quiver

Come back dull and bloody all of you
let it hold the shame inside
itself like a helmet
bring a little soil each time
for a pillow
you aren't as many as you were

Becoming the Unicorn

Go away virgin
if I lay my head
in your lap too long
they will come and lay
a knife in mine

Belladonna

The night I met you
I had the black shirt on
I had the ice pick in my boot

I climbed the tree buck naked
I swung out on a limb

I swam all the way
Under the water
With the knife in my mouth

Like a song of hog blood
Footprints you cannot track

A song that comes apart
Like a rosary
In the back of a church

O bootblack the night I met you
I quit shining shoes

The Snake Doctors

for Nicholas Fuhrmann

I   PIG

I was in the outhouse
I heard somebody at the pump
I looked out the chink hole
It was the two fishermen
They stole fish

One man gave the other one some money
He flipped a fifty-cent piece up
I lost it in the sun
I saw the snake doctors riding each other
The other man said "You lose"
He took something else out of his pocket
It shined
They had a tow sack
I thought they were cleaning fish
I looked up
I saw the snake doctors riding each other

I took my eye away
It was dark in the outhouse
I whistled

I heard the pump again
It sounded broken
I looked out the chink hole
It wasn't the pump
It was the pig

The guitar player cut them out
The midget helped him
"Pump me some water, midget" he said

The pig ran off
The guitar player washed off his hands
The midget washed off the nuts
He got a drink
My eye hurt

He laughed
He cleaned the blood off his knife   He wiped it on his leg
He started singing
The dog tried to get the nuts
But the midget kicked him

The guitar player picked them up
He put them in his pocket
The dog went over to the pig
He licked him

I pulled my pants up
I went outside

I got the pig
I walked over to the pump
I said "Don't you ever lay a hand on this pig again"
The guitar player laughed

He asked me if I wanted the nuts back
He took them out of his pocket
He spit on them
He shook them like dice
He threw them on the ground
He said "Hah"

The midget stomped on them

I had the pig under my arm
He was bleeding on my foot   I said
"Midget, I got friends on that river"

II   THE ACOLYTE

The men rode by

I passed them on the road
They smelled like dead fish

The one in front had a guitar on his back
The other one had a chainsaw

I was riding the hog
He weighed three hundred pounds
I called him Holy Ghost

The midget flashed a knife
He thumbed the blade
He smiled at me
He called me "Pig rider"

I rode over to Baby Gauge's
I was on my way to church
I had to get the red cassock
I tied the hog to the front porch
Baby Gauge was swinging in a tire
Born In The Camp With Six Toes was sleeping in the icebox

Baby Gauge said "Be at the levee at three o'clock"
I put the robe on
I said "I almost got drowned last time"

"Going to have a mighty good time" he said
"Going to be an eclipse" Born In The Camp With Six Toes said

I rode the hog to church

I took the new shoes off
I lit the candles
I changed the book
I rung the bell
I was drinking the wine
I heard Baby Gauge yell

I ran down the aisle
I saw the men at the trough
They were beating the hog over the head with sledge hammers
It was like the clock in the German pilot's shack

One of his eyes was hanging out
And the trough was running over with blood

They held his head under the water
He was rooting in his own blood
He pumped it out in a mist
Like a buck shot in the lung
It was black

He broke loose

I ran down the road yelling
I stepped on soda bottle caps
I ran through sardine cans
I tripped on the cassock

The hog was crazy
He ran into the church
He ran into tombstones

I said "Somebody throw me something"
Chinaman threw me a knife

I ran after the hog
He was heading for the river
I jumped on his back

I rode the hog
I hugged his neck
I stabbed him seven times
I wanted the knife to go into me
He kept running
I ran the knife across his throat
And the blood came out like a bird

We ran into a sycamore tree

When the cloud passed over the moon
Like a turkey shutting its eye
I rowed out into the slough
Not allowing myself to sing gospel music

I woke up in a boat
It was full of blood
My feet were dragging through the water
A knife was sticking in the prow
And the sun was black

It was dark
But I saw the snake doctors riding each other

I saw my new shoes
I put them on
They filled up with blood

I took the surplice off
I threw it in the river
I watched it sink
There was hog blood in my hair

I knelt in the prow with the knife in my mouth
I looked at myself in the water
I heard someone singing on the levee

I was buried in a boat
I woke up
I set it afire with the taper
I watched myself burn
I reached in the ashes and found a red knife

I held my head under the water so I wouldn't go crazy
It was some commotion
I rowed the boat in a circle with one oar

A hundred people were in the water
They had white robes on
Some of them had umbrellas
They jumped up and down on the bank
They rowed down the levee
They were yelling and singing
One of them saw me
I saw a horse with tassels

I put my head under the water
I thought I was dead
I hit it on a cypress knee

Two Negroes came riding through the river
They rode towards me on the moon-blind horse

One of them was drinking soda water
"Where are you going, boy" Baby Gauge said

The horse swam back to the levee
I was with them
The boat drifted away
A man said "Shadrach, Meshach, and Abednego"

III   HAMBONE

They tied his hind legs together
And hung him in a tree with a log chain

I saw them
I was on Baby Gauge's horse
I threw a knife at the midget
So they hung me up by the feet too

I saw them break his neck
I saw them pull his legs apart like a wishbone
I wished the dead came back

The midget stood on a bucket
He reached up in the hog's throat
And pulled the heart out

The dog was lying on the ground
With his mouth open

It took all day to butcher the hog
I got dizzy
I saw the snake doctors riding each other

They turned the bucket over
It filled up with blood

They made a fire

The guitar player beat his hand over his leg
He put some meat on the fire

They tried to make me eat it
The midget spit a bone on the ground

The other one picked it up
He put it on his finger

He went over and got his guitar
He tried to play it like a Negro
There was too much grease on his hands
He got blood on the guitar

The midget danced around the campfire
I wanted to cut his throat

The dog bayed at the moon
And the blue Andalusian rooster played with a snake
I was bleeding out my nose

The fish bandits loaded the hog on Baby Gauge's horse
They threw blood on the fire
And filled the bucket up with guts for fish bait
When they rode off I yelled "Peckerwoods"

I dreamed I saw Holy Ghost walking around the campfire
He was a wild hog with blood on his tushes

Along about midnight I heard a boat but no rowing
Somebody short came walking out of the woods
With a light on his head
The light went out I couldn't see

He drew something out of his boot
He grabbed me by the hair
I saw a knife in the moonlight
"Sweet Jesus" I said

Born In The Camp With Six Toes cut me down

IV   CHAINSAW

The man cut his hand off at dawn
I heard him yell
I set up in bed

He ran past the window
"Don't let the dog get it" he said

I got out of bed
I had the longhandles on
It was cold
I threw some wood on the fire
I put the dime around my ankle
I put my boots on
I put a knife in the boot

I walked out to the road
The blue Andalusian rooster followed me
It was dark

I heard the chainsaw in the woods
I heard him singing all night
He was cutting firewood
He was drunk

The dog quit barking

I drew the knife out of my boot
I looked for the midget
I saw the blood and I tracked it
I saw the sun and the moon
I saw the snake doctors riding each other

The hand was in the sawdust
It was moving
The hambone was on the finger
It was morning
The dog didn't get it
I did

There was blood on the chainsaw
I told the blue rooster
"He thought it was a guitar"

I walked around the hand seven times
I poked it with a stick
I sung to it
I picked it up like a snake
I took the hambone off the finger
I put Holy Ghost's bone in my boot
I put the hand on a stump

I danced on the hand
I peed on it
I broke a wine bottle over it
I threw it up in the air and a hawk hit it
The dog licked the blood out of the dust

I saw the fish bandit's guitar
The blue rooster pecked it
I beat the hand with it
I threw the guitar in the river

The snake doctors lit on it
It floated away

I went down to the bank
I got a pole
I put a hook through the hand
I washed it off
When I touched the wound with my knife it rolled up in a fist

Somebody came by in a boat
They held up a big fish
So I held up the hand

They jumped out of the boat
They thought I crossed them
One of them said "That wasn't no hoodoo, was it"
It was Baby Gauge
I said "No, it was the guitar player's hand"
They swam to the bank
I told them how I came by it
Born In The Camp With Six Toes said "It won't
Take another fish off my lines"

I asked them "You want to shake it"
Baby Gauge said "No, I want to spit on it"
We spit on the hand

They left

I wrapped it up in newspaper like fish
I took it home

I put it under Jimmy's pillow
And he knocked my teeth out
I put it in a cigar box with a picture of Elvis Presley
I took it to town

I walked over to the dance hall
The guitar player was bleeding in the back of the pickup

I gave him the cigar box
He passed out

The midget pulled a knife on me
I picked up the hand
He ran off

On the way home I ran folks off the road
When the truck came by the house
The guitar player raised up in the bed
He said "Give me my hand back"

When it was dark
I tied fish line to it and hung it in the outhouse
I sung to it
The moon shined through the chink hole
On the hand

I took it down
I threw it in a yellow jacket nest
I stomped on it

I took it to the palm reader
I said "Sister, read this"

A lot of evenings I listened for them
I knew they would come back

When a stranger got a drink at night
I thought it was the Holy Ghost
And sometimes a cloud went by like a three-legged dog
And the thunder was someone with a shotgun
Letting him have it

Now the moon was a fifty-cent piece
It was a belly I wanted to cut open

When the flies got bad
I kept the hand in the smokehouse

V   SWIMMING AT NIGHT

The midget ran his finger across his neck
The other one said "Give it back"

I waited in the outhouse
I had a sawed-off shotgun
The men rode off

In the afternoon they sold fish
They cleaned them at the pump
The scales dried up on their faces
They loaded the meat on stolen horses

At night they rode up shooting pistols
I slept with an ice pick under my pillow

One night they rode up drunk
The midget was sitting in the guitar player's lap
He said "Come on out"

They tied a bale of hay to Baby Gauge's horse
They poured coal oil on it
They set it on fire
They laughed

The horse with the moon eye pranced around them
He galloped home

I carved a wild hog out of a cypress knee
I made it the handle
I made four tushes out of the hambone
I used the blade I brought out of the fire
And sealed the pig with
It was the blade I put the burning horse to sleep with
I called the knife the Holy Ghost

To make me go crazy
I took all my clothes off
And jumped down the hole in the outhouse
I grabbed the yellow jacket nest
And held it over my heart
I pumped cold water over myself
And wallowed in the mud
I walked through the snake den barefooted
I swam the river at midnight
With the hand and a blue feather in my mouth
And the Holy Ghost around my neck

And the hooks caught in my arms   they caught in my legs
I cut the trot lines in two
I saw the guitar player stealing the fish

I was swimming beneath the shack
Under the sleeping midget
With the fish bandit's hand in my mouth

I climbed through the trap door
I crawled under the bed
I cut the hooks out
I believe I was snake bit
I put the hand in the slop jar
I reached up and tickled his nose with the feather

He got out of bed
He turned the lights on
He let down his pants
He reached under the bed for the slop jar
He took the lid off
He screamed
I brought the knife across his leg
I hamstrung the midget

I swam under the water
With the hand in my mouth

I came up near the guitar player's boat
He was running the lines

I swam to the other end of the trot line
I put the hand on a hook
I jerked the lines like a big fish

The guitar player worked his way down
He thought he had a good one

I let go of the line
He saw his left hand
He screamed
He fell out of the boat

I swam back through the river
I buried the knife in the levee

I was sleeping in the Negro's lap
He was spitting snuff on my wounds

Born In The Camp With Six Toes cut me with a knife
Baby Gauge sucked the poison out
Oh Sweet Jesus the levees that break in my heart

I have inhaled the fumes of the chicken feathers of death myself
I have dowsed the burning birds I have set the wet feathers afire
like the lullaby from the Russian ballet in many tongues but none of them double
none of them spliced none of them forked none of them separated by words
I carry on with myself in even the most I don't know what moments
my dreams some of them come and go like flash floods some of them rains
  that never
let up and some of them the river that remains forever on the verge of passing
out with so many batons and lost music like toothpicks
like pieces of pork and fur stuck in between like it could grow to the gums
the dreams they are strangers striking matches in the dark
they are boots that keel over to the side a definite limp for forty days
like hot metal hissing in some liquid the liquid is unnameable I
open the pages of the book without the benefit of light I walk into the bathrooms
of the catholic families and the stockings of the older sisters catch in my
eyes like webs they flutter in my hair like little wings

SHADE

1973

I too have slept all night in that stolen Cadillac.

THOMAS MERTON

Soybeans

The book is full of my father's eyelashes
He treats the pages rough
like a woman
He pinches the daylights out of them
Mud dries
up between his heel and sole
quick as spit on his thumb
You can still smell
Four Roses bourbon in the morning
through the onionskin
He will not weep He knows
most folks don't keep their word
Anyway the rain
came through like a hitchhiker

The Last Dance

Jean Follain

Save it for me
they ask you
or you asked them
what difference does it make
some guy from college
always forks over
a couple
extra bucks to the band
a little before twelve
you don't have wheels anyway
and if you still intend
on going
to school next fall
you've got to be on the gym floor
in your socks
with a broom at midnight
helping clean
broken glass and flowers

In Plain View

A white rose fell out of my lapel
outside the churchhouse
like a hand with too much sun
A horse trampled it
The barefoot rider who was
just passing through
leaned over backwards
and picked it up with his toes
He said Sorry
and I said Much obliged
And I took it from his dark foot
and gave it to his fine horse

The Unbelievable Nightgown

Of my sister I can only say
She was like a long feather
Who could breathe under the water
And snarl without lipstick
Or meaning it
Her hair was like a wildcat
Caught in some fisherman's nets
She wore it like a Cajun whore
The moon burned up
A wandering guitar player carved a song
Just a few lines of it
On the gunnels of his skiff
He tied an anvil to his good foot
And hoisted it up like a baby
He screamed
Regret des yeux de la putain
Et belle comme une panthère
And heaved it over the side
The rope wrung itself out
Growling like squashed cocoons
She would take a comb and scissors to my sideburns
And say Are you done with your dreaming
She would come in anytime of night she wanted
She would pull feathers out of the peahens
And wear white shoes
How can it be A pony and a rider
Both can drown in a slew of wildflowers without a sound
I gave my dark heart to one stone
I drank all the water I could
Those days were black carriages
It cost so much to polish

Those days drawn by a team of horses
Sunning themselves with shade
Surviving the thirst of the sawgrass
And believe it
I was crouched down like a groom
Hunting for a thrown shoe
I was sniffing out the shape of the air
Like bored out and stooping wood
Goddamn it was terrible
In the tops of the cypresses where the moccasins sun
I wrote these poems to the Sister
A fair wind
Got away with most of them So I
Start a new one Sometimes I believe
I let her have them
What's finished is finished Salamanca says
His crooning is a darted hem
And she went down shade to the bayou
Traveled there herself
Now she molts under the mud
There are still traces of her
Around where they've searched

GROUNDS

If you could do anything
You would dream
Put the slop bucket
Of twilight under the bed
Learn the blue lingo of the wolf
On a river smelling like a woman
Without opening your eyes
You'd turn up half-pints

She'd take care of the jukebox
Love you'd let your eyes
Pick out the dust of your fingers
All your children
Would send five bucks
For the flowers for the grave
Lots of love
And a saucer with Jesus in the middle
You could use it
In the mornings
Cool your brew in his eyes
In Scotland there is a monastery
Where the monks eat swans
I read that once in the prison of dogs
Strays wandered through the ruins
Pure-blooded hell feathers
Stuck and hanging from the mouths with yolk
Slick as whorehouse talcum
And pale as the bow hunter's resin
Death in four suites
Stuttering gamblers shivering in a rock barn
With some smart anchoress sewing over a bullet hole
The fishermen put out
Branches of desire and solemnity on their lips
And the locomotive of darkness
Blows cold steam through the delta
A drunk hawk in a dead tree
Night doesn't wear any of these fine clothes
And the moon is odd
Like a drifter who can't take his eyes
Off blood in a country egg
All white like an albino digging a mule's grave
While at the same time the baker
Is making his rendezvous with the beekeeper

Pulling up her black dress from behind
Touch and go
Like paying last respects to a blind guitar player
Raining on the tin roof without stopping
Faraway blisters of blackstrap in my ear
Oh yes the moon has a beautiful booty
And the sneak she loves combs his hair like Jacques Prévert
The past is slack
Like the shadow of those in a chain gang
Men among men sodding a levee
My ice tea is warm and there are no lemons
My supper is desolate and spare with regret
If the guard that queer angel brings me soup
He goes by the river first
And dips up tadpoles
With a piece of screen from my old door
Allusion to the twenty-six letters of my sentence

SOLD ANIMALS

Bring enough to buy a new dress
Enough to cut nuts at a nightclub

We used to drink ice water
And listen to music
Look at the same hawk
In the same dead tree
We used to keep an ax like the moon
And a lunch bucket full of coins
Buried twelve paces from the coop
My sister's dress was torn
Like a clump of smellgood from the stream
She stitched her days
With an eyeless needle in the morning

In the evening
The bus full of children
Goes by like a swollen man
With underwear burning on the end of a stick
Heading for the beautiful nests
In the barn where she undressed

Liaison

after Jacques Prévert

Have you seen her
what in hell was her name
all I remember
are the slips
of her writing
lost in the books
dirty underwear
lost in the cabin
where she drank like nobody's business
so she was somebody's wife OK
she never wore blue
but you could see her coming
like a dead star's light
so I can't lie
how long's it been
I'm asking you
to give me her whereabouts
so what if she's dead
I can pick up a rose anywhere
I don't care about
her children her men
just tell me
does she have a room
to lie
awake in all night
does she get gin
when she needs it
are there enough
bucks to keep her

in the kind of clothes she likes
I just want to know
if she can go out again
in a boat when she wants
like I can
friend I can understand
if you can't tell me
I know it was you and me
then we were thick
as blood then she showed up
in the joint that night
Hell if you want
just forget
those ten years
we know how it is
death and its family
reunions and salads
its puddings and the children
too old to recognize
anymore the hired bands
and by the terrific car it drives
the great swan on the front
the mud flaps inset with black pearls
the phone calls the volunteers
in the garden the trunks of letters
and roses and hair in books
where it says love
is a soaked board
splitting at the grain
the lanterns lit for living
the silent partners the dominoes
empty swings and pistols
kept in a velvet box like glass eyes
don't you remember

how she could make you
think the moon was a salt lick
for her cattle of darkness O
no here I go again
rolling up that burnt string
of sunlight and small talk
Christ can't we have a little
shade for our graves
listen are we really fucking
the people we love

My Home

Convicts and their women
could hold out in the storm cellar
The mist in the collard greens is like a boat
of dusty lingerie
The spot where my dog slept is a legend
in its own time
The hoe makes sparks where it lays
Why be so damned faithful
to the way it is Rufus asked me
sopping up his dark gravy with day-old bread
You remember that mockingbird
you strangled in your closet
I fed you its young in your dinner
and you never even knew it
And the snort you thought you heard in the parlor
You heard it
I stalked it down with a slingshot
and a cat's eye marble
It's all gone now Like my mind and your folks
Don't ever tell anyone we were friends
Well I loved you

The Cloud

Her fan is like his deep voice
when he whispers Yeah
when her hand is in his cumberbund
and he's smoking a stogie with gloves on
An orchid or a knife
Her lips are wet fur
and sometimes they are two folks peeling an apple
and a hummingbird's blood
on a french door
She is sleepwalking through our barn
Her mantilla strings along
a nasty brat
said the spider to the fly
You could see the arteries in her breasts
They were dressed rabbits

This Conflict

A body with very few clothes
An old radio
Some apples
You get to eat
as many slices of bacon as you want
the morning of a home game
The way his sweater smells
It gets so hot it smokes
After awhile
just when Sam Cooke's new song
comes on
Worms and a homely girl from Texas
who can read quicker than you
Good marks
and a lost crop
like a whole season
that passed without a letter
from my brother

Wonder Bread

A screendoor slams shut
A giggle in the bedroom
I gaze
at a cloud My other fox
can run twelve ways at once
It is the longest day of summer
almost the last
I'm so sleepy and lonely
both of them

Swirl of Dust in the Cottonfields

I quivered down the river
in my uncle's boat Lucky
someone saw me land a good one
telling me Why don't you
go to hell

Dawn

So the Mottled Houdan
stabs the Mourning Cloak
in its green heart
A few more miles
and it is
Panther Burn
Home again home again

Black Swan

Dead drunk on the fog
of a mountain pool
a child sets a fire
to the milkweed
and the dark feathers of the bird
rolling his fist at the moon

A Man Born in the Forest

Just like a light skinned woman
there was a deer
to come out of the Snow Lake Woods
and speak to my father
I saw him
take off his pants
and his panama hat blew
along the rabbits' hideout

Born There

A lake having to do
with the blind child
who inherited good looks and the ruin
around Midnight Mississippi
was where I went
swimming every afternoon
to watch it go up
in flames

Gray

Some call me River
Rat
On no one do I
pray for bad times
No gray is just a color
to let them know where you come from
Every once in a while
you might have to use a word
like chiaroscuro say
You might be able to swim like the quartermoon
lope like a swarm of flies
It will do you no good
Unless you know how to look at the eyes
at the heart of the living
A little lead alot of wood
You better know when to run when to kiss a woman
when she says No
Yes I am
like the raccoons of night
where the bull takes his long walk in the shade
and a child does her summer
sault over the grave of a footprint
clear as a whistle with singed hair
A bullet for a song

All in My Good Time

He did not leave there
even for sermons
He ground his own meal
Watching the sun rise like a weed
in the ditch
and come down with the mange
One night a hubcap
jumped off a pickup and came on
coasting down that cleared path
running to his place
He thought it was running
away from the moon
He went out to his porch
as calm as you ever
silent as blue blazes
I bet a falling star wouldn't have made him
flinch There he was to see
if his wine was chilled
He breathed on his hard hands
and wandered out over his land
That is how I came to be
born

Leer

The weeds give you something
you want to fall into
like a trap set with whittled cane
With holes in your body
something could blow
clean through you
and play a tune
and fade like some light saying Darling
Something like the wind

Drunk Song in May

All the fine snakes
woke up like vines
Their teeth are getting sweet as elderberries
When I go my way I leave
traces not prints
not sounds
That stream that stream
she rose up last night
and walked in her sleep
liked to carried me away
Her shift was black
as sin
Her legs were just as bad
My bottles they are empty
My boat it is full
Everything I got
could fit right here
like a strange lady's glove
you find in your pasture
When the water goes down with its snakes
and the morning sun rises like a mandolin
I'll pick it up

Honeymoon

I could see the horse outside the window
The hypnotist Salamanca in his store bought suit
white as Pet Milk
And the violet bow tie
like a bullfrog with its head just out of water
He was listening to his pocketwatch
The breeze was so pale and lazy
like the pigs in the sty
and the dirt daubers whispered something
in my ear
No one knows
how he rides his bicycle in the dust
playing his clarinet
the baker of regrets
looking for shade slow and rich as sorghum
how he drinks
so much sloe-gin in his hammock
throbbing his hips himself
Mumbling with his fiancée the afternoon
Come again he told her
He may have been hard of hearing
He may have meant return

The Silence the Thicket the Sniffing

Just like that
is what she meant
when she shook her head
and snapped her thick fingers
at the same time
They call it murder some places
She held on to the brush
picking out kinks of hair
like she was daydreaming of them
The foot
of an infant who is sleeping
My dick when it's hanging
And the lip of a mare
All like snow
no one expected
Tomorrow
a whole field of it can
be there and gone
before you know it

Fair Trial

The undertaker went his bail
And the chauffeur lent him
A jacket to wear
A sea blue tuxedo
It was all he had that would
Fit him
And all his friends
Showed up
Not that they carried any weight
In the town
But they came
To give him soul support
Because they knew
He didn't have a whore's chance
In heaven
You can't touch
The wife of the Law
And expect to getaway
With it hell
The paper's bound to be against you

The Hearse on the Other Side of the Canvas

I die a gigolo every night in the ballet à cheval
So my patrons can go home alone
And stay awake at their windows for hours
Writing me messages by the light of the moon
If all goes well tonight
I'll draw the most tears
I'll have another stocking for my head
It is almost time again
The clown with the black crosses
I drew on his eyes is winding the victrola
He is about to blow the sawdust off the dirge
When the tightrope walker executes
Her last bow for the evening
When the blue light hits her hand
Turning towards the ground like a wounded dove
The horses will gallop into the third ring with me
I will arrive lying in state
So I can ride out alive and on my own
I have come to know the timing of my death
Like a dancer who has finished
Every season I die in the countryside
For the same looks the same barefeet
If all goes well she will be there
In the edge of the light
Looking back over her shoulders
Undoing the ribbons of her hair and slippers
The victrola's wound
It is time for me to enter the tent
For the wheels to be moving
But all I can do is mumble to myself
Outside the wind has blown

Feathers and moths from the grilles of the trucks
And the wagon beds are clean of their hay
The dwarf polishes the mahogany with his sleeve
And the wind takes the tickets
From the coachman's palm
He is asleep
His whip and cloak are as they were
All I want to do
Is move
The earth where you sleep without sleeping
The moon another bride with child
I hold underwater
Still I'm nothing but a mime
My face is cold
As a snow that wakes up a statue
I wait with my lute like a suitor
In the brave shadows
Cast in the courtyard of the dead
I've taken away the ladies of all forms
The four of them know my horses and songs
Alone in the middle of the night
I've turned up in their hands
Like the Ace of sorrows
I bring you tonight
The same black flowers I gave
By darkness they are thrown
By light they are taken
I keep breath in my body
Wearing the tight costume of silence
I give you what I will take from you
Tomorrow night I dream
The intercepted messages
The dust in my boots
And you have to hide me out in the barn

And tend me till morning
I sleep in the afternoon
Then I travel the low road
Combing the straw out of my hair
Keeping your scent black as caviar
This is an adventure
The world is a circus I put in my ear
And I am a rider
Riding two plumed horses at once
The one is a dream the other is real
I ride inside the circle
To keep from falling
I never think about the faces
Out there in the galleries
It's too dark

Night Time

When I stand in the moonlight of the clitoris
I am like a canticle
The light years of the hermit's
ear in a conch

Sung To The Hills is what the stone says

And the breakwater goes on
making its bruises

The sleep in your eye like a bee on a rose

The things which can pass through
your mind when the fish don't bite
splinters clouds pianos
five dried up minnows like a coon's paw

There is an old seafarer
who lives in a barn over the water
two coves down

He has a photograph in a jar of oil
that shows him with a woman in his lap
She is holding a guitar
It is made from some kind of driftwood
And a breathing squid

When he gets drunk
I feather the oars

I can hear the dew
crawl down my neck like a watchchain

You can breathe
on the moon
It is a piece of butcher's ice

Because it is dark
the front end of my boat is full of leaves

I've stared at a wildcat
until it wept I really have
not knowing it was blind

Where I am you have
the schoolmistress to the east
and the Drive Inn to the west
They are all about
sixteen miles from here

I can feel the stars with my eyes shut
They are like crumbs
of cornbread
always in my pockets

To get warm I put my back into it
to work up a good sweat

Once I caught a smallmouth
trolling with an African violet

When I was twelve I had to
wash my mouth out with soap
for taking the deaf girl to the woods
and holding a lantern
under her dress

The huckleberries were in bloom

Since I could talk like an Indian
I was her only companion

The shadows of her palms were like birds
and weren't really fighting
When she kicked a sack of flour
it tucked its tail and left
Her feet would be white

We built a grotto out of willows and mussels
We found an old victrola
The only thing I could hear was the wasps

When the seafarer sang
if you could call it that
we both looked up

The whippoorwills were quiet

Anybody that would try to strum
some tentacles
must be something wrong with them

Have a daughter

At a certain hour each evening
Take a jigger of air and raise both fists
to the bloodshot moon

Wedding

In this dream I waded out into the field
like the halfmoon
They hired a man to take moving pictures
They said she would lift
her dress showing the stockings
and the bands around her thighs
I dangled like an afternoon
shadow humming like two looms
the essence of lungs hands behind my back
mild and wordless disguised like a pasture
I brought the bride my gifts two
garter snakes All of this
has been recorded

Humming This Song Trying to Remember the Way Another One Goes

For a moment the hour is two mad doves
For the rest of your life
Your blood is a sketch
I have drawn from memory
Like a missing deck of cards
Under the bed's ditch
A gardenia turning brown when you touch it
Or a stone
Sinking in the low pond's mud
It all seems
To swarm obediently
As a fugue
I am going to dream
I hear the sleep of figs and bulls
Pollinating the next second
Like a scar with no wound
There is a lightning before death
Without thunder and melody
A taproot disheveled as a shadow
And the boats remain
Waiting to be launched
A dead reckoning of birds
Flying at ninety degrees
Like lost gloves
The bodies forbear?
The bodies
Nonchalant
Burning the pillows of the sick
That have written the last lines of songs
Sores down on their knees

Begging to be marooned
The horsefly's legs the lady's cameo
A close brush with the ancients
The other one
Went like this
Night and her moon
Like a widow with child
The wood of a wild cherry will kill you
And the barefoot gypsy slicing her melon
Will kiss the ground you walk on
The rest of your life

Tryst

after Jean Cocteau

Wherever you are
you are reading
the palms of your mirror
the water grass
of your breath
grows in the belly
of the glass
sewing an insignia
on the dark
sweater of the sailor
your lover
wherever I am
waiting to drown
in the tambourine
you keep in your bedroom
your eyes of rum
to be drunk by a mutineer
the rite of your hair
the last request of a priest
I haven't seen
the séance you call
your waist
in such a long time
I lie awake at sea
it is so
quiet in the afternoon
I dream
of the hills that bleat
like the choked lambs
of your fingers so easy

to find the splinters
in the driftwood
your deadly fingers going
over my letters
like starfish making love
wherever you are
I want the last drink
of brandy which seeps
from your lips on the pillow
in your sleep I know you
fortune teller
of sinister signs
wooing the fullness
of the coastland's moon
braiding the wind through
the strands where you
can hear the doors coming
open at night
letting in the cold palms of darkness
which violate
the eleven virgins
of your candelabra
wherever you are
the way your neck lists
to the side like a ballerina
when you come near an open fire
where I am
your calves are bottles of sangria
from Portugal
poured away at the same time
there was never
another woman
dressed in lightning
like you
my lady of death

a stranger
casting a shadow
she doesn't know
waiting for someone
to pass by the window
lying in wait
for you
with a small revolver
a child I have
never seen
with no thread
in her needle
the thought of you deep
in your sleep
your hands meant
for the harpoon's plumage
meadows under the water
of the pursued
dreaming you could see my face
in the dark limbs of sails
scarred as it was
long ago I saw you
sitting at a desk
reading a book
I thought you were
playing the harpsichord
wherever you are
with your eyelashes of chants
when I return
how can I tell
these children
their mother
the mistress
was blind

Field Hands on Plantation Night

The long blue light of the fox You can't get it anymore
An old porter who's had too many women to read lips No more
Curb Service free soda crackers in the barrel or Shade
Tree Mechanics worth a damn Done with That's it Jack
Guts busted like a row Kneecaps you can't live down
When the shark bites you revive your leg swat the mosquito
who's trying to swamp your dory with the bilge of your own blue
blood Me and a man named Dark did it We did it all most of it We
have been working this ground so long turning under
shadows of the land evenly here and there we got dark
the hell we did being sharecroppers to hunger and deathbeds Partners
Us as we saw us Things Us like purple moths drinking from
a puddle having mudpies for supper with the Mooncalf No Sir
Cloudlike beholding to misery escaping mad dogs and serpents at dusk
Summoned to spring loose boards like frost nailed to get her
here Whenever machinery was broke down fish scales like dimes
Mules and socks in the gully Anything with a voice Power
Line Companies making their swatch the blue-eyed termites with sons
to look after and put through school Radio stations that don't
come in blunt tools fins like rocking chairs and stripped lumber
Spar Varnish you peel like scabs of chickenpox when you rest
six minutes like a scud and then all done Holler at Dark Sing
Is the kingdom of the fury of the dust the dimwitted ice
the dim and the rubbed and the spun fireflies and lizards
in a jelly jar your friends like salt on saltpork you cut
for bait Is the glory spilled and hewn and pulled and weighed
Bucktoothed and in pain and knowing better my belt cinched
tight as a dirt dauber I licked all of my mashed fingers
and read the books that smelled of Will Percy's stables
and Swedish tobacco swaying nearly fifty foot up in the limbs
of a whitewashed oak There like a dead and testament in a vault

I saw moonlighting singers fall asleep at the levers of a bulldozer
and cousins going steady going the whole way coast down the levee
in the backseats of their convertibles Three evenings in a row
I read Lauren Bacall's mind in The Big Sleep at Trueblood's Drive Inn
when she had to light her own smoke Two weeks later when
the Consolidated was let out for chopping a long black Lincoln
pulled up outside with no chauffeur A tall drunk man in big hat
and leather chaps got out asking for directions He was white
with a guitar fine as a Ring-Necked Pheasant slung over his shoulder
Whatever he said in a fairly good voice I never did catch He spoke
so low When I climbed down that is when I was called down
for dinner Big Emma said Child I just had the pleasure of speaking
with Mr. Hank Williams He's asking where a woman is buried
I hitched the mule and we trailed the dust his limousine was kicking
up I told Big Emma It's not much of an entourage for a famous man
but I bet we'll catch him at the Moon Lake graveyard And we did
I thought about it clear into August I kept thinking Tomorrow
is bound to be another day but the dream was like a soft-shelled turtle
that always takes your bait Hold on until you blister Dark said
But I did see Hank Williams kneel down on one leg his big hat under
his long arm in a growed-up cemetery He was like the captain
of a football team saying a prayer before the homecoming game
You won't believe me and Miss Emma has passed away but the both
of us saw a Luna Moth fly out of that hole in his guitar After
he'd blown his nose and left I winded myself running after that fly
There was something written on the stone in some crawdad French
I never did understand Je sens mon cuer qui s'affoiblit
Et plus je ne puis papier Or something to that effect It was
a queer tombstone No name and no dates Just like an abandoned boat
That tarred tree full of larvae mold ants and knife blades
struck by lightning twice and once by a speeding woman
was nearly a bed to me O I got dizzy alright With two spoons
and nothing in the bowl I could forget the nicked china on the counter
The Lord Eating Olives In Gethsemane JFK and Col. Bob Neyland

leading the Tennessee Volunteer Fight Song and some good stuff
from England rattling like snake babies when the Yellow Dog passed by
cruising full of rice and hoboes And then the water buckets would
rust out and there would be strange hammering in the barn at night
Men still rode then shallow pawed sunderers foxing the daylights
out of them Dark and I we shared quicksongs hollered at the top
of a loft and a bed We put the barbed wire's spit curls in place
Nobody not a soul would speak when he shoved open a bad door
Dark got sent up before on second degree Then he went under
the name Tom Beck But I don't recollect who he was he says
The hoot owl and the mourning dove were new gaskets for a truck
In the middle of the evening we heard mice swallow crumbs
cold latches biting the fingers of strange fellows with accents
Father Dark what was it quick tell me what was that noise
and if there was a good moon you needed wading boots and sunglasses
When things were going bad for us morning was a sledge hammer
The wideopen woods of the country a long handle to it
hitting a screwball with the label up Where do you think bats
and tablets come from Old rags and burned antimacassars and good timber
The Mills will take most anything and make it stink to high heaven
We got slugged alright In Come Back Little Sheba the smiling
Chiropractor said Dreams are funny like that Dark said Let them
like blood Let them know where you come from If a man comes looking
for you tell him or them like you was asking him but tell him
You weren't looking for me Take a wagon full of roots down the side
of the levee Be done with it As I recall Dark was a long throated man
but never said much He was like an Indigo Snake where sunlight and shade
meet He beat things to death with a flashlight slender things
living in the bedspread His feet were like grandfather bullfrogs
and they always smelled of Cashmere Bouquet Passed out he'd talk
in his sleep about his sons his trove of suck rocks and the snapshot
autographed by FDR stolen years ago He'd come to under the quarter
moon jerking his legs like a man forced to clean a ditch
with a ball and chain around his ankle liting out the first chance

he had running nearly away from the road gang leaping
from a rotten bridge when it was too dark to see the river
landing on a barge full of soybeans scared safe Women he would
say have lain down here in this field of mallards and stars
Bluetick hounds peed on us too while we were sleeping even
When it comes time I want you to lift I want you to let them know
that I have a hundred more just like you

Slow Rag of the Yearbook

All she had to do was speak to you once a word in the lunchline
and you felt like it was Friday afternoon Her dress
was like a horse you would get a creak in your neck looking
for Her body was a plantation I had to tend myself
If she came past you in the halls with someone older Shit
hit the fan I'd stroll around the Library checking out books
like a silkshirted gambler from New Orleans tipping my cap
when I had none thinking the room was mine like Rick in Casablanca
The clock was an informer It let you down like a buddy
when he lets his Mamma order a shirt from Sears and Roebuck
with the same stripes as yours Even the jukebox is utter misery
To pass the time to kill it like a mosquito that won't leave you be
you walk across the gymfloor in your cleats in the middle of the night
She has her ugly friends slip you notes saying The end of the month
is just about here Everyone knows you're poor and a bastard besides
In bad weather the principal lets the girls wear boots and jeans
The days she didn't show up for school I might as well have
gotten Oughts in the morning I quit football twice
just so I could ride to the next town and back with her on the bus
when the games were away The English teacher got me back
on the team He's got pull The season ended We didn't do any good
I got a secret They thought I was cutting firewood and hunting down
Bee Trees I had them there I pulled it over their eyes like a sheet
I made us a little shack out of rough lumber Didn't take long
It had a kerosene lamp and all A stream passed not six feet
from under the porch She could make crawdads taste like Creole shrimp
She even left some of her clothes there It was a fine situation
Four o'clock sharp every afternoon she'd gallop up on her roan
We had a garden at least we planted one and nine chinese roosters
We sent off for some laying hens but when we went to meet them
at the train they'd all suffocated in those cartons they ship them in

They say Houdini died from no air We buried them all around the little
grave In that place there was light to read by and write by
after she'd gone to sleep No one ever found out Not even our friends
Someone told me she was an Air Line Stewardess What a hell of a thing
for a woman to be walking up and down an aisle ten thousand times
a day and about that far gone in the sky A bridesmaid of buckles
laps and gin She's in a different country every night No one
Ever found out Not to this day Hell she makes more than me
All I get is twelve bucks a day guiding the lost men
I take them into the waters they want to remember
When they didn't have shit for money when they didn't have guts
I give them one chance at the big one the legend no one tells
What they want doesn't swim doesn't sound like a man full of bull
What they want they're scared to land they're scared to death
Like co-pilots with blood in their goggles speaking of dogs
Call off the hounds looking for the shade of their voices at night
Scared shitless again of the moon and its dark slop
Mistaking it for a man from the past who could drink and talk
All night long and then swing the graveyard shift with the women
They're scared of losing their lures to shadows they're scared
Of waiting on the quick and the early and the dead years
That went by like a float made of toilet paper
Somebody has got to hunt down the dog locked in the Gym
Let the poor son-of-a-bitch out put him out of his misery
Some of them are still running laps some of them
Are finding out the hard way waiting in their own ass
Hole like an owl in the dark so far from their deaths dangerous sons
Some of them are so rich I've got a hunch they can fly
Anywhere they want anytime they please O I've seen them fly over
Shining like the deep-running spoons on the end of my line

Living with Death

Long ago a man came to our place
With his daughter
It was evening when they arrived
In their wagon

They had a white piano

They asked only to stay the night
For room and board
They said they'd clean the barn

I looked out my window until dawn
Counting the peaches

The maid gave me rags
For the hot pot of coffee
She gave me to take them

I hadn't even milked
Hadn't sung to the fish
But they'd stacked sacks of manure
And sharpened all the tools

So I went to the pump
And found the daughter washing there

She said Death won't dare
Touch a hair on our heads

Called

There was only a penny
on the arm of our phonograph
but it played like a hundred dollars

Pretty soon we're all going to die
Salamanca was fond of saying
to me as he read the Bible in the outhouse

Now he's got me saying the same
words The moon mosquitoes and darkness
were in his ear
He'd have dreams

A naked white woman washing his feet
The sparrows on his eye

There were only a few chapters
left in the book He listened
to the blues and drank
He sucked ice

He yodeled at old death
when he was wanting some shuteye

Nobody on earth is like me
he'd wake up speaking
just like he was still asleep

Salamanca said he had the sparrows
on his eye
He said I am like the piano
they threw off the bridge
the snakebed and the shadetree
I'm something

He talked to death like a man
fishing in his hole

I'm something not everybody wants
to believe
He'd say sipping on whiskey I stole for him

He told death to suck hind teat

Salamanca would kick me out of bed
and holler at me

tonight the gars on the trees are swords in the hands of knights
the stars are like twenty-seven dancing russians and the wind
is I am waving goodbye to the casket of my first mammy
well that black cadillac drove right up to your front door
and the chauffeur was death
he knocked on the screen he said come on woman let's take a ride
he didn't even give you time to spit he didn't even let you
take the iron out of your hair
you said his fingernails was made out of water moccasin bones
and his teeth was hollow he was a eggsucker
you said he reached up under your dress and got the nation sack
you said the conjure didn't work he didn't smell the salt in your shoes
you said he came looking for you and you hid out in the outhouse you waited
for him with a butcher knife you asked him why not
let the good times roll

the battlefield where the moon says I love you

tonight the gars on the trees are swords in the hands of knights
the stars are like twenty-seven dancing russians and the wind
is I am waving goodbye to the casket of my first mammy
well that black cadillac drove right up to your front door
and the chauffer was death
he knocked on the screen he said come on woman let's take a ride
he didn't even give you time to spit he didn't even let you
take the iron out of your hair
you said his fingernails was made out of water moccasin bones
and his teeth was hollow he was a eggsucker
you said he reached up under your dress and got the nation sack
you said the conjure didn't work he didn't smell the salt in your shoes
you said he came looking for you and you hid out in the outhouse you watied
for him with a butcher knife you asked him why not
let the good times roll
you wasn't studying about kicking no bucket
his tongue was a rattlesnake those sunglasses death wore
I was talking to the pew of deacons theyhad white gloves on
a midget collected ears on a piece of bob wire
the black dog lifted his leg on the hubcap
the wagon load of boots and banners was dumped in the bayou
the chain gang drowned together in the flood
the disguised butterfly
the quivering masts when the hero returns
one came on horseback with the enchanted sword in the hands of the father
the magician comes into the grand court and his head is lopped off by t_he boy
so the father comes back and knights his son with three strokes on the shoulder
this was the accolade of noblemen the investiture of by the magical f_ather
the bridge burnt up the tent and the ladder and the piano are on fire I saw them
after the funeral a drunk peckerhead pulled a pistol on daddy
mother had a double bit axe just in case but daddy kicked his teeth in
if his head was cut off it wouldn't grow back he wasn't a knight he was trash
the pecker had cooties
a blind fisherman used clorox jugs he use to be Mama Covee'sman
he gets snuff on the harp I play it like when I kiss her on the lips
and she is dipping snuff she isdead
to put it out they rolled it down the bank the night crawlers
the hankytonky is burning
the piano under the water looks like a shark
O.Z. stuck a ice pick in his knee

LADIES FROM HELL

1974

The sweet dark warmth of the whole world will have to be my wife.

THOMAS MERTON

Brothers on a Sunday Night

We'd been dreaming
Or at least I had
About peanuts that grow in the river
And oozed sap
When you bit them

A woman bootlegger shook her dustmop
That was the moon

In the fields
Something barren like a journey
And echoes of salt
Sprinkled deep on the table

Where they said the young mother
Walked into the water
With her dress full of rocks
I laid down
And ate a peck of bruised peaches

A fisherman went to sleep on his mule
Riding to the store
For a roll of wax paper

Then we heard
Shouting that tore out the light.

Hidden Water

A girl was in a wheelchair on her porch
And wasps were swarming in the cornice

She had just washed her hair
When she took it down she combed it

She could see
Just like I could

The one star under the rafter
Quivering like a knife in the creek

She was thin
And she made me think

Of music singing to itself
Like someone putting a dulcimer in a case

And walking off with a stranger
To lie down and drink in the dark

Linger

The moon wanders through my barn
Like a widow heading for the county seat

It's not dark here yet
I'm just waiting for the bow hunters
So I can run them off

They put out licks on my land
Every summer

When it gets cool the animals are tame

I've fallen asleep
In the trees before

I dreamed someone's horse
Had wandered out on the football field
To graze
And I was showing children through a museum

The bow hunters make their boys
Pull the deer's tongue out bare-handed

At dusk when I hear an arrow
Coming through my field like a bird
I wonder what men have learned
From feathers

The animals wade the creek
And eat blackberries
The wind blows through the trees
Like a woman on a raft.

If She Lives in the Hills

My children died with feathers
Under their tongues
Said the woman fishing in the ponds
Facing towards the moon

A man passes by with a saw
Another breaks his bootlace
I am told how to get there
By the oozing blaze in the pine

Before I get the drift of things
My gloves wear out
I hear birds and whispers
Like water gnawing a hull

I build a fire
In the bottom of my boat
A good memory moves me through the current
My own blood and sort of wound

Women Singing When Their Husbands Are Gone

for Joan Williams

Traveler going south
I warned you
About those hidden voices in the woods
Mouths like does eating moss

Beyond that spring
Where you threw rocks
And can return
Your toenails come loose

The odor in the coats on the bent nails
Like damp sacks for a hinge
The slats down under the bed
I warned you

Flies wanting a warm place to stay
And the threequarter moon
Quieter than a child slicing a melon
Like dirt smeared over with seeds

Sudden Opera

In Arkansas the liquor costs
The wind lifts a finger
And that is all

You look over your shoulder
When you have a chance
Your bottle is empty

If I could go somewhere
I would go
Where the music doesn't have knuckles
And the dancers don't wear boots

I'll never leave here
The creeks are so cold and solo

My tie-rack is a convent
The pool hall is closed

Do Tell

everyone says it's like a dream
is it now
it was a good year for soybeans and love
Miss Lucy took her own life on the levee
with a pistol
she left everything she had
to a gigolo from Memphis
in no time at all
he bought a sailboat
and a whorehouse
and no one
is ever heard of since

Suspect

He is the one
They all know he done it
He was
Run out the country
For it
So now when they walk
Under a tree and it quakes
They look up scared
Half to death
And deep furrows
Turn over
In their brow
Like tractors
What does he do
Drink
And play moon
At the pool hall
Read the good book
And of a morning
Even before the molasses
Has had its time
He's up and walking
That long fence row
Of his farm called
You can't never go back
Dreaming
Running his hand along
The barbed wire
Chewing the life out
Of the sweet grass
Praying misery be fair

In all my trials
Saying to himself
No one knows
The trouble
That comes looking
For me
One of these days
At dark
In plain view
I'll settle all of this
The holy ghost
Willing
With a sheet of paper
With my name
And my fists

Rooms

A boy sits on the mantel with a piece of string
Tied to his tooth
A big woman rocks by the fire
With a pan of peas in her lap

On the radio they say a convict
Is loose and heading this way
The boy stares at the doorknob
Like a soft-shell turtle on a log

That coward who tipped off the law
Leans on the pool cue in the corner
He can't sleep
The hinge sings like a falling tree

Someone moves among cattle
Someone is blamed for all misfortune
The fat woman rocking near the door
Laughs at the boy with the sleeve over his eyes

Chimera

I dream I am asleep in a boat
with jars full of coins,
drifting through fine rushes.
Moss drips from my ears
and there are many swift wings
humming above me.

On the shore,
a kit fox with cataracts
paws out her eyes,
and in the cockleburs
a dusty robin moves her slow tongue.
Frightened crayfish move in the mud
like lonesome women.

I am afraid a woman
will burn my hair.

Dante Gabriel Rossetti with His Head on the Virginal

for Father Wolfgang

I give you the feeling

That you are in danger
    of a woman dressed in black
Who walks down the hall with a candelabra
    to burn the suicide notes she reads in braille

You might be drifting
    on a raft with a sleepy Negro
With dice in his boot
    and dueling pistols under his magenta cumberbund

Salome gashes the sole of her drunken foot
    on the ruby she danced from her belly
And looks up at you quite handsomely shivering in the mist
    About to fence with that smudge on her mirror

You lay your head in the carousel
    the lap of a friend's wild haired wife
And listen to the french horn putting out
    The eyes of the sea anemones

There are mountains that float like ashes
    sifted through a swatch of a Lemurian gown
And a child with her mouth full of saliva
    coming from a coffin

Blue Yodel of the Wayfaring Stranger

after Pier Paolo Pasolini

I lean my head up against the juke box in the mountains
And think about the three Indian sisters tending bar
The nighthawks come down to sleep
On the knives in my shoulders
As if I was Saint Francis barefooted and all
They come down to cut their own
Throats in the snow
Which falls like the dandruff
Of Jean Cocteau
And I go on thinking of my white horse
Waiting in the roses
I can tell by the look
In its eyes my baby is dead
All my liquor is gone so is my land
I got kicked out of school for sleeping
And I spent what I had
Going to the picture show
Where I was arrested for putting my fist through a mirror
When this song is finished
I'm leaving this place but first I'm going
Down to the Army Surplus Store
And lay away all I got
On nine guitars

Twilight

after César Vallejo

I have dreamed of escape and I have dreamed
of your laces
scattered in the alcove

Along the dock some mother
and at fifteen giving her breast to the hour

I have dreamed of escape
a forever
longed for at the ladder of a prow

A handmaiden walking the planks
with a cut rose in her mouth

I have dreamed of escape
buried on the beach
like a bowsprit

A young one drinking wine
with a black knife in her hand

I have dreamed of a mother
some fresh greens in a newspaper
and the stars of dawn's trousseau

The length of a dock...
the length of a drowning throat

Death in the Cool Evening

I move
Like the deer in the forest
I see you before you
See me
We are like the moist rose
Which opens alone
When I'm dreaming
I linger by the pool of many seasons
Suddenly it is night
Time passes like the shadows
That were not
There when you lifted your head
Dreams leave their hind tracks
Something red and warm to go by
So it is the hunters of this world
Close in

Place on a Grave

It's not hard to forget what they ate
Every winter, when the father
And oldest brother went back to do time,
Cowpeas and smoked goat, all winter
The same muddy supper, their voices
Thick as pan bread, the hollering
At dawn when the mother went out
To the pens in cowboy boots
With a bucket of feed and a roll
Of toilet paper, finding a swatch
Of her daughter's nightgown
Fluttering on the barbed wire,
The hollering and calling
The rest of them did when they
Raised up from their cold beds
And went out searching at first light
For their crippled sister, who dreamed
Walking over the mountains
In the dead of winter, the smell
Of cooking in her hair, believing
She was gone from there, dignified
Like a wooden figure on the prow
Of a ship with no horizon.

Getting to Sleep

The two sisters come home for the holidays.
There is grace, the meal, and a lot to drink.
The youngest boy goes up to change clothes.
They are all going out to visit in the next county,
All but the two sisters.
They curl up near the fire, sipping coffee.
The boy comes down the stairs, a towel around him,
Drying off in front of the fire.
He is fourteen years old now
The one sister says to the other.
After the family leaves, the two sisters
Climb the stairs to their old room.
They undress and climb into the cold feathers
Of the two iron beds.
It is a good moon out, and snow.
They lie there in the dark,
Thinking about their girlhood friend
The other farmer's wife; and the farmer,
His dark hair, his gloves, the smoke
In his clothes, and the rabbit blood under his nails.
Under their beds, holding them level and steady,
Are a few of the books they read long ago.
The two sisters lie there in the dark, thinking
This night, a pianist whose hands they can't see.
And the past, in white gloves, like the snow,
What they're hearing now,
Like a man with long sideburns
Climbing the pine stairs in sock feet,
A man the both of them are in love with.

The Paramour

don't tell me I know
the bedrooms like one
hundred rivers
that disappear underground
I know the solitary couches
with the inscriptions of mistresses
written in blood

Farewell

Is a word
That must be
Like a sword
That has worn out
The scabbard

Where We Slept Together

I open the doors of my house at night
I latch the screens

Allegory of love
Like a dog shaking all over
Like a bite that itches six inches deep

My old radio is like a toothache
Someone had in summers past
Another place set at the table
There are no longer any shotguns or guitars
In my house

There is a lotion for the hands

Each blister another
Bloodshot moon

A yawn a blessing in disguise
A branch where a bush grows
Its thorns
Allegory of love

There are bookshelves I threw together
I took the lumber
From a horse thief's barn

Go back

And there are books the dead light their stoves with
Books howling like pines on a ridge
Cats in heat

Deserted and cold
Like a handgun or a spoor
A gar looking for a wife in a swamp

A room where a raped adolescent
Is interrogated
About her past sexual life

Go back
Wearing a hat of smudge candles
Ducking back
Up the fingers of the lake
Like a ring or a cobweb

You can pass my window you can pass
My door
You can step on the blade of my hoe

All these maps
These photographs
I have wasted nails on

The cut lines it took so long to clear
Are growing back
Scars

I have looked for furrows in the dust
On the banister
And long hair in the bed

Scabs like butterflies
Standing up for the flag
Rocks in the garden of love

The clouds are like fat grandmothers
Before they were mothers
Getting ready for a dance

All these spools of barbed wire
I meant to put up
When the orchard was mine

I'm sore from mending
Small holes with tissue
Allegory of love

The rented tomb
Like a sour mash
Brewing in the ditch

They're snoring underwater
They're droning like ships departed
From the black holes of space

In the morning I'm going
To leave
A bottle on the stump

Like thunderclouds
And packages of blood
The seeds in the hardware store

Like a stew for flies
It boils down
To a slop jar at the foot of this bed

Pasture Dream

My daughter put black
Lady Fingers between my toes
I gave her a silver dollar
to buy oranges and a loaf of bread
and she came back with firecrackers
The dew was so heavy they wouldn't light
My son was jumping the barbed wire
on his white pony   Oats in his hair
drunk from the honeysuckle
he cut his morning coffee with
His eyes were deep and green like mine
like ponds of sleeping minnows
My wife was looking for mushroom and poke
Her skirt was lifted high
over her thighs in the tall grass
Her crutch was like a divining stick
It smelled like root beer
Brother Leo told me the bell was ringing

THE JUSTICES

Some dead children from other countries
Wake me u

THE JUSTICES

Some dead children from other countries
Wake me up with lamps.

They are like miners, their little white shirts
Are dirty with dark marks.

Their bodies are sore, they touch themselves.
One begins to beat a drum

Telling me the names of nine men,
Lives I have to take.

I see another face looking in my window.
They tell me she is still dead.

She will come back
But she will never be beautiful.

She will live when no man
Can make a law against another.

In the morning a bird breaks the glass
And dies on the floor.

Frank stanford

FRANK STANFORD

FIELD   The Justices
*   The Love*
*   The Death*
*   The Stone*

IRONWOOD   The Light The Dead See
*   A Milk Truck Running Into A Crazy Mt id At The Corner Of*
*   God well And Park*

I got a zero on the test a big F with a red circle around it the question was
what do you know about current events I put down
I know Elvis Presley lives up the street ten houses
I know my sister's godmother is Louise Fazenda
I know mother stayed in Hollywood with her and Hal Wallis a long time ago
I know she is secretly an actress
I know she went to the Rose Bowl with Clark Gable and Carole Lombard
I know they played oh johnny oh johnny how you can run
tennessee got beat
I know captains courageous
I know Gary Cooper's name is Frank
I know morocco mati hari lives of a bengal lancer sgt york the mark of zorro
the gaucho we saw it in a tent
I know streetcars of desire and all the Tarzan
moby dick gunga din midsummer's night dream was like me
I know I have read all those men's books that we had
I am a fugitive from a chain gang the crazy piano player red slippers
I know the girl feeling the kiss in the mirror
I know the bracelet on the wrist in the tomb
I know the horsehead nebula in Orion
I know the elders
I know Wallace Beery is not Pancho Villa
I know the melody of the song sung in the boat
I know mother has an opera Don Juan the lover
the sleep in the tree daddy makes us live like the crew in a shack or a tent
I know about the history and culture of Europe and America
I know how the carpetbaggers and the scalawags brought the colored people
          to town
head down over a horse
I know the rich are the only ones that had any good old days

FIELD TALK

1975

O go home, brother, go home!
The devil's back again,
And magic Hell is swallowing flies.

THOMAS MERTON

For Howard and Mary Crouch
and James B. Lee

Plowboy

I came up on death and love
hung up like dogs in my garden
I had no broom or cold water
just a plow and a pony
the both of them shined like a mirror
of double or nothing
so I told them
stay out of my greens
what I really meant was what do you want
I came up on death and love in my garden
lessons in paradise

Lullaby to a Child Who They Say Will Not Live through the Night

the fog worked on the coffin without a sound
like a tire rim rusting in the dark
I went around waiting for some scum to grow on the lid
I wanted to hewn me oars to take you home
I wanted to bring clean sheets dipped in ice water
and smell your curls like strawberry vines
have a one of you seen how long
it takes to wave so long or lose a crop
I plant my garden under the gradual pressure of the loveliest saddle
forgetting the undergrowth of sorrow
I make loops for the worms my darlings
I take a bath in a grave with no soap
and keep the secret of the fingernails and vortices of dirt
a pelt is taken by the sound of a lantern going out
and I tremble with the channel cat black as soot
and I pass out on funeral jazz and slow water rag
I betroth myself to the tension of the raccoon's approach
flexing my eyes with the dark
and I swear on my life
I will prowl this black island until I can return
your dirty kiss lightning's flesh and thunder's hurt
I stand ready for the spume of your cooked tongue
it is a simple ceremony
a girl has burned
her wilderness to honey but not to death
a woman will die
before the hunter rises I can hear the embers from my boat
from my bed I can see the odor of her pillows

Milksnake

Hushpuckena built him a fire
he gathered driftwood back in the shadows of the barn
you could hear
crawling through the straw
like satan's plow
or a blue river that quits
when there is a heavy frost and lemons to be eaten
some noise was heard
a hand gliding over the ruined stocking of a virgin
knocked out on the credenza
the splendor of the unfastened moon
coagulating on the seat of the coupe
the faint commotion of a priest or a thief
who walks in his sleep
a cicada on the staircase and a splinter
receding like the frontier of the cheerleader's garlic
like tights waving colors
and hair underwater
a cemetery very close to the deaf mute's bedroom
like a train
or five stolen mares
tow sacks tied to their hooves
hay bales full of evidence and mice
and the lantern blinked
so quick it would take your breath away
just like that
the devil can have both our souls
if the awnry lord did not nurse the heifer
like the chant of a dredge
he bit the teat and there was Hushpuckena with sandpaper
and smoke coming from a bucket of quills

The Long Staircase

I would like to go down it like grass
cutting shoots
leaving fumes of butter
milk and dark laurel and God knows what else
in a white suit on Easter
the brim of my hat turned down
all the way around
with my eyes shut full of pollen
I could run into anything
even the big blacksmith
with soot on his teeth
the piano
or my blood brother
sounding the hurting horn

The River Is Some Time to Kill without Warning

it has eyes
like vials of poison
in the back of its head
that is why I looked at it
when I should have really been
tending goats
doing something else
my arms went sore
until I walked with a limp
one kiss was all
it took
one kiss cold as silver dollars
holding down the eyelids
like two carpenter's measures
steady as fish
the sound of not just lead in my shoulders
righting themselves with a thirst
in my garden there is no more plowing
in my rooms there is no more sleeping
I straddled the roof I hid
the keel of a ship the river hauled me under
it was like an afternoon
you lay out a blanket for
a harpooned whale waiting for the moon
to sink
when I smelled it
I had all day
when it was time to leave
it said O Cisco

Sanctuary

a woman came to take my picture
she told me the time of day in a letter
I wanted to be dressed
fit to kill
and ready when she took it
I wanted to be lying on the edge of a pond
smoking a long pipe
and an unsaddled horse would be grazing
beside me I wanted a gaze no one could forget
without a word of warning
I heard the whirring come to an end
bumble bees sucking a rose
this woman should have told me
these pictures wouldn't be still
I'd of ridden the white horse

The Prows

I hold the knife underwater
the boats come by

Wrote Down Burns

Lay in my bed the stone
horseman with the moon going over there
towards old Turrentine's boat shack
like a cock in a den
like a green fly in the last sip
lay in my bed swimming
out of the lost cave yodeling mercy
lord jesus christ john r
evening in stripe pants leaning up against
the porch evening with a match
in its teeth evening strange nigger
following a string with a torch underwater
"only go in at night and do not wade"
lydia she wrote me in a letter they found
after she took poison
I came up along the face
of a bluff where the channel ran
my lungs were lilies
cussing out the moon hung together with dark
like camp dogs in a ditch
read those books with wet fingers
yell over to the boat of the old days
when the men chewed a match and thought
about their death
like yellow women strutting down the dust
lay in my bed with the rains falling
I remembered the rain
drive home buck naked lay
in the shade
when you walk down the streets no one knows you

The Chinese Noseguards for the Entrance of the Mouth

I don't recall what kind of sucker she'd been licking
the movie was slow to end
then someone came running down the aisle
with an accent

The Face of Love

she has one of them
like a very famous
nobody
her mother was good-looking
and drove a convertible
her father a drunk
they invited me to their home
several times
they went over my shoes
looked at my pistols
they had lovely affairs there
the grandmother
was hard of hearing
and wore a disfigured cameo
she told of days gone
when she rode an Arabian to the Landing
to meet the boat
there would be books and cologne from Paris
material and perhaps a piano
and no counts from New Orleans
as the story goes she married one
it turned out this way
and the legend continues
blood and starlight in the river
African violets and capes
Chopin and back roads
and her granddaughter was just like him
silent and cruel
always taking her beauty rest
and her best friend's
friends

Spell

I aimed to get some of my blood
back from the Snow Lake mosquitoes
my belly was full of lemonade
and my hair had Wildroot on it
I took to the thicket at dawn
not knowing where I was from the man in the moon
there were trees with so much shade
you shivered
like someone chiseling the year in a graveyard
the shadows seeped thick as smoke
when you touched them
even breathing drew blood from the wood
it was dark
as a swarm
they smelled like olives
and feet in a garden
when you bowed and kissed them

Nautilus

a body comes apart in the bayou
like cardboard
in the lid of a jar
some kind of oyster
you take out with a knife
dogs tell it
the whole night sky
is an appaloosa

A Life Taken in the Throat of the Tree Frog

I took my rest under the shade of an ice truck
that used to belong to a singer
all summer the chinaberries
ruining the windshield
for the life of me
who was it whistling those songs

Partner

some owls leave midnight is close at hand

I Would Have a Woman as Real as Death

pain my star
of all times I remember
none of them
now I do
I notice the points
of light the shoes
the ballerina wore
though years ago
now I do
nothing like
the fish
swims in its sleep
the birds patrol that dark
ness that glows
in my shadow
look
back over the
years with you
I have
the final say
so of the kiss
which goes
so alone
which knows
its destination
so well
I
no sound
I
sang
with no

passages I give you
a real blue
song the mountains hold
under their foot
on the neck
of your voice
not mine
now I know
the echo
the two bodies no
sound at all

On

there were nights I saw myself ride up in the mirror
rings slipped right off my fingers
like too much sunlight
causing you to burn
I stayed on the horse or whatever
it was
until it panted like a fisherman's wife
brushing her hair

Blue Yodel Silence You Are

You are a fourteen year old farm
girl who's done it already
you are dreaming about it again
losing your faith in the loft
in the hay of that dress you want
anybody to bring you
and the horses are sleeping
you are a dark boat
moored to the evening's
harbor and I
am a new rope
unraveling
the storm
passes by
like someone
I knew

When It's After Dark

I steal
all the light bulbs
and hide them like eggs
in a basket
going to some outlaw
I put on the best I can find
I cover them with a swatch
of something
that swells like a bite
that bleeds green
cloth that smells
of a feed store
but looks
to of been worn
I go over to nasty willy's bridge
and throw them into the creek
there in the shade I listen
for them
to make nests to escape
agony and burst

Cutting Fishing Poles for the Dead

you must do it
otherwise they will sick their black cats
on you when you aren't expecting it
break soda pop bottles on the highway
near the curve
catch the dead
laughing at the yankee's blowouts

Fire Left by Travelers

Before in our lives we have all gone down
to some river or another
and spoken with those who don't often speak
we tell them about the black fumes of our dreams
roots smoldering and asleep
and the hammer hanging on the branch
and they go on sinking long nails
into their boat's damaged wood
they make a harbor out of anything
that will hold a rope for a night
they sit on buckets
near the water's circular ruins
eating fish cooked in wine
one has a belly and keeps young ducks under his shirt
one wears a beautiful scarf
he claims the moon is a lair
under the patch over his left eye
briars take over their boots
which took journeys without walking
half under water there's a chimney
driftwood and broken oars and lost lures
floating in the flue
the current drawing them up the fireplace like smoke
there it stands alone like a stone tree
the house having burned
before the river rose
before I walked down these levees
my father's long graves
which he raised like a pharaoh
I kept coming down them
holding both arms before me like a sleepwalker

holding out my hands
trying to warm them on campfires long gone
sod might as well have been snow
I looked down the steep slope of those days
a skier getting ready for a jump
I had things to say

she said Francis I am dead from now on but I will live as long as the cloud
stays in front of the moon and I looked up and saw the black ship
like a great wolf after the neck of the moon
and she took off my pants and my cap and my wool sweater and my boots
and she stopped the bleeding with her hair and she said why do you always
        dress
in black and I said on account of all the hand-me-downs in my closet
are midnight blue for the winter and sweet milk white for the summer
but I thought about the black cloud so I didn't want to speak
and so the grass was a quilt patched by one night and though I couldn't see her
I knew she was there and I loved her I was with the girl with black hair
and when she lifted her legs it was as if
she wanted to balance the moon on her toes to keep it from falling
but I knew all along it was the black cloud that needed to stay in place
and so in that country where I was once and now and will be before I was
where I spoke the words holy holy holy Lord God Almighty all the earth
is full of Thy glory where the whistling swans ride the backs of the white
horses of the river where the boxcars and skiffs are full
of drunken troubadours where once I did lay awhile longer the pavane
of whippoorwills while the pallbearers are strutting in the ceremonies
of my sleep the passing bell nodding like a snake charmer all far
past away deep behind the woods down the road where I saw that lightning bug
in the country where my dreams are like bark
peeled off by lightning I was with her the girl with black hair
while the wolf had the moon by the throat
I said I love you in the field of honor
and she was like a colt
and she was water I held in my hands
and she was the canoe I worked through the river
and she was the flash at two-thirty in the morning of the suicidal knife
and she was a fire of pine cones who ran like a deer
and she was a butterfly that lit on the float of my pole
and she was the night herself

Baby one night somebody
Going to strike a match on a tombstone
And read your name.

ARKANSAS BENCH STONE

1975

I started Early—Took my Dog—
And visited the Sea—

ARKANSAS BENCH STONE is a *Legend For John S. Morris.* I dedicate this book to my mother, Dorothy, my grandmother, Carolyn, and to the memory of my father, Albert Franklin, legendary figures.

The Visitors of Night

This bed I thought was my past
Is really a monk in a garden

He's dressed in white
Holding a gourd of water
Because I have forgotten Tangle Eye
And Dylan Thomas
The swarthy goose
And the moon in the pennyroyal
With its gut full of shiners
And the skeleton keys to my room
And the snapshots of my land

It seems like dusk
The voice and curls
Left in the strange clothes
Roaming the forty acres of my closet

In the bow wood mountains some boats
Stray as dogs go down in the fields
Shadows yet in the land of the living

When the shade clean leaves you
To your rewards
Bad luck and trouble
Come breaking the laws and trysts
Of love and gravity

So have respect for the dead my dear
And watch your heart like a jukebox

Death coming low with its cold set of tools
But you can't jimmy love

Monk's Dog

You aren't around
Friend I might have been
Looking for you

I could have been beautiful
Like the sound of your running

Tobacco of night when I find night
Sour Mash of misery the star of my calling

You don't have a snowball's
Chance in hell

And you don't have a past

I can go into the woods
Empty-handed
And find the river asleep
And the blood under your shack like fog

Mouths Full of Spit

The gar weaved around the moon
Like a child running down the road
Towards the next lighted house
Asking help for his mother

Things move so fast
Make the dirt in the keyholes
Soft again
Blood comes back

To your blisters
And the ax blade warms up like coffee
A monk slops the hogs
And you lace up your boots

You might not tote lame girls
Across thin rivers like I do
You might not want to hunt down the dog
Locked in the gym

Their Names Are Spoken

Where the saplings come up
In the belly of the road
Nobody has traveled for so long
I found the place you bear east

And walk over the hills
Until the sun goes down
And come onto smoke and goats
And the music of no socks

For a gate they use the stead
Of a tarnished brass bed
The little winds that came up
Like a child soaping a saddle

We dream on
Now night a cool moss
On the undersides of the cold ground
Keeps growing on the stones

Lap

She pours sweetmilk over me before the sun comes up
Her dress is like a tent in the desert
Her whippings don't count

She buys the young men suits
And they cross the river with someone else
And check in at Hotel Nemo

She buries her pay in a bucket
Every new moon
She cuts her snuff with happy dust

I trace her butt in the shade
Like a Spanish Oak
We throw light bread to the fish

She mosaics the Lord's mysteries
With scales and egg yolks
Emma is a humming

Tale

The maid used to pull the drapes
So I could see dust

When it didn't rain
I bought gum and worked in the boat

There was a locked up shack down the road
With a stack of records in the bedroom

We could tell when strangers were around
From what they drank

The girls waited in the orchards
There was no need to lie

Island

Lord it was dark up yonder
Like it was night in the afternoon

Death had a smell to him
Like he had Wildroot hair oil on his head
When I was a child I slept
In a dark room
I was fond of sleeping
I didn't have worms the secret of the somnambulist

We all did we all were

Me and O.Z. walked everywhere We had a seine a compass
Liting out after death
The things we had we kept to lose
We didn't need jump cables for love

Death was like a man in a bow tie
Looking for a hubcap
We had spyglasses we all figured death ran a hotel
That was because he had keys you could send back
And many pillows
Whoa back boys oh goddamn

Lament of the Land Surveyor

Here it is the last day of November
And I am still working the hills
Without a shirt or a new pair of boots

Like the shade throwing itself
Into the river
A voice in disguise I remember
It's hard to walk a straight line

My father-in-law is coming home too
On his one-eyed tractor
Heading east of a moon
That'll be gone tomorrow

I've dreamed a lot
About a black cat
Dying at the foot of my bed
About cornerstones
I've found in the dark with barefeet

Forties of death and no bearing
Acres of sadness without death
I've dreamed a lot

And waded full gullies
Beneath a ridge where Sally's grandmother
Is shearing roses

And the smell of those flowers
Floating to the foot of the mountain
Reminds me of my hair
Falling on my own father's boots

And the smell of his jacket
And his straight razor like a lamp
Glowing in the window before me

Blue Yodel

The girl in the black sweater
Lives alone with her child
On a small body of water
And is not married

She is building a cabin
Back in the woods
But for now she and the boy
Live in a houseboat
That lists off into the evening

When you go down
The goddamn roads to her place
You know
You've been somewhere

But she is always gone
When you get there

The only place she frequents
Is a tavern in the cove
What they call it is The Quiet Night

In the afternoons I went there
Wanting to get a look at her
No way

So I took to drinking
Later than I should
And the man who claimed he ran the dive
Told me the tale
Of the girl in the black sweater
It was late when I left

He helped me in my boat
And I rowed the liquor out
Of my blood all night
Going home the moon was letting
Out its mooring rope

When I passed them asleep in their boathouse
Her sweater dried in the air
Like a black flag

Blue Yodel of the Quick and the Dead

At a time when we were sleeping
A boat drifts down the slope
Into the pond
It isn't going anywhere this is
How bluebirds die
A porch swing banging the rose bush
In a bad wind
Like a minnow net the terrapins
Stealing strawberries
Off the vine
A tornado passes over
Like an angel with a can
Of worms and then a mirror
And then a blue cock
Walking a sawhorse
Pass over the graves
A light rain falling
Up the road some children fighting
With weeds demanding satisfaction
They might be brothers
Or sisters
They're bowing
Pulling up the queen's lace
They're bending down
To the lightning it's a dream
Until a long thin weed
Opens up the boy's eye
The birds are there
Singing on the power line
The fence no one will claim
The boy lies in the dust his sister

Falls down naturally
Holding her welted thighs great storms
Coming without rain
Leaving days for nights gone and unknown
The years
Go by someone passing a drawer
With a glass eye
One winter she goes out to the barn
Her brother is fast asleep
The wind blows open the doors
But not her candle
There's an old cabinet she stares at

Will

My father left me his wool shirts
And a promise that I would take whiskey
And cured hams to the family
Of the man he shot fifty something years ago

All through high school and college
I kept his word
And wore his shirts
Until I had to go away

Well I got a Phd in astronomy
Then came back home to teach
After a while I intended to pay them a call
Soon as things cooled off

But the nights got longer
I kept putting things off
Hoping I would discover this star
I knew was there

One day in the planetarium
Word came I was a bastard so
I rode out to the country
With a kid in a logging truck

We talked over things
Ate supper and swore
I slept in a wild feather bed with two others
The next morning I walked back to town

Now I shoot pool all day
With the guys my age

And run around at night
Like a bloodhound with a lost voice

Old colleagues see me sometime
They wave me down
Wanting to talk
But I no longer have anything to say

In the tavern
The old men who knew my father
Get drunk to tell me
What a no count I am

So I gave them the beautiful shirts
The houndstooths and plaids
And the herringbone
With the sewn-over bullet hole

I do my reading at daybreak
When there are the fewest stars
And the kid saws logs in the schoolbus
And the leaves leave their books

I left the heavens for the taverns
And the shirts for the old men on pensions
My coat is black
Like the nights I have long forgotten

Shed

The old woman washed my socks
Light went through my hair
Like a school of minnows

Death had a socket wrench
That'd fit any nut
He knows a little tune
You can't carry

Death say he give you credit
You better not sign

A journey is just like a journey
The so-called mystery of death
Will run you about an even seven bucks
Go ahead and see
This includes a washtub of beer
Advice on love
Snake oil on your tally-whacker

Wind blows over our plots
Whistling up the butt of our deaths
I could be anywhere
Wind on the island at night
Not the schoolbell full of mud

Village with Dark Sun

From where I live I can see it
The dark sun over the village
It's like living in a ship
Where I do
The wind rattles my book
Like a handful of tickets
I find out I have change in my cuffs
I feel like a mate
Standing guard over a deck of cards
The red ladies look for land
And the black ones have found it
The breeze always has something
It hasn't played
Some paper with no writing
I think of the stowaway in the lifeboat
No one has made fast
Like a blindfolded prisoner tied to a chair
The wind is taking
Overboard
He goes around the perfect sphere of wood
In the whirl
Pool of the whistle
And he takes his flogging
Without blinking a eye
I live on the island the lake has made
I don't get around too much
Living here
A kind of buccaneer
On the other end of a bell rope
In an abandoned churchhouse

Inventory

A man came into the store
Told Mother he was looking for a good knife
She took him behind the counter
And let him look a spell under the glass

You could smell his new clothes
What a beautiful shirt
He had on my mother told him

It was blackwatch plaid

We all got one after that
Mother ordered one
They sent forty-nine

What kind of knife are you needing she asked
I'm needing one that'll touch bottom

He looked over his shoulder when he said that
And a man buying shoelaces nodded

He said a man don't want to go shallow
You know how it is
I'd hate to come short on a critter

That's the one I want the man in the new clothes said
It's from Sweden and it'll set you back she told him

Lady I don't care

Right then I heard a car on the ridge
Hit the bedrock
It was going pretty fast

Now how's about a nice stone
To go along with the knife said she
The man looked over his shoulder again
This time out the window

O.Z. was hoeing weeds around the monuments
We sold on the side

I mean a whetstone
Just for the steel she smiled

He swallowed like it was dark medicine
He didn't laugh
Just so it'll cut once lady
Is all I care
He told her trying it out on the sole
Of his new issue boot

Midnight or so I was down in the storm cellar
Stealing a little jam
By God if I didn't hear someone
Hit the bedrock again

Land of the Downstream People

The mules all hitched and working
The slopes of your eyes

Listening with the clock you carry
Handless in your heart
Mornings the wind blows into the children
And the moon full and flowing this side of Ozark
Smoldering like a burnt tick

Underfoot the rocks with dust in their ears
Lost roads leading
To the bad roads

Let me
Witness the mark
Of the moth in my hair

One night it rains enough
To strangle a hog

Something dead nailed to a post

In the hollow a shovel flies
Out of a grave

But in Kansas I walk with my head down
Like a sick dog

My father-in-law owns Bourbon County Implement Company
It being Uncle John country
I don't know about these people
And neither does he

They don't know when to quit they work
All night in the fields like a lake named in their honor
Everyone with their boat and their lamp
Trolling through milo maize

In Arkansas at this time of night
A man would be cranking the arm of an ice cream bucket
Or an old telephone
Bringing up angle worms out of the earth

We're installing a clutch
Welding by dark
Closely watched and timed by men
As if we're cutting something loose from kin

All men good for nothing or not listen or heed
Do not break down on the prairie
This is a living not worth selling
Parts to keep it all running

Soaking Wet

A hawk lived in the chinkapin

At night he flew
Up in the cockeyed light of our truck
And curled around the moon
When we saw it
Like Virginia creeper

I would lie in the white dust of the road
And rip out nails
From the waterlogged boards

The sounds we make of an evening
Like bulls having nightmares
Chinese geese eating minnows

When the heat of the day
Is dark and quiet
And on its haunches
I let out my nurse's thread

What titties she has
Soft as sacks of sand on the levee

A bird puts a hole in the radiator
With his beak
When we hit him at night

One morning a snake sucks the eggs
And one evening I climb the tree
Set fire to the nest

messengers bring me no messages
teachers do not raise your voices like a flag I will raise my hand
like a fox looking up on a hill in the afternoon
I will smell you out
in the dead water where my tongue is held captive
if it is to be silent it will be silent in my mouth
where darkness and the scent of roses come out like smoke
I smoke alone in the woods to be smoking so I can say
I have smoked
even after the maggots have entered the quick
I call out madam
shall I undress you for a fight the wars are naked that you wage tonight
in a bed as broad as a battlefield
as a sword I mock the fallen with
and the angel says what is dead is dead
I dream what I dream

FREEDOM, REVOLT, AND LOVE

They caught them.
They were sitting at a table in the kitchen.
It was early.
They had on bathrobes.
They were drinking coffee and smiling.
She had one of his cigarillos in her fingers.
She had her legs tucked up under her in the chair.
They saw them through the window.
She thought of his arms around her,
She thought of them stepping out of a bath
And him wrapping cloth around her.
He thought of her waking up in a small white building,
He thought of stones settling into the ground.
Then they were gone.
Then they came in through the back.
Her cat ran out.
The house was near the road.
She didn't like the cat going out.
They stayed at the table.
The others were out of breath.
The man and the woman reached across the table.
They were afraid, they smiled.
The others poured themselves the last of the coffee.
They burnt thier tongues.
They looked at them.
They didn't say anything.
The man and the woman moved closer to each other.
The round table was between them.
The stove stayed on and burned the empty pot.
She started to get up.
One of them shot her.
She leaned over the table like a schoolgirl doing her lessons.
They took her long grey socks
Put them over the barrel of a rifle
And shot him.
He went back in his chair, holding himself.
She told him her's didn't hurt much,
Like in the fall when everything you touch
Makes a spark.

CONSTANT STRANGER

1976

The title Manao tupapau *has two meanings:*
the young girl can be thinking of the ghost,
or the ghost is thinking about her.

PAUL GAUGUIN

Death and the Arkansas River

Walking from the killing place,
Walking in mud,
The bootsoles leave little hexes in the kitchen.

One summer there was a place
Where everyone chewed dirt in their supper.

It was a place like an attic
With a chest of orchids pressed in books.
Men cleaned their fingernails
In the moonlight.

Death let a bid.

And while everyone was in hipboots
Looking out for Death's forklift,
There was a shine on Death's loafers.
His poll tax was paid, so was his light bill.

In the winter Death runs snow tires on his truck,
He makes long hauls at night.
Death pays the best wage,
He can keep in touch on his two-way,
He's paid all the Laws off.

Death can afford whatever he wants.

If you listened to the ground, you'd hear
Thunder coming like a train on the tracks.
And Death would signal ahead
That the half-dollar you stole to flatten
You lifted from your father's eye.

Death dances a slow boogie.
Even the awkward can follow
Where he leads.

In my life Death has asked me
To trade dogs,
While others have asked me
How he combed his hair.

Everytime Death gets a Cadillac
He wants to fight.
He wants to run the front door,
He wants cooking that will remind him of home.

If you try to forget
Death ties a string around your finger.

Regrets and warnings
To those who don't know what's cooking
When Death's bread rises
Out of its grave.

Death, for instance, was looking
To coldcock my brother.
My brother thought he pulled a fast one.
He played the radio and drank whiskey.
He raised hell
With women already married.

Do you know anyone that's got the best
Of Death?

Some say you can keep an eye
Out for Death,
But Death is one for fooling around.

He might turn up working odd jobs
At your favorite diner.
He might be peeling spuds.

Death is fond of the double entendre.

I for one am reminded of butterflies,
Snow blowing off pines.

Death controls the journeys,
The fare and the gender,
And Death is around you
Like a lock and dam.

So don't let Death catch you
Listening to the ground, even a place
That sounds like home.

It could be Death
Would file a quitclaim deed.
Death holds a quiet title
To the land your loved ones walked.

Even if you couldn't hear
The Sound would carry
Like a truck on a bridge, like a flower
Given at a ball, a sound in place,
The tradewind called Death, gentle
As children in their night clothes
Fighting with pillows, so quiet
Not a soul is wakened.

Directions from a Madman

Tonight you better listen because I am going to tell you
What you always wanted to hear.
All you bad hombres better take a deep breath.
I shit you not.
This is the night of nights.
Take a chance on love.

Old friends making up after 200 years
Of the fine and high lonesomes
I've seen my days.

Years now I've been walking these goddamn hills,
No telling how many lies.
The love spreads its shade into the valley of your gut,
A houseboat tied to its dead man.

The love gets shed of its hard ways,
Making a bed for a stranger.

The coast is clear on my love.

Each dawn love is a captain
Without a ship.
The only instrumentation
The sad and imaginary
Sound of his voice, love with its own
Words for music, the low light
Of a fairly good star.

Love can be taken for a semaphore.
SOS, the man is wounded in his sex.

You run off into the ditch of your past
And love spins like a wheel.

An old man comes by looking for pop bottles,
He finds your love.

Evenings a young girl arrives on a tractor
To brush-hog your love.

The mouth of your love is dry,
Nowhere to roam.
Your love is in the heyday of its youth,
A sorry bastard.
Your love works off in the hills like corn liquor.

Some say love is the light form of the moth,
Others say the dark.
I say a cat always tries to cover its own shit.
Who can say about love?
There's no telling when love can have a spell.

When you were young you said you never had any
Time for love,
Now the moon no longer tows at your blood.

Your love may lie lost and deep.
You may have to hire a water witch
To break a stick
And hunt for your love.

The first day of your love
You can bag your limit, four pairs of mourning doves.

Your love goes to the centerline of the branch
But you desire all the water.

There is no way of knowing
What I tell you about love is true.
Go by the signs.

So many men try to go down into
The shaft of their loves.
They dig into the lode of their love.
They come out of their mines,
Sick to death of their love,
So much for the limping men
Heading home with a shovel on their shoulder.

The house with no woman breeds lice.

Summer nights you draw
Blood from your love, bites itching while you sleep
Alone, without lotion or a fan,
Pain becomes your lover.

This won't last long.

Never you mind, by and by
We keep returning to the early days of our love,
When it shivered like a lake.
We know what shines from the mountain now:
The roofs of chickenhouses,
Sad birds on their way to Taiwan.

Our hearts slide off the beds
And prowl down the hallway,
Looking for another door to enter.

Like a boot on a clutch,
My love is steady,

Motivating through misery or mystery,
Hitting on all six.

What you go and have in the night
Is strictly your business.
Keep it on the road.

Finally, scared to death,
You account for your worthlessness,
And the loving to death
Of your own spitting image.
You're glad to know there's enough money
To put your love through school.

For soon it will be time to go
From the one love to another,
Time to buy a home on wheels
And honeymoon until death.

Then our love comes back to us
In strange clothes,
Her breasts ever so fine and high,
Our own love ready to betray us.

I have outlined love for anybody's book.

I have compared my love to the lazy
And to the crazy girls of years past,
To a faithless truck, to a spell, a moth, and a bottle,
To the hell bending moon, if you could tell,
And to a captain—if not a ship,
And in ways you'll come to know not too soon,
But I have never compared my love for you.

The First Twenty-Five Years of My Life

I met my father in a library in Memphis, Tennessee.
Bees flew out of the sun.

The strange country of childhood,
Like a dragonfly on a long dog chain.

This is the signature of the doctor, the money from home.
Before, when each star was a minnow
Dying naturally in a tub, we slipped off
From the others in our boats.

We left in the mornings.

The mosquitoes were in our coffee
And the snakes broke ice for our journeys.
The crickets wanted to die.
Your head was in my lap.
We trolled twelve poles.

Like the owls you bulldozed into the woods,
I called you many names.
Your voice was a log under the water,
Blue channel there.
Do not reach into this wood.

Butterflies hover under the bridge before death,
I take my shade in the borrow pits of the moon.

Cloud making shadow, I cover my body now buck naked
With light, calling my name in my sleep.

The Boathouse

His raincoat. His soup. His bullets. His calendars
With women without clothes, spark plugs and u-joints for sale.
There was a wire in his jaw, a muscle gone in the thigh,
Mildew in his tarps. The corks walked out of the empty pints
Like crawdads in a dead man's pot.

A dead child, too, under the house the mouth
Full of trebles, glass under the nails. He sleeps
In a gunnysack near the same place I died.

I wanted his legs.

Some other things I know, I am dreaming
I am still alive, setting skunk traps around the cove.
Warm water drips out of my ear,
Dark water that's been there a long time.

I've carried it for years, like a relic from a holy swim.
I ache in my neck, red as watermelon meat.

In the village of the past there is a cathouse sinking with mystery.
My neck is full of places
Where the river rats bit and left their fever.
Guitars turn towards the corners
Of the uneven rooms, my Arkansas homes, like empty lamps
With long wicks.

Hum with the dumb and hope nobody has your number.

Catfish wade themselves in the shallows, men in hipboots
With flashlights looking for me, stroking my hair with their blunt hoes
When the others aren't looking, turning the topsoil
Of their own land and dead, their dreams like screwdrivers.

Groundcover grows over and from the boards and ropes,
And there is no menu to eat after a rain. The banks don't want you
To build your little raft for death.

Those lag bolts once sunken deep come out now like tree frogs
And will no longer slip in and hold. Lick
The side of the boathouse, it tastes like a snapshot, spilled blood.

Come now and take the back way, the lost road
To the old fine water where the boathouse is kept
By her dead men.

Blue Yodel of the Desperado

after Pier Paolo Pasolini

I went to New York to leave you
Flowers of blood and light
In the Picture Shows I dreamed
Of your birthmark in the shape of a pistol

There you were alone and asleep
In your bed like a lake
And your Father watched over you
And his land

As always you slept naked
With the window wide open

The down on the small of your back
Was like dust on the guitar
Holding up the pane

I believe you left strawberries
And a glass of water
Untouched on the desk
There were the ashes hidden in your drawers
And your fingers smelled like backwater

Did your Mother know
That you slept with a sachet of poison
In your scapula

You cast your shadow like dice

How many of the wealthy short-haired women
Wishing you woe

Did you visit by the dark of the moon
When they paid you a call did you allow them
To hold your hand

I wanted to ride down to where I come from
On an Appaloosa
And take you away for good
I wanted to tie your hands with my belt
And watch you stare at the campfire
In the mountains not saying a word

So it was in this dream
I gave you things to eat
So you would speak to me

I watched you grow silent and hungry
Like the middle of the night

When your leg was in pain
I saw the black seam of your stocking
Running down the side of the mountain like a creek
I put the whiskey down and listened

The first time you wept like a wooden boat
Was just launched
The sounds of the night
A dance you thought
You never wanted to attend
You were there and sullen enough to take the corsage
Without ever looking at it
As if waiting for me to do something with the pin

All that you dreamed
I would do to you I did

At dawn you said you were thirsty
Even the darkest night must give in

When you spoke
It was hard for me to say a word
I couldn't open my mouth
It was like being underwater

A bird came from nowhere
And lited on your wrist
In the dream it drank from your palm
You stroked its throat and I could have sworn
Your finger was on the trigger

The wind came up you looked away
You were always cold
I gave you a red chasuble I took off some Father
And one or the other the wind or you
Waved it in my face like a muleta
That morning there was still a moon
That was the way you parted your hair

When luck and money ran out
I deserted you somewhere in South America
It was on a Sunday I remember

I met up with this English woman with plenty
That very night
While she was in the powder room
I went back to the hotel
Stole her rubies
And stowed away on the first rig I saw
A ship full of wild horses
Bound for America

I hid below with the animals that were
To be broken at sea
More than once I put my teeth to the tapaderas
Hunting the musk of your white feet
And to think your legs are still
To be reckoned with

I thought about how a ruby would look on you
A stud for your belly
I remembered you stuck-up
And given over to what you wore

I got sick on the voyage

I had nightmares about the vessel
Going down with the horses

The smoking lamp was lit by a lad overboard
And we struck an iceberg in the Caribbean
But I knew that wasn't right
It must have been a hurricane or buccaneers

My sleep was like a long swim

I was rescued by nine women wearing black patches
Who claimed to be holding you up for ransom
Your chaperones who used to bow their heads
And say their beads on the patio
Came to bay like bloodhounds
Around the juniper under your window

I dreamed they brought you aboard
To commend you to the sea
I dreamed you rode off to your wedding sidesaddle

And the only thing you let between your legs
Was the melancholy blood of the cello

You with your instinct for music and danger
Always without escort

To this day I draw that knife
From the eyes
Of the target your shoulders
I place what is left of the afternoon
In the care of your hands
That have been kissed by so many suitors
You keep the bees in the mirror

Your calves two letters that go unsealed
Not to mention a word about a dress
Your name a night without sleep

I only went to New York to go to the movies
I got good and drunk in the dark
I couldn't get rid of the pigeon's blood to save my life

Someone really had it in good for me
At first I didn't know who it was
The killer gave you away

You were the one that was
Sending me those ten dollar bills in the mail
You paid my way into the show every night

I knew the Law was watching me
Someone tipped them off
It was Sundays and Cybele

When the movie came on
I was writing down getaway plans
In the back of that Spanish man's book

They thought they had me

I leaned over and asked the woman sitting beside me
Lady would you save my place
I want to get a drink

To make it look good
I had to leave the book and your letters
They thought I was with her
And coming right back

I foxed them alright

I only went to New York to go to the picture shows
I bought a fifth of Gypsy Rose and a horse
And left the country
I got good and drunk

As I was leaving I remembered
The handful of dirt I picked up
The cold ground you slept on

And when I got to where I was going
The place I came from
I needed a knife to clean my fingernails.

In These Rooms

after Bernardo Bertolucci

At some time the dead must come back for a few days in the country.
For now is the season when the living
Let darkness spread its butter over their hair,
And soon the rain will be poured
Into the slime we call our eyes,
Poured down the deep sockets where the slugs roam, the branches
      wayward with sap.

It will be distributed soon
Like ointment by nymphomaniacs.

At some time the dead will be recognized
As high school sweethearts who went mad in the barns,
Old girl friends dressed like a night in the forest,
Dressed in the ruins of mist and sensitive flyrods.

Nevertheless, the dead, who only intend to stay a short while.

In the Hotel of the dead there is an age-old policy against these things:

Wives and old coaches,
Ouija boards and certain cheeses,
Belts long enough to reach overhead pipes,
For now is that time of year when the hardy
Start coughing.

The management has its own garden of Thumbelina
To solace the bereaved
And in a certain time of year
Mistresses are taken to weed the grounds of wreaths.

The critics have called it a hospital where the doctors are forbidden to cut,
A whorehouse mopped with sanitary napkins,
And a convent with a trapdoor,
A door leading to a cemetery, a library of dreams.

The Hotel of pencils, loose lips, and small titties.

Where there is a constant groaning in the adjoining room,
Like an owl in the woods.

In these rooms death grows
On the shady side of the mountains like ferns
And that isn't right either
Because death is also sagegrass, belladonna, and rose hips,
Really, can you imagine a Hotel for the dead.

An inn for cold biscuits,
Windows fogged over from evening
Constitutional spiked with saltpetre.

A Hotel like a greenhouse without dirt.
Rooms and rooms of crumbs and starlight,
Drawers hard to loosen but filled with shoelaces and dark glasses,
Bibles thick as pigmeat.

There is a night man with a box of hideous keys
And a prowler admitted on sight
Who uses black gloves and spools of electrical tape.

Growing near a fountain on the mezzanine
The tree of everlasting life, wilting
And surrounded by the spoors of patron saints.

In the Hotel of the dead the bellboys must be tipped
But your suitcases are light as newspaper.

The keyholes are rusted from tears
And caulked with contact lenses.

The ceiling is an illusion of twine
And suffering from psoriasis.

The elevator is manned by a woman with pliers.

From there the postcards of the great masters have been sent in the mails
And returned, slipped under the door,
A homosexual must have tried on each shirt
And kept all twelve, a maid must have believed in voodoo,
A seamstress must have grown crazy.

A Hotel like a greenhouse of dark light bulbs
Where the wind is like a fireplace,
Water coming to a boil.

And the mirrors in the bathrooms with their broken constellations of pus.

The hours in ambush like medicine in a dark bottle,
Whereas the weekends are pillow fights in a Catholic orphanage.

Hotel of love and love the crack of light,
Hotel of tragic books and gladness to be alone.

A lamentable good time,
A pair of pants mourning your swollen body.

Impotent professors losing weight on french toast,
Old yolk hard as plastic
Locked in the dirty water of the forks.

And nothing is left of feathers but rich soil and points of blue glass.
Something is made something is lost.

In the Hotel of the dead guests are still made welcome.
Rooms opening up to a balcony with a view are still available,
Rooms that are shared, rooms that are forgotten.
In the Hotel of the dead guests clean their own windows with beautiful rags
and Benedictine.

In the Hotel of misfortune the guests cannot strike a match.

And death has a secret motor
Furnishing power to the revolving door.
A taxi is hailed, a hearse will arrive.

But the local market is kind enough to make deliveries to the old.

Sacks of magazines with soggy bottoms,
Cans of dogfood, ninety percent meat,
The pensioners can warm on the radiator, stew spiced with gunpowder.

And for those too old to open cans, there are frozen fish, laxatives, and
denture creme.
Silence, the tonic of death, which is peddled off as a miracle drug.

In the Hotel of the dead, something smells. Hotel of love,
Like a woman with an infection.

In the Hotel of the dead, there is a lobby
Where the miserable can wait,
There is a young man, blind from birth, suddenly closing an accordion.

Eyelids Noticed Only in the Seventh Minute of Twilight

after Bernardo Bertolucci

Children trying on gloves. Children in the garden of their retinas.
Children forgetting
The mystery of the ambushed clock, the mirror
Weighing down the thigh like a heavy knife.
Children like bullets in pain. Children
Like a cemetery of dreams, ships running guns.
Held to the veranda by a ghost and blackbird pie,
Held to the dark by invisible binoculars. Children
In the garden of the moon, provocateurs of meat.

Beautiful, or at least with a face,
Like a veil dropped over a pencil
Held by Robert Desnos.

Their underwear like fast rabbits,
Their little slips like spaces to rent for boats.

Blind faith in mud.

Children who drink milk and piss in the midst of the fox.
Hair like fog in a barn,
Voices like armpits, beehives in wheelchairs.

The strategy of the locked door.

Children warning, children sucking, children spitting,
Allegory of love, whistles of dust.

Buried pool tables and glue for a past.

The bodies continue, like a river, like a bottle with no pop.
Entries into a room heated by wood, midnights of plows,
Allegory of love, where these children are dressed for bed
In stones and silk.

Children imagined by Robert Desnos.

Bodies cold as rainwater
And poetry rotting like a horse. And poetry lonely as teeth.
Lonely as hats and sisters.

Flies in love.

And finally children sucked up like dust in a vacuum, and that isn't all.

Blown-up like stars or a balloon in a supermarket.

The breath beat out of them like the ticking
Of an iron watch,
The last days of Robert Desnos, impending moons
Threatening earth and its ferns, the last days
Of one Robert Desnos, buttons held up to the light,
The last minutes of the poet
Transparent as broth.

Hours that have come, hours that have followed.
The sentries of night. Thermometers
Advertising wine, nailed to an orchard. The olives of love,
Draughts to be taken for dreams, harvest
Of peaches bitten by frost, stained hands
Holding the face briars, all these devices
For intercepting the pigeons of this Robert Desnos.

Not so many days, sick man's lashes.
Not so many dreams.

Encore.

The marrow's river where the children may swim,
Where there is time
For wickedness and sleep.

Your bed is a sad cafe.

Morning, tables you've drunk from, watching women
Watching themselves curl their hair with spit,
Your childhood like an ax that slips from your hands,
Landing in the thigh of your wife, your children
Shadows covered by shade trees.

Death has been called
A run-down mansion, a drink before dinner, a group
Of musicians, it has been called an unfortunate thing,
The sun going down, the dark rider of evening.

Robert Desnos, dead and warm,
Entering a black hole in space where no light breaks,
Leaving this epoch for another, as if it were a woman.
Robert Desnos, night without dreams, plotting the vertices of . . .

Legacy of the stillborn's caul, limber as an accordion,
Incandescent, delightful, full of purpose like a house on a lake,
Clear as marbles, this elegy of thumbs,
As if love was a common grave and death a child. Encore.

Legacy of one who loved
A woman in a blue dress, a color
Only noticed in the seventh minute of night.
And legacies of those who brought sorrow for a short while,
And then were forgotten, terrible entreaties which will long remain,
Sprouts the big aphids of poetry continue to chew.

Like someone waking up alone, someone never speaking, Robert Desnos,
Trapped light, existing like dusk and love,
The likes of which we will not see, physical but not optical.

Robert Desnos whose name I promise not to mention again
Because it proves the theories of sorrow,
Because it leads to children, dreams, and this.

No Sign of Life: A Tragic Gag of Raymond Radiguet

after Jean Cocteau

Although my father's mistress called me Camille
she was not a silkworm
but a maker of silk

And so the old myths of regret are reborn
without their heroes ever knowing it
gloom is a starfish lodged in the groin

In these rooms I have listened
to a black horse tapping
over a grave

I have seen doors
through which Death comes and goes
picked clean

Paris my five hundred francs
have disappeared in your filthy river
my blood hung and in bunches like a bananatree

Long artillery of night
commanded by the lieutenants of youth
eyes half-open like wounds

I am a lie who always tells the truth
an ass bearing the Lord of dreams
an enormous parrot with no sign of life

Slim boat of the dead and soon to be dead
I have drawn my mouth on your canvas
in ink that goes away with moonlight

All my friends pretend you are dying
because I'm only pretending to weep
with no sign of life

The Forgotten Madmen of Ménilmontant

after Jacques Prévert

Do not look sadly at days gone by
days below days like a river running under the stars
Do not listen to the blues
or speak often with priests
Do not think the rich women enrolled in the college of nightfall
will always smell the same way

Everytime the tree works the leaves dream

Everytime I carve the dead wing my name
in the dark lamp of the outhouse
I said everytime I cut my name
in the old wood rotten as a tugboat
I know I am always with you

Everytime the schoolboy's bad moon
dowses blood from the virgin's stone thighs
I know I am handsome and young and drunk
eternal as a weed

It will not smell the same

Everytime I open a bottle of wine
and see a snake doctor under my bed
I know there is something coming and eternal
like taking off a white coat over the body of the dead

Poets have done this before

Poets have made love and gathered at the cheap joints
they've cut their fingers toasting one another's death

Poets have made love
and remained thick
they've gotten cold feet at the crucial moments
when left alone with the students with sad eyes

Do not die in the wintertime
for there is no okra or sailboats

It will not smell the same
that twig of blood or the chiffonier

Do not listen to hunting dogs in autumn
or tie yellow flies for the small lips of desperate friends

Poets have done this before
and they've wandered off alone and unheard of
to bury the caul of their own stillborn

Like a voice the odor has changed

Dust under the hooves of a horse
running side by side with the fog
a book in the hands of a fool

Cheese and fish and spinsters
are the body of the poet
for the poet does not eat black bread
he gives it to the poor

Everytime a mare throws a foal in an exile's country
I know I am with you
a gun in the hands of a fool

The poet forgets in remembrance of you
he is the lunatic's left hand man
on Sundays the acolyte of the moon
he is night following other nights
the eyes of the blind
the stranger your wife leaves with
when you're still talking with your youth
stowed away on the ship of death
and it will not smell the same

Everytime I see a young man
tuck his knife back in his vest
I want to say forget it and drink

At the Moment of Death

Girls kiss in the street.

The cucumbers swell on the vine
And the lame cheerleader
Is let off early after the game.

Someone is thinking: are there enough
Smokes to go around,
Who will go for the coffee,
Will the ringing bother the others
On the party line?

No one can get through
To the house of the bereaved.

The coon dogs are lonely tonight,
But not the priest.

I am still down
In Arkansas, still drinking
Charter and branch water,
Looking for a fight.

The undertaker creeps out of his daughter's room.
The janitor beats a spider with a broom.

A Black Cat Crossed the Road I Was Born On

So many have passed on.

The mailboxes keel over from the weight
Of the catalogues and almanacs
No one has claimed.

On my day off, I've thought
Of coming by with posthole diggers,
But Death knows my ass
From a hole in the ground.

The people on the roofs are drinking
But they don't brew that beer anymore.
Death is no chauffeur,
Nevertheless, he holds it in the road.

When Death beats his child
Nobody listens.

For two bits I would pull over
And lay down in the long legs of the past,
But Death is two-timing me.

Death can lace his boots
Before you can spit.

He can get all the ham off the bone.

Some people I knew hired Death by the hour.
He brought in good money every week.

My mother used to beg,
"Son, don't write about Death,

We'll cross that ditch soon enough."
I ask you to have respect for the dead.

This is the place alright,
Like a flower in the night
Death drifts over the garden
Of our shoulders,
Like a boat with no eyes,
No place for the oars, the hands.

Death has a high voice,
An auctioneer to oversee
All your worldly possessions.

He is selling a bed
That belonged to your father,
He is coming in low,
Dumping your brother's boots
In the enemy's field.

Death runs a little side show
And you always buy a ticket.

There is no doubt in my mind,
Death is a bad hog.

Death ties everything down with guy-wires.
It sends you a message every month
To keep you in the black.

The Church has a record of your birth
But Death keeps its own dossier.

When the moon is pulling its blood
From its many lovers,

And Death is caterwauling with the cold fish-
Bone in its mouth, shedding all
Its skins and secret light I, like you,
Set out a dish of milk.

Time Forks Perpetually toward Innumerable Futures in One of Them I Am Your Enemy

I am going to die.

Friends who made good,
Friends who did not,
I am going
Down into the Egypt of your sex,
The lands of your mystery and death.

Do you still want me
To find you
Somebody to love?

I cruise through the delta of your love,
Paradise on Sunday,
Cold as ice on Monday.
A hundred pounds of it on the tongs,
A butterfly at the center.

Going home I cross the bridge
And throw a bottle out the window,
Hit all my friends in the head.

The crickets under the straw
Like old folks spitting in a paper sack

Now my life the Sphinx
Laid by slaves,
My death the promised land.

A light rain falling, a split tongue
And sad eyes, no lie,
I've got you by the tongue.

I park my Cadillac outside your temple of madness.
You are worshiped there.

Look at your face, swollen from sleep.
Are you waiting for me
To unwind you from your last clothes,
Do you want me
To bury my long ship in your heart?

Your lineage like gravesites for the stars,
Way stations for great dreamers.

There is a six foot rattlesnake
Asleep in the birdhouse.
Are you taking crumbs to the warblers tonight?

Death is an isthmus, you can get there on foot.
But love had made its island.

What of the young?
I hunt them down,
Good winds in the desert,
Blue eggs in the junipers.

Tell it:

There is a fear without age or Christ
That goes through us
Like moonshine in a coil.

There is a stranger
You see more and more of
Every year, he is silt in the riverbed.
And the water tables of your mystery
Rise to their final levels,
The spitting image of your death.

If you leave a girl of your own,
Tell her to run off with your enemy's son.
If you have a son,
Tell him to run off with your enemy's daughter.
And if you have no enemies, inquire of me,
Your troubles are just beginning.

FROM "WITH THE APPROACH OF THE OAK THE AXEMAN QUAKES"

1977

from *Fifty Contemporary Poets: The Creative Process*
edited by Alberta T. Turner

from

With the Approach of the Oak the Axeman Quakes

There is a monastery in Arkansas. I was there for some years. My mother sent me there to school after my father died. There, I learned I was an orphan.

One summer I returned to the abbey with my wife. The monks asked us to come help with a summer camp for orphans. Every night the Brothers, the hundred boys, and I would swim in the Arkansas River. My wife would sit on the dock and drink wine Brother Tobias made. She would sketch until the mosquitoes came.

On these long swims to the island there was no telling what we might speak of. At the time I was envisioning a film which still isn't finished, *Deathward*. It was nearly my birthday; I would be a quarter of a century old.

I decided to begin shooting. The scenario was finished. This is the scene: I am in the water filming a monk in a boat. He is rowing from far away toward me. In the bow there is a draped casket. For the sake of rhythm I have the selection of Bach I will be using on the soundtrack. I hear this with the earphone. With the bare ear I hear commercial fishermen beyond the point, cussing the moon, listening to country music.

While we are filming, my wife is putting the one hundred boys to sleep. Suddenly, a monk runs to the edge of the water. He has brought bad news. One of the students, the son of a local wine maker, has drowned.

We are upriver about half a mile. It happened near buoy 25. We go down there. Some of the monks and fishermen are wading the sandbar. It is too dark to look for a body. But the boy is found.

Death is an old dog-trader—and like one, that night I make a title for a poem I will write a year later on the eve of my twenty-sixth year.

We traveled back in the fog. It had been a while since I'd been in the main channel. I looked up and saw a huge sphere of concrete. I found out it was a nuclear reactor. Near the water level hung the remains of a large flathead catfish. *Arkansas* Nuclear One, said the sign. A fisherman had written: The Devil's Machine.

I had a year with this poem; everyday in the woods at work I would say it. I never wrote a word down until I had it right in my mind. It became what they call a floater. That's a work song, a chant. Once I thought it sounded right, and undramatic, I wrote it down without changing a word.

Men sing when they work, or at least they used to. I'm liable to talk to myself. I try to get at the taproot of poetry, of that force drawing things upward. A paradox always—even on Saturday mornings when I might be a little low-down and hungover, but clear as a bell. I talk to myself. There is a poem that goes:

> Each dawn love is a captain
> Without a ship.
> The only instrumentation
> The sad and imaginary
> Sound of his voice, love with its own
> Words for music, the low light
> Of a fairly good star.

At the risk of sounding parabolic, I will let this go as technique. Mean and sing.

Really, I visualize the dead as well as the living. I visualize *you* whom I will never know. We are constant strangers. I imagine *you*, I stare at *you* when I write. And to think, you will never know, will never hear of those people I can no longer call anonymous. People close to me have said: I don't understand what you are talking about, but I know what you mean.…

Poetry sometimes is like going along in a big rig with no one else on the roads, no smoke, no stops by the wayside, going on with no cargo, the radio quiet, only the sound of your own voice trying to get in touch.

I really don't know if poetry can be paraphrased, set to music, or what have you. Maybe so. Many times the poem ends up down on the ground, surrounded by strangers. I believe that the metaphorical imagination can be authenticated by the cinema. I know that my wife, an artist, has "irrigated" some of her canvases with my poems.

Every two folks have their own way of loving. The poet and the poem know what they like. When a particular kind of loving is adapted, you are getting into a different and strange country.

Now when I was younger, I wrote all the time. I had time to kill. A man has to earn a living; writing has become more special to me. When the poet is young he tries to satisfy himself with many poems in one night. Later, the poet spends many a night trying to satisfy the one poem. My poetry is no longer on a journey, it has arrived at its place.

Then the poet realizes it is midnight, he is alone, and his love is with someone else. What he wanted to sing, what he wanted to mean—someone else has done it. While the poet worried what kind of nails to use, how to fasten down his love, another has hit them on the head and driven them deep....

✳✳✳

You know there is no other poet on earth like me. I know there is no other poet on earth like you. We need to be read. This is the theme of poetry, now.

In my early days I was a student of all forms. I learned everything and nothing. I practiced the katas of poetry. I listened to the blues. Having the equilibrium of a poet, I kept falling in love. Now, I believe content and form are not so much in opposition—as many would have us believe. They are one reality, in appearance as well as essence. If you do not know this, no progressive *study* of the art will provide you any insights. The poem eats when it is hungry, sleeps when it is tired.

In getting to the reasons for writing a poem, I suppose the poet can call the reader into the woods and lose him, or he can let him find his own way. I would say, though, in describing the poem we return to the place of poetry, the poet, and to the poetry itself. The following paraphrase from pages 46 and 47 of Daisetz Teitarō Suzuki's *Zen Buddhism and Its Influence on Japanese Culture* [now *Zen and Japanese Culture*, pages 70 and 71] is a good way of sending the poet on a wild-goose chase—which he may need from time to time.

> There was a great poet and teacher of the art. One day another poet came to the city to see him. He came to learn. The master said, "As I observe, you seem to be a master of poetry yourself; pray tell me what school you belong to, before we enter into the relationship of pupil and teacher."
>
> The unknown said, "I am ashamed to confess that I have never learned the art."
>
> "Are you trying to fool me? I am a great teacher, and I know my judging eyes and ears never fail."
>
> "I'm sorry to defy your honor, but I really know nothing."
>
> This resolute denial on the part of the visitor made the great poet think for a while, and he finally said, "If you say so, it must be so; but still I am sure you are a master of something, though I do not know of what."
>
> "If you insist, I will tell you. There is one thing of which I can say I am complete master. When I was still a boy and writing my poems, the thought came upon me that as a poet I ought to

in no circumstances be afraid of death, and I have grappled with the problem of death now for some years, and finally the problem of death ceased to worry me. How does that sound?"

"Exactly! I am glad I made no mistake in my judgment. For the ultimate secrets of poetry also lie in being released from the thought of death. I have trained ever so many hundreds of my pupils along this line, but so far none of them really deserve the final certificate for poetry. You need no technical training, you are already a master."

I don't think it matters how a poet plants his garden; it is the quality of the yield which matters. Just like the stars, there are so many things to be said about poems and their poets. I can say I don't want my work to be obscure or vague—I also must say that sometimes I don't mind this trait in the work of others. I am not content in just *suggesting* things by the use of words, I want to *show* the origins, the metaphors of reality, the free movement of the spirit. Poetry is a body, all right, but in spirit it is the function which oftentimes creates the organ.

Jean Cocteau said mystery exists only in precise things—people in their situations, situations in people. Because I believe the visionary life has nothing to do with a necessarily transcendent existence, I *like* most of the poetry I *read*. I believe most poets know *this* is the world; and when you try to lead a special life or write a special poetry, you are dancing with an imaginary partner at a meaningless dance to which you have invited yourself and no one else.

So I think the visionary life is commonplace for the poet, the hair on his head, the pain in his rotting teeth. And I think there is a fear of all this good poetry. The spokesmen and spokeswomen of various constituencies of poetry are on their bulldozers, clearing away perimeters around a vast forest of poetry. This is a way of laying claim. You know what happens. They all meet in the center; everyone else is gone.

I don't believe in a tame poetry. When poetry hears its own name, it runs, flies, swims off for fear of its own life. You can bet your boots on that. Jean Cocteau said a poet rarely bothers about poetry. Does a gardener perfume his roses?

Truthfully, it is the lure of the other fields, of other forces which draw me into a poem, not the techniques of a self-conscious poetics. A book like *The Secret Life of Plants* would have more influence on my poetry, add more in explaining and understanding the other systems of poetry, than would certain texts.

Every poet has a field of force not presently understood. Someone with no experience with poetry over the last thirty years says he is confused by "Death and the Arkansas River."* If I had the time, I would take him with me somewhere. I would give him another poem to read from one of the ten books. The truly confused are good and fair to deal with. Twisted minds are another species of folks.

A carpenter can tell you how a table is made, but can a medium joining hands with us over this table tell us what it is? Hug a tree.

We go back to the poetry, the poet. I see a figure in the field. There is genuine moonlight shining on his crowbar. He is prying stumps out of his ground. Poetry busts guts.

* See pages 289–291 for the final version of "Death and the Arkansas River."
—Ed.

I was driving Miss Nevus down a lowroad
in the dead of winter
the haze rising out of the kiln of her blouse
like breath in a meadow
the small animals crossing the road at night
swooning in the headlights of the black car a V-8 mudfish
that rode low to the ground like a nasty pair of bluejeans
the song on the radio was something
the Prince of darkness could swallow
I wanted to grind charcoal into fine powder like a lens maker
I wanted the soot that looked purple at night
to pry into the flesh of the snow apples
I thought about setting fire to the cold fields
I wanted her tongue to stick to the mirror
and the owl buried deep in the head with an odor of blood
lisps like a female prisoner speaking in her sleep
taboo
something flying up to the side
an invisible horse that reared up on the other side of the fence
a little cyclone of mystery
crazy like a girl looking at the moon in the water
with thoughts of tangerines and a fading light
a girl with the cold-blooded eyes of a lizard
that goes for the fingers in the crevice of the cliff
a girl with a streak of meanness
like the dark lateral line of fish
who can feel death through the water
and maneuver by the sound of dust settling on land
there are vibrations in the weeds before dawn
like a rattling of dishes in the widow's parlor
like a crust of bread which gives away a visitor
there are faraway voices that come from beyond

the constellations we have not named
strange noises of light that quiver like tropical slime
that arrive through the bedroom window
when the sons and daughters are into the woods of one another
there comes a knowledge of the deaf who dream of tentacles and beaks
a sediment which forms around the tracks
where the dead have often ridden together
really I think of simple things
of ordinary acts and nights
that take place in the desolate minds of the very common
words like water or a pile of branches
gestures with the rhythm of plankton
and the heartbeat of birds and hooves
the steady growl of the wildcat about to pounce
and smooth running cars
hitting on all cylinders
with rearseats that can sound like Tarzan's monkey
I think of the intimate steps the dancer can make
bold as the letters of the stonecutter's inscriptions
that beautiful weapon the knife an instrument of peace
the calligraphy of the seed and feed lists
the crow on the horizon you see in the eyes of the Trappist
who has gone so long without sleep
broken glass perseverant lips the apostrophes of the man in the fire tower
the woman who will drown herself
touching the inscrutable fragment not the statue
I think of the simple things of the spirit
the last rites of the snow
and the lovers who go to bed with a child in mind
and when they wake it is so
should she plait her hair with warnings
I will forget my vagueness in the midst of the rose
should she remember my ugly face which brought her to ruin
I will live in the old bell like a vine and a burden

I will envision the desert's laments
when the going gets rough I'll take my eyes off the road
I'll look at the body of my passenger like a small ship underway
the crazy one with eyelids of semblances
who can camouflage herself with shivers and the iridescence of fish
who can utter milt and seaweed
I think of the simple girls from the country
who can get out of their clothes as fast as a thoroughbred
and a sailfish
I go down the road dreaming drunk as a coot
when she says to slow down boy I think of a throat under siege
and the motto of a horn
I think of a pyramid and an hourglass a voice that gives off its own light
my life I love it
in the dark
under the water of my shadow music
my form
and substance lonely and blue as ever
I give away my deluded clothes
I fall by the wayside
only the stones for throwing
across the river
and the girl who transfigures the predator
know how I listen
for that boat full of melons and sorrow
alas was the word
they used in the old days
they had been friends in youth
I wandered through the hamlets
barefoot at times
a two-bit troubadour
going very deep in debt to the canebrakes
they called me fisherman then
and my pockets were full of blackbirds

I dipped the good snuff of the delta
with its boiled coffee and crawdads
the sailmaker sewed me tight pants
for my bandy legs
the gravedigger broke ground for my arbor
I took roses to the panther
twice a week I came in heat
I dragged a cottonsack full of books
up and down the levee
like a litter the Indians used for the sick
and wounded
oh well the cook mammas jingled
their cans full of fishhooks
they picked buckshot out of the churchhouse door
with carving knives
and used it
to sink their lines
and concocted bait
deep into everyman's blue hole
I am the ones who have arrived I am
delivered by the dark light of a thousand glowworms
that stand fast in the tree
suffering I know the spinning wheel the Negroes turn
I who take money from no one
with the touch of the virgin's crucifix
in the palm of the dispossessed werewolf
the query of firebirds blackberries and female tigers
creedless and risking my ship I go quite phallic
starting with the backwater of your corpus
I discover myself beyond the laws
aware of the ribald the sublime and the reckless
taking holy water leaks in the big river of unconsciousness
which flows elemental under my shack
taking my hounds and roosters all over again

I exist in the natural musk of the farmgirl seer
I exist in the miracles of the nebulous clitoris
I exist beyond symbols and two-bit concepts
beyond shadroe never accepted by the high class
I assume the skill of evangelical beasts the good and the bad as well
I fade away in my quivering limbs I fade away black
and lighthearted on the wild seas of what I want you to do
I utter in sad blossoms I admit the visitors with tears
I wait for the schoolgirl who waits for me
clear and strange I plot my garden in yours
I live in the sung root
of good-fortune and death on cue with the fodder
I as fierce as the dust on the rose
I loom in the hours where the dragon swims
I jump from the barns of wasps and castrated ponies
I dress like the holy spirit and smell just as bad
I stink with the night of the snake
I sleep with my arm around whoever is sleeping
I motley boy on the loose with the mad and the rabbits
I am taken for you at my age
I suffered and earned twelve dollars a day being a guide
I pivot like the runaway who sees his girl
I stride through the grass not nearly as good as you
I ride an old horse in the creek
I marry the unknown in the poolroom
I make out the great thighs of the shark
I undo my pants looking for trouble
I interpret dreams like Daniel I focus the bee
I tarnish
the mirror with slang and redeal the cards
like a sonneteer of chalk and sapphires
I glow with the venom of the lover
moving forever and ever shall be without antidote
I am the fair lead of the air's noose

I invade the gutter and Louvre
I strike deep in the drunken paws I link the naked
I atone for nothing but her pink plectrum the moon
I smile in the blackstrap syrup I blow like secret wind
it is as simple as that
sexual and frank
I tinge the bold juice naive and delirious I welcome strangers
I go down easy and solid like whiskey and found knives the Indians traded
I appear insane and on fire
I died in prison like Reich
I wear an ancient cape that trails like a maze without cause
I the hunted
I the mocked
I who carry the stones from one cemetery to another
I who was most certainly mad
once upon a time by contemporary standards
I a shadow among shadows
your chapters of faults in the valleys of death my stead
I a fake and a starfish
I who can hold the wounded hawk to my eye
without fear of losing it
I who bed down with your daughters and beg for their alms
I the liar
whose only curse is the sadness tying your lips
I who was the richest poet in town I who was always the only
I who never set foot in a city see what I mean
I whittle wings and whore with the beluga
I who know there is nothing for me beyond this world
I with enough friends to bury me
I who will go unread by the warrior caste
I who keep silent with the feather and no further retinue
I who deny the most noble truths because I dreamed them singular
I eat with the hogs and contend with the ages
I drink with the mighty clouds of joy out of Tishomingo

with a physique of pure lava
I side with the daffodils and the foetus
with a physique of a catch in tragic winter a keeshond on board
I say with a lava physique I pass bastard of frankincense
O stutter again friend of the ax
O draw a branch across your arm
O jelly of hell seldom on duty
O paradise riding a mule
O poets who sleep I write never never windswept and incredible
O orchards for now
O pasture in unison with a dozen naked women from Lemuria
O wreckage of milk and tiger lilies
O moon smooth as ever in the bull
the unworldly which is worldly and rain
the sadness habitual
I pass out in the wagon of cotton
I live for the day
with bruises in the lighthouse and the very scent of honey
steeped in blood
I say let this be a movie and you will live forever
in the beginning there was the sound of the word
and I spoke nothing of myself how long sister
say I told you
when you are gathered together
let each one take a line to himself
or herself or both
let no one read me alone
say I like the beautiful coal in the pulpit swamp
say I like the king snake
say I going round to your friend
say it again

A woman in walking town one end of town,
A man in driving town the other,
~~They~~ drink a either at and ~~look~~ at the stars ~~the~~ ~~[crossed out]~~ *watch*
til when the moon covers up.

She wants to say something   *a dollar*
But he ~~only~~ ~~first~~ asks for ~~a dollar~~ ~~with~~ some change.
                                              ~~to play~~

She plays ~~and~~ songs she never heard of before.
He's looking at her.

He says look, it's like this
She says No, it's isn't.

In a place no one wants to go to
But when you're there no one desires to leave

CRIB DEATH

1978

Duplications and variations of "Death and the Arkansas River" and "Fire Left by Travelers" appeared in more than one of Stanford's published volumes, including *Crib Death*. Both poems have been presented only once, elsewhere in this collection, unless an alternate version was available. — Ed.

One's country is a group of rivers that flow into the sea. The sea is death.
There you are . . . to die for one's country.

LUIS BUÑUEL

For the Dead: Pier Paolo Pasolini &
Rahsaan Roland Kirk

And the Living: Muhammad Ali &
Pharoah Sanders

Amaranth

There are no starfish in the sky tonight,
But there is one below your belly,
And there are cold evenings in your eyes.

If I could get to your house
I would look under the bed of your childhood,
The tongueless loafer without laces or eyes,
The cave of your young foot
With its odor of moon, its dampness
Coming from underground, your shoe
Which also bled and is now an island.

You have to remember these are the memories
Of a survivor, you have to remember.

You could be looking for clay to haul away,
Fill for the deep washouts of your love.
All your old loves, they bled to death, too.

Your hair is like a cemetery full of hands,
Fingers in the moonlight.

When you come down to the heart
Bring your posthole diggers and crowbar.
Do not set a corner, a fence won't last.
Do not bury our first child there,
Or set a post,
Although I have tasted blood on the lips of a stranger,
At night and in the rain.

A Woman Driving a Stake into the Ground at Midnight

God, I have not forgotten you
For sending all my children into your old iceboxes.

I remember that goat
You let them follow with a compass,
Those wooden wheels you let them roll
And break their first silence on.

I watched those beautiful kites you let them glide,
Their hearts all balls of string.

When they were young and unfucked
And old friends with the moon
Spreading its cream over their lips
As they slept, you came in
The window with the light
Like a cat on their necks.

You leave
When you want, the dark honey
Of their breath you store
In the catacombs of your lungs.

Alone and licked, their dreams
All rat-bitten and full of fever,
They remember your words,
Droppings on the white sheets.

Where are the dead?
In my arms, their panties pulled high,
Their eyes and teeth all small and even.

I remember your sadness, too.
A pan of wash water.
I threw it out in the chicken yard each evening.

I wanted my love to be an orchard,
Rows of thornless berries.
I wanted my love
To be death for the suffering.

Like you, I knew a woman once.
She was carrying a child.
One night she cut it
Out like a vine
With her husband's razor.

I didn't want you
To forget my love
Is a dark and rotten fruit on the ground,
A deathbed for your dreams,
And I don't know you, now,
Your sadness or your mark
On everything we bury.

Taking Your Life

The man's tongue laid down beside him when he slept.
The man did not know it.
He thought his tongue was safe and quiet
In the pillow of his mouth.
The man thought his tongue was his wife.

The man did not know his tongue
Dreamed of touching others,
Longing with pain, moaning with pleasure.

One night the man woke and had no voice.
He felt his mouth, saw that his tongue was gone.

He went through the bars looking for his tongue.
He wanted to drink, but he couldn't.
He wanted to sing, but he couldn't.
He envied the musicians.
He heard his tongue was with another.

He went home, sad and imaginary
With desire.
He dreamed he was a musician,
That his tongue heard him one night,
Fell in love with him,
Came back to live in his mouth.

This was a dream.

His own tongue, the soft root of his death.
It would fly
Out of its lair, light in a tree,
Cast its own shadow on the man.

The man in the darkness of his tongue,
The man with no voice, no lovers.

Strange Roads Before Light

At midnight I am alone
And my love is with someone else.
The moon is like a woman in a red dress
Standing on the beach.

I listened all evening.

All I heard was a one-legged boy
Looking for his coon dog.
He was looking at the moon, too.
It was like a plate with no supper.

And a route salesman in a saloon
Was looking at the moon.
It was a clock with twelve numbers,
But he had no arms to hold her.

And the child who was supposed to be
Practicing the piano
Was looking at the moon.
He was already thinking of a woman.
He wanted to sleep beside her,
Not with her. Odd, but not bad,
He thought the moon spilt the key to her room.

The woman blowing smoke in the dark,
Her fingers looking for the ashtray,
She thought the moon
Was a piece of stationery
In a drawer she would not open.
She would have written there was no moon,
That I am screwing somebody else,
Trying to remember your telephone number.

Lost Recipe

The water boiling rabbits and onions
Fogs up the windows of my house:

Why does the old fat woman
Let me come around here,
Drawing long words on her glass.

A woodwind solo,
She keeps putting those empty blue bottles on her sill,
Living alone in the woods
Like a spayed stray.

She reads her twenty-pound bible
Full of secret ancestors
And the recipes of youth and luck,
While I lick plates
And grind out the ice cream.

When I open my closet
Dust blows in my washed hair.

Birds have nested in the cast iron.

That book of hers, like a slab
Of cured bacon, words carved in meat
Smelling like hickory.

Water that is boiling to disinfect sickness
And scald hogs.

Water boiling in the locomotive,
Hauling its full cargo of death and soybeans,
Like windows bending in a storm.

A burning tree.

The matinee postponed due to lightning,
A long-lost cousin making good.

I buried the afterbirth in the sawdust
On the floor of the barn.
And sometimes, when winter becomes
Such a deadly shot, I push away my supper.

Men go out at night, trying to sweep up the stars.

And women grow weary of the cold weather in their men.

They need a friend on the lake with a sailboat.
They need to take medicine and be alone.

Bad food and dead children are not forgotten.
They smell like cod liver oil
In a thimble on the fingers—
A fat lady in a housecoat
Walking through rooms with a cage,
Calling a bird.

The Angel of Death

A man came down the road.

I told him he better watch his step.
He asked me what I was doing,
Sleeping in the middle of the road.

I said I was an orphan.
See these suspenders?
They hold up my pants.
I sleep where I please, says I.
My pillows come from the best roosters.

The moon went back into its night
Like a blue channel cat in a log.

The man cast no shadow.

My shoes wore out
Like a thousand years in the desert.

There was a snowdrift in my heart,
And in the broken mountains of the South
The smoke rose
Wet on the edge with blood.

I am getting out of here, I told the man.

He spit a fish bone on the ground.
He took off his glove.
He laid it on the bone.

What I wanted to do was run.

The moon beat like bait on a black hook.
Then there was a new fish
Sucking wind in the road.

Take off your pants, he said.
He had an egg in his hand.

Anything for the angel of death.

Knew It Was Love, Felt It Was Glory

after Pier Paolo Pasolini

Here is where we went out in the boats, listening
For the dogs and children, for the girl laughing
When she lifts her dress, for the open casket,
Strolling through the wet libraries of moonlight.

You could smell horses, some kind of flowers.

This is the way it was before they started pissing
In the guitar player's cup:

We tried to catch wind
Of the wars
Like a fly in a book
And those who believed
They were still dreaming

In the old days a man chewed a match
And thought
About his death like a woman

He told his son to quit drinking
He told him to see the priest

He marked his bottle like a bee tree
And he wanted his wife
To stay quiet in bed

He dreamed of the rains a good bull
And his daughter
Coming in late at night

Holding her shoes
In her fingers

He stared at the fire
Waiting for the voice of his best friend

He cracked open the window
And put sugar on the sill
Like the moon was an animal

The man counts to eleven and the pain comes
Again, no wonder all of them went crazy.
After all the beautiful and clever dreams
A man ought to be able to say nothing.

You can smell the dead bird, but not its song.

In This House

They go to sleep at the big table.

They doze off working,
Teaching french, castrating horses,
Putting up preserves, polishing silver,
Whatever the ledger says they owe for.

They drift off with rags in their hands,
Spoons and switches and hoes.

Not too long ago I sat on a pop bottle case
And got a conch job, dreamed
Baby Gauge and I were following
The long spikes of a hundred pound flathead cat.

We were on a cottonwood raft,
Had carbide lamps
And a heart that was still beating for bait.

This was in Panther Brake, what some
Call Panther Burn at Luna Landing,
Where he held the light, and I held the spear,
Where he held the spear, and I held the light,
Where we all dreamed the cold sleep and wake
Of the black fish moving under us,
And we had the rest of the camp
Dreaming with us, like a prayer meeting.

None of us told the truth, we didn't lie.

We found shirts with numbers on the back
In canebrakes, we found wristwatches on bones.
We looked for bootlaces.

When it rained, we changed our names,
Something bloomed in the eye.

The mosquitoes got drunk
And laid out on the moon's lounge,
So we stuffed light bread
Through the holes in the screendoors.

A wild horse, a new tool, an eaten melon
Full of rainwater and tadpoles.

Things loom up right odd,
Like a dark truck with hay, a room
The wind blew out of a tree,
Room for the voices and bodies
We hoped for, a woman putting jars
Over seedlings.

The draperies are pulled apart
Like a bone under the table
And the wet fields give pleasure.

Forget everything but the dining table
Where he went to sleep
Polishing a silver platter,
His head on it, shadow in a clean mirror,
Feathers from another country in a vase:

A nine-year-old girl is driving
A team of mules down every road,
Hauling a coffin of honeybees.

Every soul hears a bee in their window,
And the lips won't move.

The ones without men are carrying
Portraits of men
Up and down the stairs.

Hats blow down the road like dandelions.

The Boy Who Shot Weathercocks

At first I did it with a shotgun,
But that blew out windows,
And went through chests
Full of dead people's clothes
In the attics.
It would wake people up
And I had to run through the woods
Swallowing cold weather
A fish hook at a time.
Now I do it from the windmill with a rifle.
I like it best in the spring
When the fields are smoking
And the flies are thick.
I don't kill them, I just knock them off
The iron branches of the houses,
And they fly off, ahead of the bullet even,
Until they see the first cemetery,
Then they light, feed themselves
On the dark earthworms of shade,
Then they swoop over orchards, mess
On the lovers, then they are far away,
Such a distance a cripple like me
Can't imagine, man, then they are gone,
Laying their cold eggs all over the sky,
Rid of the wind.

More Biscuits

He took a match out of his mouth
And sucked some old meat
From beneath his teeth.

He didn't spit nothing on the ground,
He swallowed it.
He struck the match on the side of his pants,
Threw it in the yard
And let it burn.

There awhile, he soaked his feet.
Then he picked up and left,
Went off down the road
With his bucket of Delta brand dark syrup.

A Milk Truck Running Into a Crazy Maid at the Corner of Getwell and Park

They pull a coat over an old woman's eyes.
They ask one another who the old woman was.
No one knows but she worked everyday
And was carrying a sack
Of newspapers and a carton of eggs.
So they say what happened
And someone says she got up
Off the bench and shouted,
When a cow drinks water we get milk
When a snake drinks water we get bit.
She lifted her white dress
And waded out into the intersection
Like it was a river.
They lick their thumbs, write down what is told.
The other maids are getting off work
Standing around wondering what got into her.
The cats from Memphis State are sitting on the bench
Talking about the new Ornette Coleman album
Waiting for the bus,
And the servants of the people are pulling out of parking lots
And into their driveways,
A beer in their lap
Smoke from a dead cigar in their eyes
And desire and desire and desire
Like a long way to go in a bad war,
So they eat a big supper tell everyone what to do
Send the children to bed early have words with their wife.
They set the clock and lie back in the sheets.
They think of toes being slit
And blood that can be heard like a bad tap.

They draw their coats over an old woman's eyes
And think about standing in a warm pool
A white sheet wrapped around them
An old woman holding them
Taking them down into water.

Island Funeral

Mama Julinda is let down into a hole
Her sons have to dig minutes ahead
Of time or the water will rise up
And make a channel around her,
And then it would be like having
Bad dreams, standing in a circle on the bank,
Throwing shovels of dirt at a boat.
The oldest is wearing a new blue suit.
It shines for night, like a fish.
The white gloves he had to cut the arms from
Are a tad soiled, like gardenias
After you touch them, and there's dust
Glowing on his long-toed shoes.
He's breaking the seal
On the bottle, breaking the law,
Drinking untaxed whiskey, the oldest
Son taking a deep, stiff drink,
And the grease on his head runs down
His temple, and everybody is going
To the glove compartments of their cars,
Like acolytes for their pints,
While the goat is turned and burned,
Deep in the moon of the delta,
An island funeral
Where days passed like a barge,
Around us many stars sinking in their light.

The Home Movie of Those Who Are Dead Now

Fourteen years ago a Negro
Rode into town on a one-eyed mule
He had a long coat on
It was midnight blue

A woman was telling another woman
With sign language
In the honky-tonk near the river

I went to sleep with a catfish
Under my bed
A dog licked my toes

The chauffeur combing his hair
With a red comb

The bride shading her eyes
Like a run-over hawk's wing
Embedded in the macadam

And the Host blowing out of the priest's fingers
At the Morning Worship
Celebrated out in the garden

Mule in the ditch
A man afoot

Boats cutting through pure dark

Nobody hearing the deaf and dumb children
Burning wasps under the bridge

My mother changing a tire
For Martin Luther King's father

White gloves for the pallbearers
Cold drinks for the rest

Why the Moon Is in the Outhouse

We shall not all sleep
But we shall all be changed,
It says in the Bible somewhere.

When I was young I didn't owe any doctor bill.
Now they send me statements, special delivery,
Envelopes of X-rays I hold up to the moon,
The cancer swimming up my guts like tadpoles.

In the orphanage the other boys would
Put minnows in my underwear.
I wouldn't wake up.
I would dream about a green cat.

A wealthy lady loved the cat.
She gave money to the Church.
The priest told her she could love the cat.

Her chauffeur would drive up,
Get out, and light his cigarette.
This was the signal the lady wanted the cat.
One night the cat said I could go with them.

We drove through the delta in a black Cadillac.
In those days people asked why do fools fall in love
And they called the place we went niggertown.

There was a blind man out front of a juke joint.
He sold red carnations.
The cat always bought a flower for the lady.

You had to say the password
And the blind man knocked on a door with his cane.

The cat did all the talking.
All hell broke loose when they opened the door.
Everybody was carrying on.

There was a waiter who could dance
With a silver platter
Balanced on his finger.
He brought me a pop.
I told all the people I wasn't spoken for.

The cat and the lady went into another room.
I could hear them throwing their dough
Against the boards, making their bread.

I could smell the blind man behind me.
He said he wasn't blind, he was hypnotized.
I drank soda and looked at his watch,
The waiter twirling the platter.

He said when he snapped his fingers
I would open my eyes.
I wouldn't remember the orphans,
The green cat or the lady.
I would be older, set in my ways,
Holding something black up to the light.

Blue Yodel a Prairie

Whenever I think of the shadows
Two oranges cast on the piano
When the sun drives a horse mad in a dry spell
I think of Virginia Day
Hanging up sheets in her backyard
She has a pair of blue jeans and a brassiere on
Holding the prairie
With a clothespin in her lips
Her husband is putting a new coat of lacquer
On his canoe
He still wants to kill
Whoever it was stole his birddog
It's been a long time
Since I smelled new laundry
The days have gone into the ground
Like rainwater strangers wipe from their eyes
When they meet again
In these drinking places

Memory Is like a Shotgun Kicking You near the Heart

I get up, walk around the weeds
By the side of the road with a flashlight
Looking for the run-over cat
I hear crying.

I think of the hair growing on the dead,
Any motion without sound,
The stars, the seed ticks
Already past my knees,
The moon beating its dark bush.

I take the deer path
Down the side of the hill to the lake,
Wade the cold water.
My light draws the minnows,
Shines through them, goes dead.

Following the shore
I choose the long way home
Past the government camping grounds,
And see where the weeds have been
Beaten down,
Hear the generator on the Winnebago purring.

The children of the tourists
Are under the wheels
Like a covered wagon.
They scratch in their sleep
Until they bleed.

When I get home
I drink a glass of milk in the dark.

She gets up, comes into the room naked
With her split pillow,
Says what's wrong,
I say an eyelash.

The Dead Man's Fiddle

A long time ago
A stranger rode into town
On a stout white mule.

The same day my brother
Who was mad from birth
Took a notion to swim the river
After a blue luna moth
Taking its own kind of journey.

He must have thought
It was a butterfly.
He spent time in front of trucks
Stroking the radiators.

He was always getting lost,
Climbing bee trees,
And putting up angels in the barn.

I still think he pretended to die,
Because we all pretended to weep.

Some boys shooting marbles
Tended the man's ride for him.
He gave them instructions to bite its ear.

He went into the hotel
And got a room.

His upper lip looked like a hawk
Gliding in the distance,
Coming towards you.

He went into Big Woman's Supper Tent
And came back out
With a slice of cornbread,
Wrapped in a silk paisley scarf,
And a quart bottle of sweetmilk.

When I think of my brother
I think of a white sheet with a hole
Left out on the line overnight,
The fiddle player drinking milk.

He ate and drank
On the boardinghouse porch,
His pocketwatch opened up like a mussel in the mud.

Evening shined and was quiet
As the blade of a broken-down bulldozer.

But he must have heard something
Drifting over the sharecroppers' dark fields.

The moon was swollen up
Like a mosquito's belly.

That night I found him
Facedown in the river,
I don't know if he was
Drinking or listening.

The white mule had the fiddle
Harnessed to him, like a plow.

Between Love and Death

I watched the woman in the room.
She moved in her misery
Like a pine in the wind.
I could hear the woman sweeping her floors,
Boiling roots, and drinking milk.
I could watch the woman
Turning the tap of her bath
Through the hole in the wall.
On the summer nights I whistled,
Wanting her to hear me.
She would look my way, sometimes,
With an apple core in her mouth.
Working late, overhauling her truck,
She would drink coffee and hum,
Go to sleep with grease on her fingers.
God I was crazy for not
Going to her door,
Tapping on her window,
Following her to the river
Where her dory grew wet like the moon.
A bird sick of its tree, I despair.
Leaves without wind, I lay
Damp and quiet on the earth.
She bled through the walls
Into my side of the house,
And they came with their lights
Asking did I know the woman,
And I said no, not I.

Dreams of a River I Waded with Others Long Ago

She died in the river, she died stepping back
Into the shadows, she died under the bridge
With her pants down, she died with a tongue
In her ear and a dark cigarette in her lips,
She died like heat lightning and milo,
She died like snake doctors on the windshield,
She died in the spring in a dark house
With a storm, she died with her cats and saxophones,
She died with the dead niggerlilies
And the fan belt part number on the nail,
She died first like the wolf
Then the snow in her paperweight,
She died with toilet paper in the screendoor,
And she died with a flyswatter and she died like a window
That turns into a mirror at nightfall, she died
With chowchow and dead flies on the tablecloth,
She died without a hand
On her forehead, she died on the side of the road
In the arms of a stranger.

Would You Like to Lie Down with the Light On and Cry

My nights are like valleys
Where the night falls soon
And the mist rises early.

The work I do is not easy,
But it is not bad.

When the white barns of the afternoon
Are dark and quiet
With their wasps and snakes
I wonder why we lie to one another:

Spots on the aged
Are called little flowers of the cemetery,
On the young they are marks
Left by the teeth of beauty.

The dying
Clutch their genitals
And shake like trestles
When the locomotive of death passes by,
And lovers
Like their trains
In the trembling bridges of their beds.

When no one is looking
We touch the thin underthings
Of our death to our lips.

I remember my death
And I remember desire,
And they are not the same.

Nine months from tonight
A woman will be holding
Her belly in pain.

Blue Yodel of the Lost Child

You're so dusty,
Like a nightgown
Thrown down from the attic.
Always late
And used to dark places
Like the beautiful white spider,
The moon.
What would I do with you,
Give you a fan
To spread in the theater
When you're blind,
And have the wind
Make its legend at your back.
I've thought about letting you
Search for your death,
Dowse for yourself
With a forked stick,
But I keep waking up wet
With a twig of blood
In my lips.
I can't find you.
Now you're quiet,
Like a loaf of rising bread.
A letter to the condemned,
You came too late
Like the snow
Who calls you his wife now,
And your breasts will never be
Heavy with milk,
And your voice like an owl
On every fence post.

The Lunatic

Somewhere out there a craft is traveling
Through black and final space.

It is built of light wood
Darker than this desk.

The dead trees of silence
Spread their naked legs,

Lying to us
Through their teeth.

And so our senses lie,
Forming the capillary systems

Of night and the universe,
A still moon of fire

Like a willow near the water,
Or a quiet bed.

An ancient stone
Is following this ship,

Music
Like a weightless anchor

Of form and line,
Caedmon's dream.

But we are deaf,
Timeless engineers of sleep,

Draftsmen of space
Designing toolsheds for death.

Listen,
All I know is this desk

Is a swarm of stars,
Tadpoles in orbit,

And Nothing on earth is solid.
Innocent blood

Passes between light and myself.
So far

As I know,
It has not risen,

It has not taken my life
Or a journey without me.

Death and the Arkansas River *

Walking from the killing place,
Walking in mud
The bootsoles leave little hexes in the kitchen.

One summer there was a place
Where everyone chewed dirt in their supper.

It was a place like an attic
With a chest of orchids pressed in books.
Men cleaned their fingernails
In the moonlight.

Death let a bid.

And while everyone was in hipboots
Looking out for Death's fork-lifts,
There was a shine on Death's loafers.
His poll tax was paid, so was his light bill.

In the winter Death runs snow tires on his truck,
He makes long hauls at night.
Death pays the best wage.
He keeps in touch on his two-way.

Death can afford whatever he wants.

If you listened to the ground, you'd hear
Thunder coming like a train on the tracks.
And Death would signal ahead
That the half-dollar you stole to flatten
You lifted from your father's eye.

* An earlier version of this poem appears in *Constant Stranger* (see pp. 199–201). — Ed.

Death dances a slow boogie
Even the awkward can follow
When he leads.

In my life Death has asked me
To trade dogs, take a fall for love,
While others have asked me
How he combed his hair.

Everytime Death gets a Cadillac
He wants to fight.
He wants to run the front door,
He wants cooking that will remind him of home.

If you try to forget
Death ties a string around your finger.

Regrets and warnings
To those who don't know what's cooking
When Death's bread rises
Out of its grave.

Death, for instance, was looking
To cold-cock my brother.
My brother thought he pulled a fast one.
He played the radio and drank whiskey.
He raised hell
With women already married.

Do you know of anyone who's got the best
Of Death?

Some say you can keep an eye
Out for Death,
But Death is one for fooling around.

He might turn up working odd jobs
At your favorite diner.
He might be peeling spuds.

Death likes the double entendre.

I for one am reminded of butterflies,
Snow blowing off pines:
Death is around you
Like a lock and dam.

So don't let Death catch you
Listening to the ground, even a place
That sounds like home.

It could be Death
Filing a quitclaim deed:
He holds a quiet title
To the land your loved ones walked.

Even if you couldn't hear
The sound would carry
Like a truck on a bridge, like a flower
Given at a ball, a sound in place,
The tradewind called Death, gentle
As children in their night clothes
Fighting with pillows, so quiet
Not a soul is wakened.

A Beautiful Woman Came Down to the Sawmill One Friday Evening

Hello, I'm a teacher from the school.
Is there a man by the name of Drusky works here?

He'd be over on the saw, lady.

Thanks, I've got some bad news for him.

The woman came over my way.
The sawdust was blowing in her eyes.
I cut the saw off
Just when she was yelling.

Are you...

I'm Drusky.

I'm sorry to break this to you
But a child of yours was killed today.

Which one?

Your girl.

What happened?

The schoolbus hit a chicken truck.

---

* The poem "Fire Left by Travelers" began this section of the original edition
of *Crib Death.*—Ed.

Was it quick for her?

I don't know Mr. Drusky,
But the others said there wasn't even a mark.

What about the others?

They're all fine.
Your child was the only death.

Was it anybody's fault?

We don't know.

I never lost one before.

I'm sorry Mr. Drusky,
I have to be going now.

She walked away.
I seen a light on the hill.
Trouble is, there ain't nobody home.
I took off the safety glasses.

Hey, lady, I called.
I'm proud you didn't come down here
With a whole lot of goddamn fancy talk.

She kind of smiled
And must have told the boys,
Because they all come over
And took off their caps.

Boogen said I guess you won't make it
Up to the dance hall tonight.

No, tell them I won't be there.
And do explain
It ain't that I don't feel like singing,
It's just some others
Will be wanting my voice this evening.

The boss said I didn't have to show Monday
And handed me a fifty dollar bill.

I told them all
Let me remind you trouble will find you,
Nobody can ride shotgun on your love.

I took to that lady.
I was proud she didn't come down here
With all that goddamn talk.

The Neighbor's Wife

Four a.m. and she's still gone
But I'm not going to call.
It's not so bad, until just before morning,
When I see a truck driver
Take a smoke out of his lips
And throw it out the window
And I watch it go to pieces
All over the road.

Terrorism

While my mother is washing the black socks
Of her religion,
I climb out of the washtub,
Stinking clean like the moon and the suds
In my ass,
The twenty she earned last week in my teeth,
My shoes and my pistol wrapped in my pants,
Slip off the back porch
And head down the road, buck naked and brave,
But lonely, because it's fifteen hours
By bus to the capital
And nobody will know
How it feels to nail down a heart
Black as tarpaper.
Mother, when you beat out my quilt tomorrow,
Remember the down in the sunlight,
Because I did not sleep there.
Remember, come evening, the last hatch of mayflies,
Because I won't.
They are evil, Mother, and I am
Going to take it all out, in one motion,
The way you taught me to clean a fish,
Until all that is left is the memory of their voice,
And I will work that dark loose
From the backbone with my thumb.
Mother, the sad dance on fire.

Only One Set in the Singer's Eyes

He got drunk looking at a woman from his past
And this is what he wrote down on a paper sack
In the tavern one night while I watched him:
Your body is a plantation
I worked on for seven years, all of them solid,
Deep in summer it's uncleared timber, backwater
Ditch and slough, the years of the bad-assed
Sax, the years of bad cotton, nights and crops
I went shares on, evenings with gars,
Lord God Almighty didn't it rain,
So long, say love, say night honey, pull
A stump, court with your crowbar,
The bedrooms like trembling bridges,
Like women holding mirrors in the spring,
And here I am, the snow all around me,
A match in my mouth, like the high water,
Crazy, sad, and dangerous, a log
Chain on your floor, what love
There was, bee on the rose, buried in the year
Book in the attic, common and pretended sleep,
No one loses their shadow because no one
Is a boat on a river without wind,
And there are screws on the window sill
Never will be sunken to hold a pane,
You can listen to the rain, you can lie
Yourself back into bodies you never
Touched, cruelty, cruelty, cruelty,
That's what I told her.

Living the Good Life

There is only one locale for the heart
And that's somewhere between the dick and the brain.
I don't believe love is for chickenshits.
It's low, dark, and cold-blooded, like a cottonmouth.
Children are often involved. They stink
When they sprout in the garden of light,
And they stink mulching their way back down.
Coldhearted women, work, madness, and death
Are the things separating the nuts from the shells.
Everything else is strictly a pile of shit—
Except for childhood, which we moon over
Because it smells to high heaven. So, go it
Alone. Solitude is a constellation:
People can't connect light anymore,
The only code they can break is darkness.
You can get a file in the heart
But you can't jimmy love—a woman once said
It'd take a shotgun to open my heart.
All the time I was on my knees in the bathroom
Crying like a fool. No one knows
How to love anybody's trouble, nothing will
Deaden the chiggers of pain sucking
Blood in your sleep—oh beautiful tree frogs,
Sonic in the nasty oil of evening, I love you,
Sounds by yourselves a star's life away.
But it doesn't mean a goddamn thing.
Death isn't cold, dark, and quiet.
It is a love letter written on an X-ray.
Better still, it's a manta ray
Squealing in your wife's drawers.
Is this where your will is kept?

What sleek doing is she dreaming of tonight?
How much money do you have in the bank?
Are your early years filed away
In another bureau under another name?
Ask me no questions, I'll still tell you lies,
My father would sing like a bullfrog.
I thought my father was a flat-out wonder,
A faraway and constant stranger in my midst.
He wasn't even my father, the cuckold.
So do Lord help the bucket mouth son
Doing a job on doom and eating banana flips.
I for one leave the transcendence of language
To the auctioneers on the widows' steps,
And to the truck drivers with ears
Looking for the smoke on the road.
As for the snow that drifts ever
So silently into the eyes of children,
It is all full of shit from the north
And radiation from the west.

The Light the Dead See

There are many people who come back
After the doctor has smoothed the sheet
Around their body
And left the room to make his call.

They die but they live.

They are called the dead who lived through their deaths,
And among my people
They are considered wise and honest.

They float out of their bodies
And light on the ceiling like a moth,
Watching the efforts of everyone around them.

The voices and the images of the living
Fade away.

A roar sucks them under
The wheels of a darkness without pain.
Off in the distance
There is someone
Like a signalman swinging a lantern.

The light grows, a white flower.
It becomes very intense, like music.

They see the faces of those they loved,
The truly dead who speak kindly.

They see their father sitting in a field.
The harvest is over and his cane chair is mended.
There is a towel around his neck,

The odor of bay rum.
Then they see their mother
Standing behind him with a pair of shears.
The wind is blowing.
She is cutting his hair.

The dead have told these stories
To the living.

I would like to quit school and go back and live in a tent I would like to
dream again sometime I am afraid one day life will give me its Sunday punch
I am afraid after reading all these so-called initiation books that some
cortege of bootlickers will enter my room while I am sleeping and suck
my eyes out with soda straws they will be older men and women much like
the amanuenses with bad breath in the principal's office who call
up and tell on you the Unferths of the world better beware
I know Jesus would have kicked your teeth in you couldn't pull that shit on him
he was telling his buddies one night boys I'm glad y'all decided to come on up
and eat supper with me I hadn't got much there's a few things I'd like to say
at this time Matthew says to Simon I sure as hell don't know what he's got us
here this time for I'm beginning to wonder you talked to him lately
yeah I was shooting the shit with him on the mountain but I want to tell you
this Matthew don't never come up on him when he's alone he jumped on me
I thought he was going to kill me he was just walking around just talking
to himself waving his arms like he does he's worse than John
Jude put his hand up to his mouth and said down the table I think Jesus is going
off his rocker get Simon to tell you what he asked me
Simon says he didn't want to talk about politics or dreams or nothing he
               just said
Jude next time y'all are over in Mesopotamia why don't you pick me up a few
bottles of that wine they make over there
sure thing Jesus I says
well now the boss is talking he is saying I asked y'all up here because frankly
I've been feeling a little sick lately and I want to make sure y'all know what
to do in case anything happens I know one of you is going to do me in I know
that but goddamnit y'all know those people in town are after my ass
the other night I walked down the streets in a disguise and I seen a couple
of you messing around and drinking with the soldiers what's going to happen
if one of you gets drunk and lets it slip where I'm hiding out then I'll
be in a fix you know if they was to find me they going to cut me y'all ever
think about that and Peter ain't you ever going to get it straight what you're

supposed to do give me one of those biscuits Judas and go outside and take a
look-see I got you Jesus Judas says
John leans over he says been catching any fish Peter
oh well I been getting a few of a morning they ain't biting too good now
        you know
on account of this blamed weather nobody is even listening to Jesus he's just
talking to himself like he was crazy Matthew says I believe he's been hitting
that wine a little too hard don't you reckon
Jesus says another thing I told all of you it'd be better if you didn't get
involved with women
now just listen to that little two-faced bastard James the Lesser says
we all know what he's up to shacking up with all those town girls
the other night he was dressed fit to kill and drunk as six hundred dollars
a rolling around in the mud like a hog kissing that whore's foot why shit
I wish he'd let us in on what he really does
Thomas spoke up for once he says I know what you mean the other day Andrew
and I asked him about some scripture he said leave me alone I don't know
nothing about that shit and then we seen him cussing out a priest over at the
temple he knew more about it than the elder did
another thing Matthew says I wish he'd start writing what he wants done down
and do it so I can read it you know as well as I do that damned Peter can't
keep it straight he won't get anything right
Bartholomew says don't make no difference atoll cause Paul is going to tell
it like he wants to that's for damned sure
all the time Jesus just mumbling to himself wine spilt all over his robe
the rest of them chattering and cussing trying to figure him out
John the Baptist about the only one Jesus can count on except for crazy John
is banging his goblet on the table he is saying now ain't this a sight
spitting in the lord's face at his own birthday party I'll swan
Brother John why don't you tell Jesus what the real problem is
the crazy one says everyone of y'all is chickenshits you are afraid to look
those elders in the eye and tell them what you think y'all get up on a rock
to talk and you see a soldier coming and you say anybody seen a stray mule
Jesus is saying to himself I'm going to pull those temples down if I have to

get me a rope and tie it to a pillar and a jackass and do it myself
wake up Jesus Philip says
Paul who hadn't touched a drop gets up and gets his paper out and says
the nature of the problem Jesus is this the people don't believe you
those fellows in the temples have got it all organized all they have to do
is send out stooges and hire a couple of rednecks who make out like they're
crippled they have a big gathering they say the same things you say they
pull off a fake healing the redneck's wife stands up she says LIE he ain't lame
he's just drunk and so all the people go home saying those christians what a
bunch of wind see Jesus they are using your material but they ain't coming
through so that is making you an enemy of the people we just got to get
organized as is proved here today by your followers carrying on as they did
so I'm getting sold down the river by the elders and their hirelings uh
that's right Jesus ask anybody here why I didn't think they'd do that he says
I told you a long time ago not to keep talking with them temple people
    John says
you should a know'd what they was up to ain't nobody going to understand you
why you ought to know that when we first run on to you we had second
    thoughts
we thought you was crazy there's probably still some sitting down here right
this second that still thinks you are a crazy one but Jesus you should a known
we been through a lot together we go a long way back you should a listened
all they wanted was you they liable to get you yet then they won't have no
competition they want to keep feeding the hogs the same slop
they the ones that want to get fat man you listening to me Jesus
he says ok if that's the way they want to do things at the temple
I'm going to change my tactics I going out after these chillun more than I have
been they'll know I'm telling the truth I still got a few things up my sleeve
left what's that Paul says
I'm going to do a few things can't nobody follow
we could always go back to biting the heads off fish and chickens Peter says
why don't you let us in on it for a change Paul says we follow you around
like we were bunch of sheep picking up your tab bailing you out of jail
coming up here all the time for supper and what do we get to eat nothing

why can't you have a little faith in us Jesus
ok this is what we going to do he says hold on who is that walking up the steps
it's just Judas
how does it go boy Jesus says and the other one answers just fine Jesus just fine
and John the Baptist turns around he says to the one who has just slipped in boy
didn't I see you talking to some white folks the other day
here endeth with a chord on the guitar that's how the men did Jesus like he was
old like he was young just like Elvis did to Big Boy Arthur I know
just like another blind singer the men come down to see with their equipment
they get his song they pay him twenty dollars and he don't hear from them ever
again except sometimes in the mail on Christmas when one of them might
       send a
five dollar check there won't nobody cash oh tell me brother how do the old men
feel who were young as purple flowers from Hawaii once when they listen
       to their
songs coming in over a borrowed radio tell me don't they take up a notch in
       they belt
don't they tie another knot in they headband don't they wring that sweat out
have mercy Jesus deliver me from the lawyers and the teachers and the preachers
and the politicking flies can't you hear them buzz can't you hear them bite
       another
chunk out of me oh brother I am death and you are sleep I am white and
       you are
black brother tell me I am that which I am I am sleep and you are death we are
one person getting up and going outside naked as a blue jay rolling our bellies
at the moon oh brother tell me you love me and I'll tell you too I want to know
how do they like it when the ones who sung shake they leg on the Television
I want to know Jesus don't a blind man count no more some by signs others by
whispers some with a kiss and some with a gun and some with a six bit fountain
pen whoa lord help me and my brother help us get through this tookover land
we are poor wayfaring strangers bumping into each other in the dark
going to the outhouse like the picture show in the tent in Snow Lake
that old marquee tacked up side the whiskey sign it ain't ever right
everybody specting once upon a time one thing and ain't getting such a thing

when they get there they might as well turn around cause it won't be on
less you want to get a pint and buy a ticket and take a chance
you can't never go wrong on that sign it always got the good show playing
I tell you I'd rather put my faith in a fishing pole instead of a word
many a time in school I've had my mind like a circular table like a mirror
ready to be set with hope but when the teacher opens her mouth she besets
it with TV dinners when I had a feast in mind a feast to feed the world
of my dreams and I had them and I had one oh lord help me my ship is spinning
round and the women and children is still on board those fuckers in
      Washington D.C.
done grabbed all the lifeboats and they ain't letting no more board
I tell you one day in the unknown county where my dreams jump and shout
a train will arrive and it will arrive like a General

YOU

1979

You can piss in my face, just don't tell me it's raining.

ADOLPH REED

Bright moments is like seeing something that you ain't never seen in your life and you don't have to see it because you know how it looks. Bright moments is like hearing some music and ain't nobody else heard and if they heard it they wouldn't even recognize it if they heard it because they been hearing it all they life, so when you hear it and start popping your feet and jumping up and down they get mad because you are enjoying yourself but those are bright moments they can't share with you because they don't know even how to go about listening to what you are listening to and when you try to tell them about it they don't know a damn thing about what you talking about.

RAHSAAN ROLAND KIRK

Circle of Lorca

When you take the lost road
You come to the snow
And when you find the snow
You get down on your hands and knees
Like a sick dog
That's been eating the grasses of graveyards
For twenty centuries.

When you take the lost road
You find woman
Who has no fear of light
Who can kill two cocks at once
Light which has no fear of cocks
And cocks who can't call in the snow.

You find lovers who've been listening
For the same roosters to sing
For twenty centuries
Roosters that have swallowed stones
Out of each other's tracks
But have never met
Anywhere on the road.

When you take the lost road
You find the bright feathers of morning
Laid out in proportion to snow and light
And when the snow gets lost on the road
Then the hot wind might blow from the south
And there is sadness in bed for twenty centuries
And everyone is chewing the grass on the graves again.

When you get lost
You come to the moon in the field
The light all lovers soil
The sheet no one leaves clean
The light cocks are afraid to cross
The same moon woman danced under
For twenty centuries
With blood on her face.

When you get lost on the road
You run into the dead
Who have broken down stones
In their throats for twenty centuries
I saw two little crazy boys crying
Because it was morning
And when morning comes it comes
In the morning and never at night.

I saw two security police taking out a man's balls
And I saw two little crazy boys
Crying by the road who wouldn't go away
But two has never been a number
Because it's only legal to pass one at a time
It's only a drum you can carry but you can't beat
It's the evidence they need to make you disappear.

Source

They found a body in a field
But no one claimed him.

There was a full moon and late snow
On the jonquils
When the train came in.

A big man with a bass slept in the depot
Until someone came by
And took him to the home
Where the body was.

He played all night until train time,
Just my brothers and I listened.

When he quit my father came with a bottle of whiskey
And they went off.
They left the motor running in front of the station.

I asked my father who the man was,
He said you'll know him one of these days.

Once on the coast when I was sixteen,
I met a beautiful woman.
She knew who he was.

And before my brother got killed in Cuba
We got a message from him.
He knew who he was.

People come down and play music at his grave,
Never say anything.

I grew up wondering,
Sometimes I thought I knew,
Like when I see dirt washing down the river
Into the gulf,
I think I walked over that ground.

Weariness of Men

My grandmother said when she was young
The grass was so wild and high
You couldn't see a man on horseback.

In the fields she made out
Three barns,
Dark and blown down from the weather
Like her husbands.

She remembers them in the dark,
Cursing the beasts,
And how they would leave the bed
In the morning,
The dead grass of their eyes
Stacked against her.

Wind Blowing on a Sick Man

Men with no headlights drive up in front of a whorehouse.

They get out of their car,
Wipe the dust off their shoes
On the back of their pants.

Then they go upstairs and hang a woman.

Summer is almost over, the river is down,
The sun comes loose
Like the bright orange thread
I used to bite off a new pair of dungarees.

The further they drive down the road
The closer their voices get.

Desire for a Killing Frost

In the hours when the animals are making their calls
In the fields, and the men are making theirs in the cities,
I remember dressing in the dark,
Serving the early mass at the orphanage,
I remember the hoboes and the faces of those
Who passed them on the road
Without looking into their eyes.
All the good rides we missed
Like a summer and the summer before that.
My sadness waves back
Like the heads of grain in another's fields.
It cannot be combined and no one is hungry.
It is the quiet before the hunt,
When the hunter touches his eyes with cold water
And stays by the creek and does not hunt again.
The head of the varmint
A hired man nailed to a joist in the barn
Is remembered, but the hired man is not.

Everybody Who Is Dead

When a man knows another man
Is looking for him
He doesn't hide.

He doesn't wait
To spend another night
With his wife
Or put his children to sleep.

He puts on a clean shirt and a dark suit
And goes to the barber shop
To let another man shave him.

He shuts his eyes
Remembers himself as a boy
Lying naked on a rock by the water.

Then he asks for the special lotion.
The old men line up by the chair
And the barber pours a little
In each of their hands.

Faith, Dogma, and Heresy

It was Sunday, before dinner.
My uncles were listening to the opera.
O.Z. and I carried my brother in
And laid him on the table.
The women started screaming.
My brother raised up on his side
With dried blood on his hands,
We killed those goddamn Canale brothers
And nobody is ever going to touch us!
The men shut their eyes and danced.
We drank until morning
When everything was quiet.
They wiped their eyes, kissed us goodbye and left.

What About This

A guy comes walking out of the garden
Playing Dark Eyes on the accordion.
We're sitting on the porch,
Drinking and spitting, lying.
We shut our eyes, snap our fingers.
Dewhurst goes out to his truck
Like he doesn't believe what he's seeing
And brings back three half-pints.
A little whirlwind occurs in the road,
Carrying dust away like a pail of water.
We're drinking serious now, and O.Z.
Wants to break in the store for some head cheese,
But the others won't let him.
Everybody laughs, dances.
The crossroads are all quiet
Except for the little man on the accordion.
Things are dying down, the moon spills its water.
Dewhurst says he smells rain.
O.Z. says if it rains he'll still make a crop.
We wait there all night, looking for rain.
We haven't been to sleep, so the blue lizards
On the side of the white porch
Lose their tails when we try to dream.
The man playing the music looks at us,
Noticing what we're up to. He backs off,
Holding up his hands in front, smiling,
Shaking his head, but before he gets halfway
Down the road that O.Z. shoots him in the belly.
All summer his accordion rotted in the ditch,
Like an armadillo turning into a house payment.

They Really Do

Three years later the same man
Came back to our town. Everyone says
He must have had a twin brother.
He comes back just the same, except this time
A fairly good looking woman
Was driving the truck; he was in the back
Leaning over a blue organ. And there was a bird,
A cockatoo, perched on it.
We all had to pay two bits to hear him.
He kept looking over his shoulder at us.
Some young boys, our sons, gathered
Around the cab while we listened to him.
One by one, the young lady pulled them in the door
And pulled down a little black curtain.
Hell, we didn't know what was coming off.
She kept each one for about fifteen minutes.
I know my son couldn't stop talking about it,
All his life—which only lasted a week
Or so from then. The whole bunch of them
Pulled out of town in the middle of the night.
We were having a special vigil at church.
Going home that early morning our wives
Told us the weathervanes were spinning.
And every woman's broom lost its straw.
Later in the month, we all got black envelopes
Delivered at night, challenging us to a duel.
Either that, or send him snapshots of our daughters
And the second mortgages on our farms.
As I gave away, to the T all our sons died,
But our daughters did very well for themselves.
Mine all work in a whorehouse in Joplin, Mo.
And they send us a check every month for the Home.

Allegory of Youth

I suppose that at one time there was a ship
Called Night, named and painted on the bow
In blood by a girl that went by Lucy,
And it had a great cargo, the moon,
As it sailed past all points
East and West of the dark hearts it broke.
On board the blowflies were bad, but the music
Was lovely, like a cat in a wet field.
The sleek ship Night was known for its french afternoons,
Its decks dark as hell and Vermeer, the portholes
Free of horseshit and sad eyes,
The harbors it loved to forget, its duels,
And fantastic library of sin,
The Science of Imaginary Solutions
Written in disappearing ink.
One morning a storm formed, an owl flew
Itself to death around the mast.
Naturally, the ship sank, but all
Was not forgotten, only the warnings.
Ever since, the air's been thick as the dreams
Of migrants polishing their shoes.
And Elmo, the black driver who raised me,
Knows he's getting on in years, knows
What he needs is more sleep,
That he's not long for this world,
But he still has me
Latch down his dark helmet
When he makes the nightly descent.

Allegory of Death and Night

When he comes home from work
He washes his hands
And sits down at the dinner table
And eats. He doesn't say much,
He drinks from an old bottle.
What he doesn't eat, the dog does.
And while the hound is licking
The man is snoring at the table.
The woman slaps the oilcloth
With a flyswatter, and he comes to.
A milksnake is crawling
Along a rafter in the barn
And a storm is making in the east.
There is a bird flying high
And the shadow of smoke
From the last fires in the moonlight.
He's laying crossways over the bed
On his belly. She's taken off
His pants and unlaced his boots.
Whatever he dreams he keeps to himself,
Like a prayer sent up for rain.
When he's dead to the world
She reaches into the pocket
Of his trousers for a white pouch.
She rolls a cigarette with one hand.
She smokes in the dark. Clouds
Go by, turning under the soil.
She turns a flashlight on
The man's body, looking for seed
Ticks that have been there since dawn.

Instead

Death is a good word.
It often returns
When it is very
Dark outside and hot,
Like a fisherman
Over the limit,
Without pain, sex,
Or melancholy.
Young as I am, I
Hold light for this boat.

When the rest of you
Were being children
I became a monk
To my own listing
Imagination.
Nights and days floated
Over the whorehouse
Like webs on the lake,
A monastery
Full of noise and girls.

The moon throws the knives.
The poets echo goodbye,
Towing silence too.
Near my house was an
Island, where a horse
Lathered up alone.
Oh, Abednego
He was called, dusky,
Cruel as a poem
To a black gypsy.

Sadness and whiskey
Cost more than friends.
I visit prisons,
Orphanages, joints,
Hoping I'll see them
Again. Willows, ice,
Minnows, no money.
You'll have to say it
Soon, you know. To your
Wife, your child, yourself.

The Wolves

at night while the dogs
were barking
Baby Gauge and I crawled under the fence
with knives
we made out like the rattlesnake melons
were men we didn't like
the new moon ones were wolves
I would cut a belly this way
he would cut a belly that way
the flies
came around the sweet juice
it was blood to us
we tasted it we licked it off the blades
we decided not to kill the wolves
we wanted to be wolves
we stuck the knives in the ground
the moon shined on them
we turned the pilot caps inside out
so the fur would show
that way when we crawled
under the bob wire
a little piece would get caught
we wouldn't though
we wanted to leave trails
but no scents
we tore the melons open we licked the blood off our paws
we wanted to be wolves
and in the morning all those dead men
with their hearts eat out

The Burial Ship

Jimmy's wolf died
it wasn't nothing but a cub
O.Z. built a coffin ship
he made it so the head could look out the prow
the river was going to be his grave
we held services there
everyone wore a black mask and we cut ourselves for old times' sake
he was laid away
buried in the little ship
there was no sacrifice no dead chickens
we broke a NuGrape bottle over the hull it was full
the ship was about four feet long
Ray Baby and I could have fit in it if we were dead
for sails we stole a tent flap
Six Toes painted it red with a black cross
each one dripped some blood over the wolf in the boat
Melvin said the cold weather set in
we brought the blind child with us to tell the fortunes of the future
he always carried a frog gig and wore a top hat
he reached out his hands and wiggled his fingers
that's the way he knew
he said I need two bits and a little music
he didn't talk right he made it all sound like a song
everyone had dirty white gloves on
we had a jug a guitar and a oil bucket
someone said woe is the wolf
we thought we heard Mose playing a fife away back in the woods
I was on Ace comb and Stage Plank wrapper
Baby Gauge sang Back to the Dust he wailed
I wanted to sing The Blood Done Signed My Name but they
      wouldn't let me

the blind child said he'd have to go to Newport to see Aunt Caroline Dye
ashes to ashes dust to dust the devil be had if this old life don't get worse
it was getting cold
he said some river rat was liable to use the wolf for bait
better keep watch
the smoke was coming out our mouths
Jimmy wasn't shivering he was just staring at the water
I poked him to see if he was in a trance
he said come on O.Z.
they rowed out to the coffin the ship bearing the dead wolf
they set it afire and watched it burn
there was one big spark that cracked like ash in the dark
it must have been the wolf's eye
it kept on going towards the heavens
it was a shooting star

Blue Yodel of Her Feet

Times I can't look you
In the face you're a wolf
That's killed things I once loved
So I look at your feet
Dark from summer like paws
Soft as buds
Hard as branches they hold
The weight of your body
Cold naked statue I like to frighten
Your waist is a place of solitude
Briars in the forest
Your chest gives ground
Like an island on a river
And as they yodel in the song of songs
Your nipples taut as raisins
Killdeers try to fly from your eyes
I wish I could nail your shoes to the floor
And lose your socks
Good plants bearing in bad soil
So hard to raise my eyes
Over the rest of you
So I looked at your feet
They walked over the ground when you found me
They'll cover the same terrain
When I lose you

Blue Yodel the Many Evenings

Your hands
Passing for a stranger's
Everytime I come home
To you young lady weary
Of the fiddle the other woman
Who stays so long in the mornings
In your bed
Saying let us
Wander
I keep two kingdoms of firewood
Two loaves of cornbread and two key
Holes the drafts and weeds
In the shack
The boy four sheets
In the sweet wind
Your old hands tuning the screenwire

Dreamt by a Man in a Field

I am thinking of the dead
Who are still with us.
They are not like us, they are
Young and beautiful,
On their way in the rain
To meet their lovers.
On their way with their dark umbrellas,
Always laughing, so quick,
Like limbs flying back
In a boat before night,
So constant,
Like the glass floats
The fishermen use in Japan.
But for them there is no moon,
For us the same news
We do not receive.

Search Party

All lovers listen and sleep, turn back
In your dream before it's too late.
The water's up and the hills are steep,
Christ is not alive but the she blood is.
Slow down and swerve to miss her.
The ground is easy to dig
And the sun will rot you fast.
Your passion is blue and white
Like the eyes of a child in the last hours,
Like a small white building
With a woman lighting a cigarette
In the window at the end of a rain,
Like a hatch of mayflies.
Brother and Sister there are fish
Under the water lilies
Laying their eggs like moonlight
Watch out or you'll slide
Like a pickup on a curve
With nothing in the bed.
Desire has a soft shoulder, better to
Stroke the beast than to hit it
And forfeit the eleven stars of your youth.

You

Sometimes in our sleep we touch
The body of another woman
And we wake up
And we know the first nights
With summer visitors
In the three storied house of our childhood.
Whatever we remember,
The darkest hair being brushed
In front of the darkest mirror
In the darkest room.

Shutdown

There was going to be a dance
For a hardworking girl from my hometown
Who didn't give a shit after the day
Shift ended on Friday who was passing
Blood in their urine that evening
And someone had broken her birdbath.

She only wanted to get her dog out
Of the pound and crawl into the sack.

She had it and she knew it
And the birds were gone
Like that man who gave her
The clay whistle shaped like an elk
You blew through the stifle.

And so was that girl
She swapped paperbacks and fruit with at lunch sometimes.
She fixed her wiper blades once, remember
The soft dead wings on the windshield
Bright as a sewing box.

She was alone on her hideaway
In her shoes listening to something
That kept getting darker and going around
And glowing like morning on the oil
Spilled under her truck, there
She was drifting through
The rosewater of her heavy red hair.

She only wanted to be rolling
Off a swollen river sliding

Out of a clean slip turning
Over in a deep drum trailing
A shimmering thread like a slug
Under a pile of wet leaves,

There she was in her river without birds,
The struck matches of her blood
Going white and stinking like smoke
Closed blinds a ceramic floor a white blouse
A shard of glass collecting the white light in her belly
Waiting for the snow.

Handling Paper with Cold Hands

It is almost not there,
Like a watch with a black face
You dropped down the well of your childhood.
Nights rummaging
Like a barn cat in the root cellar,
A prowling relative left out of the will.
And then you are married, again,
And the cuts are thinner than ever.
The moon is your old shirt.
Fruit and vegetables
And a new bar of soap on the chopping block.
Only barely there, oak on the cliff,
And the wood in the iron stove
You fetched yourself
Turning grey like ashes of black paper,
Whining like a pup on a dry teat.

Jonquils

A woman who has been dead a long time keeps sweltering
At a piano she keeps singing one kind of music
In a hot church that smells like old fruit
Peeling itself as it ripens
She keeps calling for a child who was going
To blow on her fingers when she walked across the room with wet
       nails to change the LP
A woman keeps singing in a long piano
Without ivory or ebony
About the way they laid her out
A single white rose
Fastened in her fingers
A shade of lipstick on the very first time
Her mouth sewed shut
It was angels spoke to precious
And she was wearing the prettiest red shoes.

Spirits

The fisherman's child is dressed in white
Small and beautiful on her box
And nobody is not alone or remembering
The double music of rivers and nets
Or nights with other women.
What they think is the cemetery's
Like a cheap hotel they paid for a room once
But did not sleep
The beds were all small and the same
Standing straight up and white
You had to let them down with a cord.

Postcard to Lucia

Low the moon, high the wind,
I for one
Am coming between
Like a boat locked and damned.
Make, love, your sorties
Into the Havana of my heart,
But bring back rum.
Hold, friend, your soirees
On any beach
The storm is driving us all to,
But let the enemy sleep.
Remember what you will,
I will, the air looking for the sky,
The moon in your dark hands
Like the body of Christ,
Or a doctor in a shack
Beating a child's heart with his knuckles.

Epiphanies

Two people are sitting at a table in the afternoon.
It is summer outside and dark
And cool in the room.

She is dizzy from the light
Swimming through the reeds
Like shadows of minnows.
She is sad from sipping the flat beer
Of her own voice.

She is tropical, she knows
If a man is sand,
Those who walk through the desert
Are men.

He is a carpenter, he knows
The soaked down tree he drives nails in every night.
He thinks of a stone
That flies in the dew of the moonlight,
Easy for a sad man by a river.

Wonder if it was night
And they left like strangers.

He would think of her hair
Coming down her waist.
She would be in the jungle
Making her plans from the enemy's sleep.

In a room like this, together,
Looking into a table
Wet from its own darkness.
What do they need, what can they say?

Boots

My grandfather and his men
Would ride their horses
Into the swamps
On nights that sung and flew
Full of blood like mosquitoes
And draw their pistols to fire
At the snakes that struck
One terrible circle after another
All so we could come later
With knives tied to broomsticks.
This was the reason for mud, whiskey, and the river,
Also bad debts and weather,
Mysterious birds robbing the orchard
Who disappeared like favorite daughters.
This was the reason for women weeping after a rain.

Braids

At the end of the war there weren't many
Men left.

So the widows traveled
To the gallows on hanging days
To look for a blindfolded man.

Any woman could save a bandit then,
And maybe two
If she had a thousand acres or a daughter.

All she had to do was bring another horse
And tell the sheriff, him.

Parole

A man takes his daughter to buy white shoes.
In a few seconds they walk out of the store
He touches her shoulder and looks around
The girl sees something taking place on the street
The father explains
Some things are forbidden and breathes on his hand.
They attend a movie
He is careful where they sit.
He checks the time in the dark
Smells the garlic on his breath
And later in the afternoon
Waiting on a waitress to take their order
The father hands his daughter the old shoes
Tells her to unlace the new ones
And put them back in the box.
The daughter does not understand
Some things are forbidden.
The man disappears to make a call
In a few minutes he returns
The white shoes set on the table
His daughter is gone.
The man looks around the room
Rubs his hand over his mouth
Thinks how he could wipe them all out
In a few seconds.

Freedom, Revolt, and Love

They caught them.
They were sitting at a table in the kitchen.
It was early.
They had on bathrobes.
They were drinking coffee and smiling.
She had one of his cigarillos in her fingers.
She had her legs tucked up under her in the chair.
They saw them through the window.
She thought of them stepping out of a bath
And him wrapping cloth around her.
He thought of her waking up in a small white building,
He thought of stones settling into the ground.
Then they were gone.
Then they came in through the back.
Her cat ran out.
The house was near the road.
She didn't like the cat going out.
They stayed at the table.
The others were out of breath.
The man and the woman reached across the table.
They were afraid, they smiled.
The others poured themselves the last of the coffee
Burning their tongues.
The man and the woman looked at them.
They didn't say anything.
The man and the woman moved closer to each other,
The round table between them.
The stove was still on and burned the empty pot.
She started to get up.
One of them shot her.
She leaned over the table like a schoolgirl doing her lessons.
She thought about being beside him, being asleep.

They took her long grey socks
Put them over the barrel of a rifle
And shot him.
He went back in his chair, holding himself.
She told him hers didn't hurt much,
Like in the fall when everything you touch
Makes a spark.
He thought about her getting up in the dark
Wrapping a quilt around herself
And standing in the doorway.
She asked the men if they shot them again
Not to hurt their faces.
One of them lit him one of his cigarettes.
He thought what it would be like
Being children together.
He was dead before he finished it.
She asked them could she take it out of his mouth.
So it wouldn't burn his lips.
She reached over and touched his hair.
She thought about him walking through the dark singing.
She died on the table like that,
Smoke coming out of his mouth.

The History of John Stoss

for Ginny

People were going around with chickenfeet.
People were going around with bibles.
There were many strangers waiting in the rain.
There were thieves ancient roads and women from other countries.

The lamps smoked the dogs shook under the houses.
The farmgirls stood on the front porches
Holding their aprons over their eyes.
They did not want to see the witch scatter her straw
Over their fathers' fields.
They did not want to hear their mothers weeping
Over their cracked plates.

There were footsteps in the graveyard
And hair being combed in front of mirrors.
The men stayed up all night in front of the stoves
Holding the dropped calves.
Everyone who had new snow in their heart
Held their pillow
And spoke to the feathers.

Someone heard their words.
It was not Jesus.

It was a man who fed the beautiful geese
Of the pioneers,
It was a man who tracked scoundrels with the Chippewa

It was John Stoss
Coming across the prairie in his wagon
Playing his tuba.

His bed was full of pretty dresses new jackknives
Bags of seed for the lonely to pass around at night
Thread to patch the winter's strict teachers.

John Stoss gave away his lunchmeat and buttermilk
And drove on
Getting heavy on his love.

He spit in the dark by himself
And the wind broke like the rivers of Kansas
That disappeared in his heart
And the moon was his white piano
And his children went around stammering
And warm in the evenings about to cry.

in my new movies there will be a child
walking to town barefooted.

He is carrying ice for to love you.
when he sells the ice, he buys a pair
of ~~good~~ walking shoes
10 rq tea

For to kill the spider in the
corner of ~~my~~ house.
you

And there will be a big black woman
toking a shotgun, coming
~~thru~~ the fog in ~~~~ the
Bow of a rowboat.
she got her sawed-off pistol
and her dead man's fedora

those of you who can put
2+2 ~~together~~, will devour
this the boy will the new glass
in rowing the ful woman
~~though the~~ God ' down the
rain.

Him making
At gtri. got her d. in Anstelam on.

in my next movie the wife of the c ??? poet woman.
she's sewing the sweater for,
and runs off with a welder from c >

in a cabin in the ozark a husband
is waiting to his cat.

YOU

skeeter
forget

new poems
by

FRANK STANFORD

"You can piss in my face.
But do not tell me its raining."

THE LIGHT THE DEAD SEE

1991

The Kite

Before he stole Mr. Charlie's sedan
Chinaman rocked along the cuts dead easy,
Chopping cotton, singing like a katydid.
It was a long time ago on a low turn row,
When he took his bimbo for a ride
In the bossman's car. They saw someone
Getting buried in the Bogue Phalia River.
When Chinaman got picked up for stealing,
He told his gal to keep her mouth shut:
"Don't say nothing, till I get out of prison."
They paroled him once, he knew he wouldn't fall,
But his Pine Bluff jelly-roll flew in a kite
That keyed off the captain to bring him back.
Now he's hoe-time floating for life.
All his tunes have lost their hinkty licks
And he can't keep up on the grassy rows,
He doesn't think about bimbos or parole,
Just a panther tail popping at his back.
It was a long time before knock-off.
The dog sergeant was twirling his bat.
But *his* youth was jumping in his chopping
And he wasn't going to waste it on grass.
He thought, one more time, he wanted to be:
Flatweeding, rocking dead easy.

The Brake

I saw them coming down the back road
In a black Ford. We weren't that far away
And we could feel their dust settling on us.

"They gonna do the Man's business tonight,"
Ray Baby says. "I seen them do it before."

Born In The Camp With Six Toes says, "Uhuh."

"No they ain't," I says. "They just going
To Aunt Julinda's to get the suck rock."

It was almost the first day of August,
My birthday, a full moon rising,
And time for the mad dog season to start.
Aunt Julinda Bayou had the only
Suck rock around.

          "Now what you think?
Even if she do got it, it's been out
The buck's belly too long," Ray Baby says.
"You seen that nigger in the back seat."

"That's right," I says. "He got mad dog bit
And they taking him to Aunt Julinda's
To get the mad fever sucked out."

Ray Baby and Six Toes stood there
In my hand-me-down elastic band shorts,
Lightening up with the dust,
Shoulders back and bellies out,
Shaking their heads at their navels,
Pushing out like other little peters.

"I seen them do it before," Ray Baby says.

We were over our heads in good cotton,
About a dozen rows from the road,
And on our way to raid the Sorghum Brake,
When the police passed us in their black car.
We had to cross the road, another cut,
And then, hack through a thicket of briars
Before we'd even come to the woods.

"There's gonna be a nigger coming up
Out of the blue hole I say," Baby says.

We walked through oak, holly, and gum,
And found the clearing before the brake.
We were looking for the lightning bugs
On the berry bush to show us where the bogue
In the center of Diamond Woods was.

"Fire bush," Born In The Camp With Six Toes says.

We passed the sawgrass, cypress, and cane,
Where there was only one alligator left,
And looked for Mose Jackson's Sorghum Brake.

"Go right," Ray Baby says, "or they gonna find us
In this here swamp tomorrow morning."
"You got to take a right at the fire bush
Or you gonna walk right into that bogue.
What you keep jumping in the ditch for, Six Toes?"

"Cause my feet is hot!"

                    "You better shut your mouth
And quit jumping in that ditch! You hear me?"

"Better listen," I says. "That might be quick mud."

"Now I'm telling y'all my feet is hot."

The moon was high and the whippoorwills
Were looking for nymphflies in the switchwillows.
Way away, black and tan nigger dogs bayed;
The clouds were the shade of an indigo snake.

"Hey! What would you do if you got dog bit?"

"I'm going straight to Mama Julinda's
And ask her for that deer rock," Six Toes says.

"What you gonna do, Baby Ray?" I says.

"Same thing."

     "Thought you said it was too old."

"I did. That dragline oiler from West Memphis
Killed that deer with the rock in it last year."

"How come you won't go to a hospital, then?"

"What you saying? Ain't no colored person
Gonna go to no hospital. Shoot man,
They give a nigger fifty shots if he's bit
And they always give him one anyway."

"I think we're getting close," Six Toes says.

"I'm going to the hospital," I says.

"SWEET JESUS!" Ray Baby says. "We got to leave!
We got to get out of this place right now!"

He pointed to fresh cut sugar sticks
And a blue shirt with a number on the front.

"*STATESVILLE* too! SWEET JESUS!" Ray Baby says.

"I'm getting my young ass out of here," Six Toes says.

"What are y'all talking about?" I says.

                                        "Shit!
Man, I told you nobody got bit," Ray says.
"That weren't no bit nigger in the back seat!"

"It sho was a crazy one though," Six Toes says.

"They going straight to Aunt Julinda's alright,
But they ain't studying about no sucking rock.
Mose Jackson is out of the penitentiary
And we standing right in his sorghum patch.
Man, we got to leave!" Ray Baby says.

"What is the matter with you, Ray?" I says.
"If that's him, then the police have him.
And you know they gonna lock him up."

"That's what you think! Mose Jackson is smarter
Than both those peckerwoods put together.
Already made them take him to his Mama's,
And she gonna conjure them peckerheads
As soon as they walk in her door," he says.

"There won't be no *nigger* coming up
Out of the blue hole this time I bet,"
Born In The Camp With Six Toes Lewis says.

The Lies

There are ships leaving tonight but I don't know where
my bed is like a harbor of dreams
it is the port of sleep
I always go it alone and get drunk
with the words under the water
because I've never seen
the ocean I see the heads of the horses
swimming through the river
I see a ship departing with the secret dancers of death
don't worry if you see me
throwing knives in a chinaberry tree
in the middle of the night
you might be sleepwalking with the lightning bugs
you might be dreaming
and step on the blade of a shovel
it is only me standing vigil by the slough
I hop around on one leg like a gypsy
if I had a violin I'd make you cry
I can feel the rafter in the old mansion settling
I can feel the minnows swimming in the great swan's belly
and all my wolves are hanging
upside down on a barb wire fence I can feel
the wings knocking the fog off the pond
while I sing to myself the mosquitoes give their soliloquies
I am like the hunchback in the woods
hacksawing spurs while men are asleep I touch the horses
and the clouds are like a cortege of howls
there are so many bottles floating in the river
the fishermen must be drunk by now
I swim under the dark men's shanties
the catfish are eating supper under me

someone left the radio on I got the blues
I swim through imperial night like a long lost
prince in a black cloak
good night brother I say to the water moccasin
in the mud I rest on a turtle's back
I watch the devil's needles darning a shroud
I hold drinking water in my hand
and when the wind comes up it lists like a moldy compass
I strike out in the direction of my spit and the moon
the boatswain yells lad overboard
and I listen to the prows go past me
I see the ship of the hundred rivers of sleep
and the ship of the lookouts passing out
the ship of drowned infants the ship
of tortured stallions
the ship of dreams sighted by blind riders
I watch the bowsprits
come and go and I hear the men on the docks
closing their pocketwatches with a sigh
ships are leaving this moment
but I don't know where
night has put her coins over my eyes
I don't know my past
like the back of my hand
I have forgotten what flag I fly
if I am drowned it is all the same as a tarnished looking glass
so at night I roam the decks
looking for fights
the sailors see me in their dreams and call me captain
of ghosts
I heave out my guts on the lee side
I lean over out of breath and touch
the hull the invested body of advancing wood
there are no splinters in dead timber

the ghost captain knows
I walk along the wharves like a wanted man
I see all my children stealing rope
one of them comes up with sores on his head
he asks me to open a tin of shoe polish
I give him two bits and tell him shove off
I smell it on the balcony
along about twilight a hubcap flies off
and a Negro pulls a fish bone out of his mouth
with that look in his eye
in a cove on the other side of Spoon's Landing
somewhere I don't even have bait on my line
all my hooks are snagged out except for this one
and the fish I get I ought to throw back
when it gets dark I'll dream
about a ship's wheel
I'll look at the moon like a bleeding toenail
the dancers will pass by

Sun Go Down

I spent many afternoons
On the shore
Looking at my boat

Especially in the fall
I breathed on my cold hands
And watched the clouds

Mosey over
Like blind men
Picking apples

You have the feeling
The past
Is like a woman

Who ran off
With everything
But your belongings

There were never friends
When the weather was bad
Just visitors and books

Sometimes strange birds
Flying south
But nothing stolen

The water lied through its teeth
Like a draft
That seeps in at night

Making you sick
When you go to bed
With wet hair

I can't remember
What afternoon it was
When those men showed up

Other boats
Landed in our cove
The crawdads

Under the rocks
Told each other
To keep quiet

One of them wiped his nose
"Step back boy
A dead man here"

They Were Society People

I was a cook in the Army so when I got out
that's what the VA got me a job doing at
this country club. I worked there a couple
of months and thought I was doing pretty good,
but there was this one woman who kept complaining
about my steaks. At dinner parties sometimes
they'd make the waiter bring me out and they'd
bawl me out in front of the other guests.
Pretty soon it got to be a joke and kind of
regular. It didn't matter how good the dinner
was, they had to have their fun. I went to
the hospital on my day off and told the doctor
what I wanted to do. He gave me some pills
and told me to forget it. Well, the next day
I went to work planning the party. I had it
all laid out when in walks the woman in charge
of the benefit. It was her. She was the hostess.
She said for me to change everything she'd plan
it all. She ran everybody out of the kitchen
but me and started telling me what to do.
She said now I'm going to teach you what I
learned in Paris one summer. I put a fish in
her mouth, and tied her up to the cutting table
and told her I was going to show her what
I learned in Vietnam one year. I fixed
a dinner none of her friends will ever forget.

Death and Memory

When poor women died
The undertaker would close the caskets early
And roll them in a room
To cut their hair.

My brother and I knew this.

So when they had our sister
We hid one night in the funeral home
And waited on the man
To come back from supper
With his scissors.

We heard him whistling.
He was cutting the clothes off a boy in another room.
He was washing a body.

There were other visitors.
The mother came with her daughter
To trade
Their hair for a coffin.

My brother said it's bad
How the rich go on
Living and wearing the beautiful hair of the dead.

I knew what to do,
I knew.

I'd been walking for ever so long thirteen miles I bet
I's heading to Snatch's for chicory coffee
it was a saloon and short order cafe on the side of the state highway
the big trucks full of cotton and folks
who were moving furniture back
they turned me around like a top
I found a broken drill bit
the sky was the color of a working man's shirt
in between Semis I did around the world with my yoyo
I had cardboard in my soles
the blue vapor light outside Snatch's place couldn't make up its mind
a 52 black ford with sun visor and halfmoon fender skirts
pulled off the road beside me
where you going one of them said
t'ave my coffee I said
up there at Snatch's they asked where else I said
you won't believe your eyes when you get there they said
I believe anything I said
you better be with your eyes when you open the door they said
I see through them says I
they peeled off
and one of them called back he's big
the only car sitting in front of the place
except for the dead man's station wagon
was Snatch's rig wine flashed blue and GOOD
EATS flashed yellow Jax Beer IS SOLD HERE
Premium Prices GOOD RIVER CAT TOO
usually folks was there eating that time a evening
it wasn't that bad a cold wave
my throat was kindly sore
a little lemon and queen bee honey in my coffee
would do it good

it sho wasn't going to snow
Snatch's wasn't one of those rolling kind of places
just a few drinks and pin balls and eats
a lot of truck drivers and family men went there
I was thinking they might of had some action
a fight to run folks off maybe the state boys closed him down
Snatch was outside by his car down on one knee
with the door open listening to the radio shaking his head
he had on a day glow furlined cap
and was smoking the last part of his cigar
what's up Snatch says I
he let me call him Snatch instead
of Mr. Snatch because I's good on Big Leaguer Pin Ball
he didn't answer
like a man who gets served a grease white egg
when he wanted the thing done with lace
down in you side I asked
he still didn't answer
come on be a sport I says
why he never lifted his face from the ground
just shaking his head slow back and forth
well I know you got some coffee on
a cold day like this
I'm going to get me a cup
I'm going to make me some hot chocolate
if you got any marshmallows by god
the bells jingled on the door when I opened it
but there was something keeping it from opening
you got this thing latched from the inside Snatch
how come you done that
it was getting dark I had to go around to the window
what I saw I thought I didn't see
I turned around five times and spit
on my floor with both hands over my eyes

I cleaned my fingernails
and turned on the hydrant to slick back my hair
I needed sleep
I ran back and forth jumping up in front
of the window like a deer
I tried looking with one eye
thinking of dreams where the wagon comes unhitched
I looked for cotter pins and washers
and tried to get Snatch to talk
what's he doing here I was studying
shadow boxing with blackbirds
this is how he looked
he was a big black monk all dressed in white
the way the hood on his sweatshirt was
I could just see some of his chin
with black hairs under his bottom lip
like he was the stock of a shotgun
pouting over who was shooting him
there was a crack in the window
Snatch was losing money on heat
says I to myself mosey on around to the other
window and take a good look
the air was slipping out or in I don't know
which of the crack like someone who doesn't
know how to play a woodwind
I got me a sawhorse and rest it upside
Snatch's quick stop
I nearly caught his attention I made so much
noise dragging it over to the other window
everytime a Mack truck went by
I like to lost my balance
he was an awful big man
sitting at the round wooden table all by his self
he looked like a knight come back

empty-handed and beat from the crusades
lions and gnats wouldn't have bothered him
the moon was down and out on the other side of the building
I could see it coming through the glass
on the other side in mine
I breathed on it and it turned to oil
I smiled at him but it was like he didn't see me
that made me afraid
you know how I am I thought maybe a artist was
drawing his picture he was so still
like a bear taking deep breaths under ground
in his sleep his hand was a dark squid
wrapping around the quart of Stag
thumb reaching clear back over to his knuckles
there was two empty Falstaffs beside him
and a big mug with a see through bottom
that's how I saw Sonny Liston crying in a short order cafe
steam was rising off of him like a ridden horse
he made his own kind of fog
the way a destroyer dies when it leaves a enemy harbor
his running togs were grey
he had a white towel around his neck for an ascot
sweat was hanging off his forehead
it was little loads of buckshot on his brow
I thought about women coming home from church
a few sundays after Easter wearing the same clothes
he had honey in his beer
about nine plastic wrappers off those containers
were scattered all over the table
that stuff ain't no good he should of asked Snatch
for some real honey on the comb
there was the smell of dressed game soaking in water
his eyes seemed to be floating
Sonny Liston belched

I bet I could drop a window weight on his chest
when he was sleeping and he wouldn't feel a thing
I raised up the window
it didn't make a sound
I could smell Sonny Liston
he was in his sock feet
his black tennis shoes was on a chair to themselves
like guests
steam rose out of them too
like genies from lamps
a trickle of blood ran from his left nostril
some of it dropped into one of the honey cartons
his eyes were half shut
you been running too hard Sonny I thinks
I looked at my white knuckles
the first move he made I missed
when he picked a booger from his nose
he seen his blood then
wiping it on the side of his sweat pants
moving his toes
I lost my balance
and almost fell through the window
I jumped off and ran around to Snatch's smoke house
where he kept his jars of honey
I couldn't open the lid
I told him I was going to get some
of his bee honey so you couldn't exactly say
I was a thief
was on my way to take
Sonny Liston the jar of apple blossom honey
and on my way says I to Snatch
you got a real guest in there don't you
Snatch he don't say a word just shake his head
and fiddle with the radio

it's getting colder and darker now
and I still hadn't had no coffee
here goes is what I tell him
he turn around at me and beat some of
his ash off gritting his gold teeth
I climb through the window
and take hold the lid again but I can't
open it Mr. Liston I say I'm bringing you
some good honey here see if you can
take the lid off try the comb
you know how he take it off
no hot water or knife handle
I just barely could look him in the eye
he was so mean looking
you mind if I sit with you
the blood wasn't running anymore
he didn't answer
what brings you training down this way
Mr. Liston how many miles did you jog
I wished I'd a known you was
a coming I'd a had somebody fix you
a proper training supper
not no beer and hot sausage
Mr. Liston look like he didn't hear me
well I reckon you too tired to talk
so I went I drew my coffee
and got the can of pet milk out of the
bowl on the bottom of the beer cooler
it was good coffee
I told him boxers ain't supposed to drink
no coffee or beer are they Mr. Liston
you was bleeding while ago
there your blood is on the table
he was still evaporating

he was like a fire
until he got the chills
shaking all over he taken his false teeth
out and set them down
and reach in the honey jar and take
the comb and bring it to his mouth
holding his head under it
like a platter
honey dripping down his chin like tears
he sucked some off it
how you like it Mr. Liston
he kind of smiled
told me one word energy
I went and got the bedspread
off the couch where Snatch took his naps
there was a big Flamenco dancer on it
I threw it over his shoulders
telling him best not to get too cold after a run
a few things I said to him
the coffee scorched my lips
while he wasn't looking
I got the little empty honey carton with his blood in it
maybe I should have told him I had it
he was chewing on the comb
I pulled the ace out of my back pocket
and poured apple blossom on it
I had me a comb too
the coffee was doing me in
I looked at the dirt on the floor
he dropped the honey on it
I kept making little circles of pet milk on the table
Sonny Liston stood up and yelled
at the top of his lungs
a four pound shell cracker hanging on the wall

fell off in back of the counter
the chandelier rattled over his head
he looked like a king
who'd just lost his kingdom
I had some slide pictures in the back
I thought if I brought them out Mr. Liston
wouldn't be so down in the mouth
a champion ain't supposed to be like that
these slides was taken in Paris back during the war
I ask him you ever fight in Paris
I got the slide show and set it on the table
this is what I figured
if he wanted to see them he could
I didn't have no money for the jukebox
it was silent and good as it was
I asked him how about a massage Mr. Liston
he kind of give me the eye over that
I said I'll give you one no charge
you been running up and down the levee ain't you
I tried to get my fingers into his back muscles
but they was hard as a barked tree
I nearly broke my thumb trying to rub him down
the coffee kept me crazy as a loon
I began to dream that Sonny Liston was dying in my arms
Rudyard Kipling had hauled off and shot him
I mean assassinated him from the galleries
just when Sonny was about to knock the other
knight off his horse with the jousting stick
it was made out of white pine
with all the rough spots lathed over
the grounds was getting bitter in my mouth
he seemed to be going asleep
snoozing like
I got him in a head lock

not to tell nobody I got Sonny Liston
in a hold but just so's I'd know it
like a handshake like we was friends
I wasn't going to tell no one
besides it was getting rid of the pain
in his neck I was applying a gentle pressure
I know Snatch wasn't looking and he was asleep
so I kissed Sonny Liston on his black neck
I let him sleep

                                          he laid down
I sat in his lap and ~~sat down~~
(to their big place on the river

I ran into ~~brother~~ Alan Ginsberg
to their big place on the river

One night I ~~see~~ a man inside there
He jumps to my window and came in

One Night God tunes eye in my room
He dug at my heart with a pitchfork
And threw it out the window

(

Box 97
Tr&uro, Mass. 02666
21 December, 1974

Jeffrey Mitchell
Assistant to the Executive Director
The Academy of American Poets
1078 Madison Avenue
New York, New York 10028

Dear Jeff:

I just got a letter from Frank Stanford saying "The Am.
Academy of Poets wouldn't accept for consideration my ms.
for the W. Whitman award; said it was too long to read.
Horseshit."

I think you have made a mistake. Stanford is a brilliant
poet and just because he is ample in his work, like Whitman,
is no reason not to consider his manuscript. He has had this
difficulty often in trying to get his poetry published. Again
I say that I think that he is a brilliant poet and he should be
encouraged in his amplitude rather than rejected for it. I've
been reading his work for the last four years or so and I'm
convinced of his genius as a writer.

If the competition has not already closed, may I urge him
to resubmit his manuscript? I should add that he has not asked
me to intervene on his behalf.

Give my regards to Batty,

Best,

Alan Dugan

P.S. I'm sending a copy of this letter to Stanford.

A. D

Vision

the cruxfiction   A hundred bob whites around
crusifiction   Cruxsifictions

Christ surrounded by one hundred bobwhites.

minutes or so ago on a clear night, and now another squall is blowing through, the rain pounding down on the bulkhead outside this dining room window and right now the squall is passing ~~toward~~ toward the north-east and out to sea. The insects, as I said before, are confused about this weather because there was a big red-eyed fly walking around this ball point pen on this piece of paper without any notion that I could kill it. The weather is confusing. The fly is drinking from a drop of beer I left on the table, and now it is sitting on my thumb. It annoyed me, so I killed it and send it to you. This is

the relation between human beings and certain types of flies.

The rain continues. So does the wind. Mike Ryan's interview with me should be out some-time in August: I want to say something about tape-recorded interviews: I think that it is a cheap way of doing things. I have, on hand, the galleys of Michael's tape, and I find the ~~resulting galleys~~ galley-proofs reading as being chopped up as hell; tape-recordings don't make for continuity, but rather for dis-continuity, so I'm not going to do it again. it is too fashionable and too easy, and as the galley-proofs show, it makes the

They came to get you in the middle of the night
when the moon was a dead child.
The Black cook danced naked wild.

~~It had to be at night.~~
~~some of the children would get on their knees~~
~~kneel on the floor, in the~~

They gave ~~another week~~ ~~~~ a thousand dollar cash
and she gave them a jar of holy water, another.
we drove off in a big car
to a little chapel in the woods.
He undid her garters, pulled ~~~~ down to his knees
leaned her against a tree.   She put her arms around the
                              tree, he just leaned and
It was a long hush.
I looked at his black and white shoes
in the hood of the car.
then they prayed.
then they ~~looked~~ at me for the first time,
~~~~ Brantley like ~~~~
                              in the morning,
into smile.
I took hold of him like a live oak.
He felt me from behind, wept in my nearly hair.

UNPUBLISHED
MANUSCRIPTS

PLAIN SONGS

after Jean Follain

Many of Stanford's unpublished poems were organized by the poet into manuscripts of varying sizes. I've attempted to present the poems as the poet apparently wanted them to be gathered. However, numerous poems that appear in these manuscripts also feature in other books, sometimes in slightly different versions. "Plain Songs" gathers "versions" and "improvisa-tions" influenced by the poems of Jean Follain. — Ed.

Schoolboys and Their Hound

For the hell of it the schoolboys
break the ice on the pond
near the tracks
they're all bundled up
in army greens
stained with axle grease
and dove blood
and chalk and cum
their belts hang down
like snakes on a fence
the leather is coming apart
clear up to the last hole
they poked through
with an ice pick
the dog on their trail
is too deaf and lame
to hunt no one
will feed him
his age they never did get
exactly their own

Fox You Are My Convict

From time to time
whether we know it or not
a fox as red as fire
as black as a keyhole
goes through our evenings
across the shadow
we cast on the side of the road
in fact the ground
sleeps the color gray
and dreams smooth stones
the night of nights without love
earning a dangerous living
following us like sand
like books
we make ourselves
chewing sweetgrass and feathers
at the same time
and from the longest dream of water
breath on the river
in the fall of the year
giving us zeros
when we hairless and guilty
stuffed with the mystery of cornbread
and the fire in the shack
wake up thirsty

Desperate Song of One Who Has Gotten Rid of Some of Himself

I guess it all floated south
like a ghost ship to Antarctica
I strike out at twilight
and get back at dawn
my coat labeled botany slung over my shoulder
like a lamb or a bat
I lope through the stomach
of the killer whale the delta
taps on my soles not on my boots
I fill my gizzard with precious stones
I drink too much of the night's blended whiskey
I smell like the moon's loud fart
and shoot the moon to strangers myself
I float and sink and walk
I feel the tiny shipwrecks in the girls' tanned bellies
crazy dogs come chasing after me
I feel shade on my face   swirling and unexplored
when I walked past a barn and the sun is going down
I like those grapes I want to climb your vine
I ask people for a ride
I pay my way by asking questions
I'm nothing but a rope of smoke
tied around the stars
and you're bound to see me
I don't carry around clocks or knives or cameras
I ask you to do the same
don't turn me in
let me keep going my way
peeling this peach
eat it brothers and sisters

it's dedication to the memory of Shelly
eat the sweet red middle let me keep the cores
I'll poke eyes in the cold ladies of the snow

The Divorced

The burned field bends over the moon
the black smoke like flies around rinds
faces rotted dark by the river
shoes fed up with night
curtains like blankets over the drowned
like thunder we wait for in summer
summer we wait for too
leaping over the cradle with its mirror
returning with cold ears like a bandit's envy
the air

The Future

What we see down the hill
isn't the end of the hill
but the waist of the hill
if all my friends would get on their harmonicas
you would have gumption enough
to reach in the hole of a dead tree
and risk the stanza or your hand
in the dead wood you find a locket
you shut your eyes and walk with it
further down the hill
you talk like a fool to the slope of the hill
you wet your feet in the branch and look up the hill

Cotton You Lose in the Field

Some bad whiskey
I drink by myself
just like you
when this wind
blows as it does
in the delta
where a lost hearing aid
can be taken
for a grub worm
when the black constellations
make you swim backwards
in circles of blood
stableboys ruin their hands
for a while
and a man none of us
can do without
breaks his neck
jumping over some hill
chasing the fox
of a half-pint
and a fine-blooded horse
is put out of its misery
even the young sisters
of the boys we run with
we would give our fingers
to touch them again
but this war
seeps back into us
like insecticide
and the white cricket of those days
drags itself off the hook

there are no more fish
there is no more bait
the rivers are formed by the tears of sports fans
we try to pour a trail of salt
as if making a long fuse
with a gunpowder keg
we try to swim away from the gym
like slugs with gills
the girls from the other school
step off the bus
the clouds are weighed in at the gin
there is a pattern to all this
like a weave of a skirt
we all go crazy from looking

The Dark Child

Left alone
in the mansion
the boy wanders
through the black corridors
and rooms of books
and swords and mirrors
and portraits that follow
him everywhere he goes
the storm has knocked
out the wire
the brass jaw of the lion
falls like a star
the servants have grown
afraid and left
in the town the parents
are very well off
at the picture show
the father has worn
black evening clothes
the mother sleeping
through death's long montage
and the dark mistress
sipping gin in the balcony
worries about the child
at home alone
in the darkness
running into the mahogany
and glass
but nothing is broken
lightning makes it through
the rapids of his eyes

like a gypsy's crystals
he can see his good looking mother
sprawled out
the canoe waiting
to be cut loose
from her throat

The Deep Sleep of the Fox

Dogs barking and men coming out on deck
to take a leak and look around afraid
afraid the stranger will come back and walk
in their simple gardens in his black coat
and large hat and iron mirror shoveling the loam
from the pasts scattering it all over
the beehives and old boots the hemispheres
of the wise and lonely who ruined their names
echoes of the farmgirl calling her slow
rooster filled with light like a virgin's head
trapped under the earth which is also deep

Sister

There are roosters
quite beautiful
that will drown themselves
drinking
if they do not blink
and infants who suffocate
in their sleep
shoes wear out
the blind peel their apples
the young feel their nipples
without a care
a lifebuoy
and a soggy rose
mark the spot
where they heard her

Second Thoughts on a New Tattoo *

When you like you can leave
with blood
all over your hands
you can walk a long ways
and remain there
remote as a lost cork
floating in sorrow
without string or a hook
moss its only message
and when you rest
on the cold damp ground
you will still find dust
at the top of your socks
like mute starlight
your gardener will follow you
he will hail down a traveler with his shovel
he will open the door for you
take off his hat
and ask you to remember him
you make a mean deal with night
and the moon still has you
under her thumb
hay flies out the rear
of the girl's truck
she asks you where you come from
why you're wearing gloves
you've seen her before

*At least two other manuscript versions of this poem have alternate end-
ings: "with this red word on your wrist" and "with this red word on your
arm." — Ed.

don't I know you she says
in a voice smooth as a curve
looming a few miles up the road
her boots are beside her
her feet are leery as snakes
as innocent as doves
she shifts gears
going into the turn
her skirt hiked up to the elastic
on her flank
your old home has been sold to hunters
the garden is thick with rabbits
you go to sleep in these pickups
tired of work near the water
fond of the instant
you travel with no lights no license
through the country you know
through the countries you forget
with the word free   red on your arm

Night of the Following Day

Daylight is also between the feet
of a virgin
you get invited
to go to a movie
and spend the night
with a friend
what an odor in their home
a swordfish over the fire
a fig under the piano
and a lot of books
his sister comes in later
she leaves a crack in her door
she takes off her clothes
she turns the radio
of our childhood back on
and leaves it playing all night

The Way She Was

I get up when the night is the coldest
and darkest and put green wood on the fire
so the room won't be cold in the morning
the wood is wet and sour like stale beer
or a pillow in a baby's white room
I listen to the split sticks groan like boats
going their way overhead somewhere else
on the long lake last summer when I was
under its body and singing like fire
thinking about those rooms I was in last
winter holding my breath looking for a window
a murky glass of wine on the table
like a weird mirror of blood and
bad fortune in the bedroom where I could
see a bird in a cedar tree keeping
out of the rain and smoke gets in my eyes
and she goes away wet after her swim

Branches Pushed Away by Scarred Birds[*]

My mother used to pour me ice tea
from a pitcher so heavy she needed
both her stout arms I know we are
supposed to forget this country
and its illusions of water
coming over hills in uneven land
but I remember among convicts
and guitars among the lovely rituals
of the three-legged horse. Fox
or the dust in the carburetors
of even my grandmother's childhood
I forget nothing like a sawhorse
or a bucket oh these bleak trees
of winter must be death's capillary system
no matter what the company
or how thirsty I am I still cannot
pour without spilling a little

[*]Although this poem never appeared in a published book, it is assumed that
the poet meant "scared" instead of "scarred." — Ed.

The Purpose of Sin

Everywhere I look after it rains
the branches of the trees
the weeds at the edge of the slope
they've all had too much to drink
if I were to take a knife
if you could see me mean at the glass grave
and dig it back into my thigh
searching for its curved point
the papers on the desk would flutter
and the ferns hanging from the ceiling
would sway like they were stowed up in a storm
simple air would pour out of my wound
like the soft and the hard bugs on a summer night

The Dream near the Witness Tree

Death uses a beautiful rock as its perch
you don't know what it feels like
how cold and bright it is
until it snows and a blackbird leaves there
the wind blows through its crag
and holds up a branch in the night
like the last peach on the tree
or a woman who has lost a breast
and thinks she will lose you too
Death makes a point of saying I
will lose you

Wages of Fear

He came to work late his boots still in his hand
a ways down the road we could see him coming
barefooted the dust rising like silent runners
were stealing bases under him we watched him
cut past the turn row taking his time to catch
up with us in the stuff on the ridge gone with weeds
all he said was has the ice man gone by
I told him no and he said good
when he does remind me to give him a dime
for a sweet cake I don't want any pop
we worked until noon
the ice man came late
he said he was held up
near the bridge
he was tired of drinking cold water
so he stopped for a little while near the creek
he laid down on the ground and dipped his hands in
and a stranger came up behind him and said
I want one hundred pounds of ice or your life
he said he said you can have it I'll help you
carry it anywhere you want to take it
so I helped him load in sacks over his one-eared mule
I didn't want to mix words with see I saw
what he had in his pocket the fact is it was a pistol
so I won't be back today so there's no use
giving me any change y'all just have to do without
today the ice man got his truck in gear and left
we laid down in the cool dirt around the cotton stalks
thinking we would take the rest of the afternoon off
that's what we thought Willy the man who came left
hollered like he was going crazy he said I'm going
to town they got a circus and a side show so long folks

Raids

An owl comes from its roost
in the loft
to drink the holy water
from the churchhouse
so it is said
if its throat is still
dry it will swallow
the lamp oil
with its scent of nerves and eyelids
and go screech
near the candles
lit for the intentions
of the perpetual dead
so it is told
the wide bird flies
through shattered stained glass
through the belly of the Holy Ghost
in the dead of night
while the easygoing and the bitter sleep
while vanity and lust wear through
while the fire bugs draw close
the bird winds up,
winds up its wings like an absurd commando
and goes back to the rooms of children
who drowse and swoop

Bells and Whispers

You know they have worked
their fingers to the bone
just ask them
they've been let down
and taken up
like the hem of a gown
kept in the attic
the same ritual on the stool
some things are not touched
the relics behind the altar
passed around on your saint's day
the collection taken up for the nuns
who care for the orphans
there is golf and croquet
and invitations to the dances to send out
the evening goes slow
just listen to the talk
like a slug taking salt back to the mine
why quibble over the affairs
of the ladies
they could care less
in one room sit the professors
ambassadors of lard
in another stand the local officials
authorities on gas
they keep tucking in their shirts
rolling up their fists
waiting for their beautiful daughters
to come down the stairway
a butler is scolded
for not dusting the banister

nothing is to soil the long white gloves
the whole country club sways a little
like a chandelier
a shadow moves over the draperies
of the french windows in the ballroom
coming from the garden
is the silhouette of a stranger
brushing dust off his evening jacket
a silver flask
flashing in the moonlight like a dagger
the ladies go over the lists
of those who have been invited
wanting to know who hasn't shown up
the men smoke and lie to one another
the help eats fish eggs and drinks cold duck
while upstairs the girls wave out the windows
at the drunken guest
who was never invited
the dark guest dancing alone in the cool evening

What Luck

A man at the end of his rope
and dead broke
runs into a couple
of his former mistresses
having drinks together
in a dark cafe
they're fit to be tied
they're so glad to see him again
in the same shape
they left him

The Last Boat

An exile
happens to be passing by
the winds he loved
leave him cold
as lines
recited in the name of the lord
and the notorious earth of his country
lying in wait
like a woman
an ambush

Floating Bridge

The blind man gets up and tends his stove
he puts on his water then goes outside
to split kindling and gather eggs
the black cat sleeps at the foot of his bed
he cracks one egg for the cat
and gives it to him raw
and lets his soft boil
the blind man prays
he plays the guitar for thirty minutes
he goes out on the porch and shaves
the rain beats down on the tin roof
like August sun
he holds out his hand
washes off the soap with rainwater
and checks the long strings
running from the porch
to the outhouse and pump
and mailbox and garden
making sure they're taut
he goes over them like a sailor
inspecting the rigging of a ship
in a few days he'll cast off
the river is rising
coming to a full crest
like the moon on a cloudy night
his chickens will lay
on the swing and window sills
and he'll sound the depth of his yard
by throwing marbles in it
and when the water has gone down again
he'll go out with a spoon

and dig them out of the mud
hold them up in the sunlight
and he'll plant some bell peppers there
in their place and from that time on
he'll eat and sleep alone
by then the black cat will be gone
drifted off with the bluebirds and mosquitoes
taking other shelter
in the rafters of the bridge

The Strange Boy

The first day I went to school
The schoolhouse burned down,
So they turned over the undertaker's parlor to us
Seeing how he had passed away.
There was a victrola we all wanted to play
And a room of ferns
And a closet with odd pillows,
But the teacher combed our hands with a brush.
There was a girl in the high grade
Who had failed several times.
Her breasts were beginning
To show signs of danger.
She was cautioned, as was the dark-eyed orphan,
For whistling late in the afternoons
When all you could hear were the flies
And the boys drinking up at the store,
But warnings did neither of them any good.
Quite a few times they found them
Together in the barns. He knew
How to speak in a different tongue.
But he didn't know why, nobody did.
They just took it that his real folks
Came from some other country,
But the girl's folks all came from the county.
She liked it that he drew
Bodies asleep and angels on the blackboard,
Drew them with the blue chalk
He stole from the pool hall
Where he had a job racking balls
And sweeping for his keep.
He liked to walk at night with a broom

And a book of pictures by Hieronymus Bosch
Past the girl's shack and whistle.
Then, in school one day, a wagon of odd people passed by.
The boy shut the geography book,
Spit on his ink pen.
He stood up and moved through the desk rows
Where we were doubled-up like life rafts
And he cranked the arm of the victrola
And a music no one but the undertaker
And the dead had ever listened to
Quivered through the parlor like a swarm of bees,
And he and the girl left the room
And jumped in the back of one of those bright wagons
Which never have passed this way again.

I was rocked to and fro like a careening boat
I dreamed with my eyes half closed about the practicing carnival workers
the violinist and the juggler thinking about stretches of sea
through their windows where they were born
I saw them in time I saw them going to sleep at their work
I saw them as children before the wars with extra spending money
along a coast in Europe
climbing cliffs and talking about the days to come
the handkerchieves tied around their necks and the sea below
I felt like the wounded man being painted by the drunken artist
in the picture show Odd Man Out
I felt like he did when he remembered the words from the bible
and he stood up amidst the stares of the living paintings
and said his piece
I felt the two words Power and Dominion had been betrayed by the lawyers
of property I dreamed that these days the union carpenters
in the suburbs have joined the same houses together for the sake of joining
            them
I believe there is no sanctuary for me and my strays
in the subdivisions
and I dreamed the cathedrals built by the unknown
I am like grass cracking their concrete
I am a horse confused on the highway
I am carved by a blind negro in the shanties where I learned to speak
and the ones from town are automobiles made in the assembly plants of
            Detroit
and my brother is the bleeding child of hit and run
he is bleeding in his sleep
I am the rider called death
I sit in the saddle with Dark the negro
and his crazy blues sinks down like a diver into my belly of dreams
like terrible adventures like unknown poets going down with their ships

SMOKING GRAPEVINE

after Nicanor Parra

Homage to Jacques Prévert

The truth is we both attended
The same boys' school.
Reformatory, whatever you want to call it.
You were a big dick—I know you don't remember me,
Always stealing coins
From the collection for a Sunday matinee.

You used to confess you fucked the young maid
So much, she really had to lay you,
So you wouldn't lie to the priest anymore.
Then you spent your nights playing with your meat,
Weeping, drinking mass wine,
Listening to the queer monk's records of the blues.

You ate chicken legs in the alley
With orphans and criminals.
You, dressed fit to kill, your cape,
Your beret, your shorts, all one dark color.
And the ragged copy of Villon in your hip pocket
Like a handkerchief to cough in.

You weren't like the other boys,
You were like me, but I was too young and ugly for you.
You could play the cello well,
But no one ever heard you,
Not even the whores in the dives
You stole off to on free weekends.

Oh, I can read to numbskulls in the Southwest,
Make a few bucks at a cockfight with a bald-headed poet,
Watch some hillbilly cornhole a mule,
Then go back to Chile, with plenty, on a boat running guns,

But you, you can dream forever,
And still not remember who I was.

Translators

Blindfolded surveyors walking around a cliff
near the sea
looking for the cornerstones of death
brothers and sisters
fucking each other below on the sand
near the sea
near the sea
teachers stealing gum
from under shipwrecked desks
offices full of missals and TVs
sad feet
no gas
checkbooks washed up on the beach
acres and acres of hogshit
every foot of which has to be stepped off

Stinking Feet

I went to the United States and read and drank
and fucked and made enough hard cash
to book a ship back home
halfway there a queer told me
the President was dead
this couldn't be possible
this was possible
death takes the song
as well as the bird
so I hired a navigator
bribed some mate for a life raft
and in no time flat
I was back in the USA
with the first draft of a new and selected
I planned to call it *death yes funerals no*
I based it all on my old home town
I read and drank
and fucked and made enough hard cash
to get within the cordoned off boundaries
of my country
where I found out my name
was mud again

Assistance

Help goddamnit my pants are on fire
the whorehouse has been
bugged
the church has been looted
the church has been congratulated
water water everywhere
and every drop on the brains
eavesdroppings
where am I
the new Vice President kisses ass
like each one was a ruby
on the Pope's ring
Nixon looks like a foot
his mouth smells like an old lady's cunt
a can of wheat soaked in gasoline
the Secretary of Agriculture
cannot read is allergic to shit
is a known transvestite
how the hell did I get here cocksuckers all of them
a Fulbright
a purge
I weep in the streets
with my friends
Alan Dugan and Andrei Voznesensky
we drink like night
is an abortion we got for our mothers
we drink until we dream
the yeast of Berryman's home brew
I weep yes I weep
the name of my country over and over
I hold out a bowl

a punchdrunk waitress asks me
with or without beans
the last time I was there they shot a hole through my hat
I'm talking fast like an exile
there have been orders from above
there are no more butterflies in Chile
there are no gardens
no dreaming an anti-female policy
once more no dreaming no teeth
no brooms no poets
just last straws executive actions
full of green shit

Colleagues

They kissed the moon's asshole
then they spit minnows when nobody was looking
they knitted socks
they thought Hank Williams was Wagner
they never cut sugar cane
just stinking farts
they paid for operations
they screwed in less than thirty seconds
wearing neck braces
they lifted barbells
and sent off in the mail for toupees
they buried pencils to make up for lost time
they wrote like mad
they were just the way they were

Where's the Graveyard

How else are you going to explain
all these lawns without blankets
perfect formations of rock
houses without beds
a woman can't even have an affair

No rubbers in the parking lot
just stationwagons full of disturbed children
all these books and black light shadows
we're probably in hell
let's look around for a bar

No doors
no hair or mirrors
not one goddamn drink in the place
only a few bucks under a cross
so there's bound to be a church close by

I Put the Screw to Another Bottle

The same old habit
of smelling the cork
like it was my finger
I do the fox trot without looking at the clock
I don't give a fart

I take a drink in the bathroom
I take a shit
the day goes by
I take off my shoes
God they smell good

I throw one of them at the moon
bury the other near a girl's window
my wife calls me from the office
she keeps asking do I know what time it is
I'm not budging until I get a raise

Past Times

The earth created from nothing
without purpose or reason
just to screw things up
what the hell for
don't ask me

Untuning your father's guitar
whacking off with rose petals
stealing from your little brothers
writing surrealist poetry on the walls of the funeral parlor
kicking an old cripple

Lying to the police
lying to your lawyer
picking lice with professors
throwing spitballs at the priest
during study hall

Giving your steady the clap
pretending to have a fit in mass
slobbering for the family photographer
playing with a cat's balls
submitting poetry

Calling blacks niggers to show off
throwing the game
unzipping your fly during class
setting fire to a nursing home
asking for anything you can get

Crucifying Jesus Christ
playing with your meat

giving a political speech
without purpose or reason
just for the hell of it

Editing a film for death
spitting on the floor
shooting the Czar's children
slicing up the unborn
smelling your finger

in a word taking a dump on the piano

An Individual Above and Beyond Suspicion

Looks over his shoulders
puts out his smoke
and ducks into the labyrinth
taking off his clothes as he goes
in the first place he looks like a cockroach

He talks your head off
I mean he won't shut up
he smokes and runs at the mouth
laughing for no good reason
his vocal cords look like slugs

Bags of liquid salt appear under his eyes
he jacks off instead of cutting his throat
he throws mirrors at stones
nasty sores develop
he fiddles with his private parts on the bus

He won't read any of their papers
he grades by dice
until they report him
he's asked to leave
he leaves

He gets circumcised
later in life he coughs up blood
he talks with his hands
they quake like dead leaves
he translates modern veterinary techniques

He gets a divorce
married again

quits whacking off
dreams then apocalypses
holds out his hands and is defeated

really they catch the low-down son of a bitch

The Arkansas Prison System

Is like a lyric poem
with seven basic themes
first the cottonpicker
dragging behind it a wagon of testicles
a pair of pliers which can fill in
for a cross in a pinch
then there is the warm pond
between the maiden's thighs
next we have some friends
of yours and mine
who shall be with us always
Pablo the artist
the pubis of the moon
Pablo the cellist
panther of silence
Pablo the poet
the point of no return
and in case of emergency
the seventh and final theme
of this systematic poem
is the systematic way
death undresses in front of you

The Cross

Before long I'll be going back home
to the wide open arms of the cross
I'll weep promising never
to do it again
I'll get down on my knees
and kiss the foot of the cross
what a whore
what a mother the cross is
turning me on like my daughter in dance class
I married the cross
because I knew I could leave her
anytime I wanted
and she would always have me back
I had to
she was three months gone in the belly
she waits up nights for me
with wide open arms
and I creep into her room
my room
tears in my eyes
I crawl into her bed safe again
then there's an eerie sound
like wind through a tree
the creaking of a ghost ship
or a ripping tool
the dark cross passes over the moon
like an airplane
carrying the egg of doom
for now the cross is an airplane
a woman spreading her legs.

Somebody behind Me

Is reading everything I write
through a hole in his building
he makes fun of me
like a bitter guardian angel
he keeps whispering dirt about my family
he looks like Harpo Marx I think
when I look over my shoulder
all I see is a star
shining through a chink hole
making the sound of shears
but I know he's around here somewhere
down on his knees laughing at me
what will he do when I'm dead and buried
who will he pray for who will he look after
I ought to make arrangements with my publisher
to leave a flashlight in the outhouse
after I'm gone
so he can worship the lord of the flies

Flies on Shit

To the gentlemen from the south
to the tourists from the north
who write poems about the south
to the dumb-ass students
I'd like to ask one lousy question
have you ever seen a regatta of flies
sail around a pile of shit
and then come back and picnic on the shit
just once in your life have you heard
flies on shit
because I cut my eye teeth on flies
floating in shit

No Grudges

So you can see I'm not carrying anything
in my pocket
not dancing with your wife
not playing your daughter's bongos
I'll give you the moon
I'm not poking fun at you no shit
I'll give you the moon
you ought to win the National Book Award
a new car from the Super Bowl
for what you did
I'm taking off my hat
you still think I'm trying to pull something
go to hell
I tried my best
if you still want it go get it yourself
maybe your daughter will get it for you
Christ I'd like to grab a handful
of those butterflies in her panties
come sit on your bald-headed uncle's trick knee
if I have to do all the work myself
if I have to swat the flies
and do all the thinking and bending
you can kiss my ass at least

The Truth

I'm not going to lie
Through my teeth to you
Like the poets from Minnesota,
The South, and the West,
And New York City.

Most of all in life
I would like to fuck a thirteen-year-old again,
And I don't have any hesitations
About saying I'd rather be Marlon Brando
Than I would T.S. Eliot, etc.

I have more respect for Muhammad Ali
Than any other living man.
Of course I've tried *Esquire*,
But my shoes aren't platforms
And I don't know shit about canoes.

Although I can't prove it,
Most poets work for the highway dept.
There are more of them than there are
Flies and engineers.
And I stink like a dead mule under an overpass.

WOUNDS

One version of this manuscript carried the subtitle "Fifty Poems Vanquishing the House of Momus," yet the manuscript contained only twelve untitled, three-line poems, presented here. Perhaps the book was never finished or some of the poems migrated to other manuscripts. — Ed.

These poems are like starlings.
You creep up on one to catch
it and they all fly away.

*

This poem is a chainsaw.
Why don't you like it? It fells
trees you are afraid to climb.

*

This poem is like smoked glass.
You think you can see it and
yourself at the same time. Fool!

*

"I was John Kennedy's shoe.
I'm lonely. I would rather
smell his foot than kick your ass."

*

This poem is asleep. I
don't want you yelling at it,
waking it up. Let it dream.

*

This poem is so far a-
head of you you will never
catch it. Don't wear yourself out.

*

This poem is a faggot.
It's like a mirror. You
make it so it will make you.

*

This poem is so old I
doubt if anybody would
want it. I certainly don't.

*

This poem is undiscovered
as of yet. If you are what
you say you are, let it alone.

*

Raise this poem like a sword.
It is the last to make a
move, the first to land a blow.

*

I want this poem to be
a crane, so it will stand on
one leg and watch you look for it.

*

A poem looking for the
image behind the bug that
rolls the shit along the road.

he's dragging the cat up on the bank the pole is broken so he grabbed a holt
of the line now I can't even talk right with this rope gagging my mouth
I bet you ain't never had rope burn on the lips and my hands is bound to the
oarlocks and my feet is stretched out to the stern and I can hardly breathe
I'm telling you I ache but I know there's people on this earth bound to be
hurting worse than me so I'm going to quit feeling sorry for myself and look at
BoBo now he's pulling the catfish up the bank he's down on his knees
with the knife in his mouth the dog is trying to get a hold at his throat
so BoBo jerks his head around and gores the dog again I mean a good one too
the dog is lying in the mud whimpering BoBo has got a hold of the fish it's nigh
as big as he is about two hundred pounds about the size of that alligator gar
we was riding the other day and I see the catfish whiskers that look like
indigo snakes I've felt them brush up against my knees at night when I was in
the water I know BoBo is trying to stick his knife in the soft spot on the fish's
head all he needs is a piece of wire like those sapsuckers twisted me up with
that's right bob wire BoBo is going to try to paralyze it but the catfish
rolls and sweet Jesus the spike that big fin on top of his back it went clean
through BoBo he's hung up on the fish it is like the fish had it in him to spear
the nigger who run him through I can see it sticking out of BoBo's back
and just when BoBo was grinding the knife in him turning the blade around and
around but the negro he still ain't found the cat's brain you got to hit it just
right that dog is just gnawing and now I can't tell the difference
between catfish blood dog blood and BoBo's blood come to think of it
I'm bleeding again myself I'm going to have to yell in a minute
but I'm mostly scared too I don't know if I got no tongue left or not
I ain't got no feeling of one but sometimes I think I can see it
I see the negro pulling himself off the spike and the dog he done chewed
down to the bone pulling his guts along like a king's robe
BoBo is on his back I think he's crying I hope not cause the salt will be
running down in the cuts he is looking at the catfish and it's growling
like a bobcat I know that cat is smart but I think the fisherman is smarter
and I think that dog can smell what to do now I have to tell you something

I don't really have to when BoBo lay his head back in the mud that pillow
we all want to comfort us most he saw me he saw me twisting my head
he saw that I had on the aviator cap that use to belong to his son he gave me it
you know that cap saved my life the fur of some Japanese animal inside it
and the soft leather outside the calligraphy that says something but I don't know
what so it says whatever I want to white band sewed inside now dark with
the child's sweat from his play and his work in the field the child dead now
and to think when BoBo got it long ago there was only one stain on it
a small sphere of blood where the pilot was shot a stain directly across
from that other red moon that rose for his nation and its gods the moon
that is black now like the rest of the head band and in it I can still
smell the odors of BoBo's boy I can smell the kiss of death in the sky at dawn

The Slaying of my Father in Nineteen AND Sixty~~four~~ Three

The nuns came down the ~~halls~~ aisle of the orphanage
Dragging their rosaries
Like the portaguese ~~men~~ man-of-war,   (MAN-OF-WAR)
~~Flipping to adoringly coming into our~~
patrolling our sleep, saying their words
To themselves when they found us hard
or deeply rich,
They ~~floated~~ around our beds,
Soft, ~~and~~ ~~something~~ mean,
But only when our ~~fingers~~ ~~stunk~~,
~~A stick was wet,~~
T

AUTOMATIC CO-PILOT

VERSIONS & IMPROVISATIONS

Dressed in Black

Comte de Lautréamont

I have seen him in the taverns, quiet and tired,
Leaving alone, strolling the piers after midnight,
And entering the seclusion of his estate at dawn.

I have seen him brushing the crumbs from his wooden table.

I have seen him give lavish parties, and never show up.

Most intriguing of all, I have seen as many as seven
Beautiful but dangerous ladies
Calling on him in one evening, and not the slightest bow.

He may take off his gloves, but he will not bow.
He may look at his watch, but he will not speak.

Listen, he carries no weapons. His cane is a cane,
He has no companions, like twilight, he announces himself.

His cape is a cold shadow, shade wearing a mask. His garment
Drawn around me like a clean bandage for the wounded,
These kind knights who will see to it Ducasse is not forgotten,
Black and untouched like the belly of the guitar, these last nights,
A cape drawn around me like the sea, dark rag I was swaddled in.

Orphans

René Clair

We lived in the big house, we lived
In the ditch like a hubcap. We stole
Eggs, we stole flour. In town they accused us:
Dreaming without sleeping, of wearing our hands.
We swam with our hair, we sold black wind
To soldiers who went by in summer,
We held our breath, passed on the road.

Dreamers

René Clair

Death, sleep, and the lovers. The clock and the coffin,
The crawdads, the stars. The great satisfaction of night.
The outworn clothes, the currants sunk in the earth, the invaded
Butterfly weary of flowers, weary of forests, like a footprint
Full of blood. The calm umbrellas, territories of sound
And no sound. A gown, anything that will survive. A knife
Drawn in the desert, someone in the streets, someone in love,
In the empty river, someone vertical; putting out a fire,
Putting out in a boat that has no silence, no death, no solitude,
Another traveler sleeping beneath the horse, beneath my own journey,
Like a mirror warm as pudding, the thirty tombs of Judas.

Cafe of the Poets

Man Ray

The wind cocks its thirty-ought-six
Comes home again like a three-legged dog
And travels the worn boards near the pump
Bullet of light and lightning bug and hound
This odd boy walking the haymow
The stalks digging bait from the soles of his feet
Moss trailing the perfect rocks in the shallows
Between mouths there are counties of tongues
My friends were telling me
The same things that the wind was a bolt
That a dog was a dark ship
That a starfish was a pillow
When I remembered this whippoorwill in the meadow
That kept calling like a dead jew

Stranger Stop and Cast an Eye

Yukio Mishima

Death can do many things: atoms and whores.
Time-lapse photography, even undress those quite bored with undressing.
It makes a patron saint out of a fool, turning the sleek
Idiots into monks, more mysterious than Rasputin,

Growing out of the midsection of a sunken ship, growing and everbearing,
Pollinating itself, like one of those strange plants
That lived on smoke
Jean Genet used to blow in the eyes of sailors from Senegal.

What a place to drink, the casino death runs.
Nothing fancy, nothing beautiful, a blind man called Mud Island
Taking requests on the piano, slow betting,
And the keys are worn down dull as bone handled knives.

The jellyfish, renegade priest, stinging the dark earth
Under the snow, the diver beating oil from his liver,
The writer running his mouth late at night, mountains like pyramids,
Brooms and worn overalls that have come from America.

All these eyes: plucked out by the blind, long strings of guts
Fantailing out like caladium roots, wet and strange, hell,
A place the lost can find, work, graceless and sea-like,
And without a living, all these odd jobs the dead can do.

Cemetery near the Sea

René Daumal

The word has no luck
And continues to wander

When it is almost morning
I drive a stake in the ground

The sea
The street where I tangled with your shadow

The sea
Like a great tent of sad tigers

The grave like a rope ladder
Left by a thief

The tide sifts out my eyes
Prison without hammers

Perhaps this is the root
Singing in time

And this is the crime
Living and dreaming

Stigmata

Oskar Kokoschka

The man lives on the side
Of a hill
Other goats would starve on

He only drinks wine
He only eats bread
The bad sleep well

And yet the young women
Are fond of his skin
Sown with black seeds

He's let his body go
To ashes like a snake
He dreams with the conch

He wears a white worm
Behind his ear
Like an aid for the heart

Forever wearing white gloves
He never changes his style
And the bad sleep well

Play in Which Darkness Falls

Raymond Roussel

Two girls run away from the Home. They have a revolver
In their possession. The Sisters of Our Lady have given up
looking for them, returning in the night with soft candles.
The sleek clouds have thrown their riders, and the bees
are returning to the honey, the clover at the edge of the
cliff black as eyelids, damp as blue mussels flexing at the moon.
The girls look in the stolen mirror, then throw their shoes
in the sea. They take off one another's dress, posing
on the rocks that jut over the faded water of the last days.
The clover beat down from their splendid feet, the clover
quiet like a vault. Nearby in a ship named for early death,
I drink wine like a city. Anchored far off the continent of love,
Strange, but bees do not die in their own honey, and how the dead
are toted off, how the sweet moons are deposited in the catacombs.
The clover at the edge of the sea like a chemise, place
where animals have lain. They help one another with their hair,
their dresses blowing back to land. They look over the
cliff, spit on the beach. Birds I have never seen going by.

Lacuna

Dziga Vertov

Then we could use night

Boy dipping his minnow
And the moon would not finish
Its great elegy

A ghost ship might cruise
Like a garden
Of statues closing their eyes

Sack of ashes
And a ballad

The ballad of the midnight bees
Gramophone of shade trees

How they keep dreaming
They are dreaming

In Another Room I Am Drinking Eggs from a Boot

Hans Richter

What if the moon was essence of quinine
And high heels were a time of day
When certain birds bled
The chauffeur is telling the cook
The antler would pry into ice floes
Swim with a lamp
And we'd be shivering in a ditch
Biting through a black wing
There would be boats
There would be a dream country
The great quiet humming of the soul at night
The only sound is a shovel
Clearing a place for a mailbox

Door over the Water

Salvador Dalí

Your ear in the wave of dark hair
Tall cross of bandits
Owl without eyes
Glass stained with wheat and stones
Outlined by nudes
Divided by night
And traced in loam
The name I give you portal of silence
Lost sand
At the bottom of your neck

Sometimes a Cloud Was Filled with Air

Pablo Picasso

The dark train of childhood
Black breath of a bone moth
Like a man on his deathbed returning a sock
Asking for fish a man wearing eyeshadow
Blue as the geography of sad letters
The pianos of snow because they are rugged companions
A man without friends like a man no longer knowing
Who he is if his shoes are polished
A man like those mirrors passed over the mouths of the dead

For Those Who Sleep and Those Who Die

Antonin Artaud

Return to the house where I drank pot liquor of love
Return to the field in evening where the mowing is laid by
To the lots of string without a kite or a hand
The same street the same dock of flanks
Dark river beds where a fellow can piss
Where a man passes his dick turns into a rat

Cave of the Heart

Federico García Lorca

Night falling around you like a lonesome animal,
Struck matches to plait your hair, dark loaves
Cooling your belly, moaning like a bloom, domain
Of the fourteen year bird, the cloud without sex,
And sweet rags warmer than a melon, soaked in echoes,
Drenched in the lost blood of the moon, yawning
In the furrows turned after dark, your thick legs long as feathers,
Stout as brooms, the earth you sleep on
Too young to call a grave.

On Foot

Robert Desnos

Who is that in the room
Sweeping my fingernails
Not knowing   their shadow
Smells like a nun
An empty doorway
Their face a cold star
Dark as a pond
Stolen horses owned
Swings without porches
Who is it coughing
Who is that man asleep and wooed
His hair in the guitar
Floating with weeds
Who is that lame child with a monkey
Who is that dark gardener
Coming towards me with a smile
With a cold biscuit
And who is it in this room
Turning like a woman on the end
Of a shoelace

Snake Oil

Yvan Goll

I'm going to sell you a comb
A plot for your children
I'm going to give you these slugs
To hold over their eyes
At night someone will appear
At their window with a sack
And a lamp and a clock and a map
And the comb will turn
Over in their bed
Waking them up
Barking like a cricket
Then it will turn black
Then it will turn green
Like a fish like a jade
The wet moss on the stones
Filled with feathers
Then it will fly around
Like a boot a bat
A cap with the insignia of dreams
Then it will die in the palm of your hand
Like a wound that never was

Slender Means

Julien Torma

There is a bird
And it sings all night

There is a fish
That quivers like a breast

And a river who's lost
Its memory

A liniment a shirt
That smells strongly of love

There is a man a woman
Breaking clocks at dusk

I say at dusk there's someone
You will not remember

In the Inn there's a dead man
A traveler at the window

The Horse's Blood

Yukio Mishima

Black jelly the lonely steal to lick with the deaf,
Light bread my father put in his shoes,
Like a fan or a screwdriver, a lost garden,
A swan's heart beating in the palm of a mad child,
Bride too beautiful to be had, forgotten water
Stricken with lips, like rain in a boat, like a cock,
Anything to stir the memory.

Rendezvous

Raymond Radiguet

Soon, the moon will lie on the tongue of the actress
Like a host, like a sleeve, a litre of german wine
Spilled in your lap, starving, lost, and filthy,
I still remember to spit on your name.

Dead Orchard

Raymond Radiguet

Like seven birds sleeping on the plateau
Overlooking the shipwreck of love, mystery
Of the drunken visitors wandering off
With your wife, men who talk with a bad accent,
The condemned the abandoned, one day of silence,
Two days of silence, dreams shattered and protected,
The more blossoms the more you suffer.

Whorehouse

Comte de Lautréamont

My eyes are minnows, cruel peacocks
Suddenly finding themselves at home again,
And my hands don't reach in my boots,
And my hands are spending the night with you, dust
Bedrooms, white melons, my unfortunate hands
And my father looks at me swimming the river
And my eyes rot.

Wanted

Luis Buñuel

A white bull, a cassock, an antique mirror
The famous ones have passed hours in front of,
A midnight blue tuxedo, a fainting couch, a key
To a box of lewd photographs, a swastika,
Twelve bales of hay, three grave plots, a statue
Of Christ holding a heart pierced by a dagger,
A black patch, all kinds of utensils for the sick—
Including thirty-nine feet of catheter tubing—
A houseboat, a dog, a baby grand, an oar
Said to have been carved from a lovely river
And a woman's hat by Alfred Jarry, a mattress,
A shotgun, a diving helmet, an essay on The Art
Of Taxidermy and a clitoris mounted on a ring
Like quartz, a crescent wrench, a bulldozer.

Starving to Death

Bernardo Bertolucci

An unmarried woman comes into the bar with a child.
She sits down, she looks at the fan overhead. She
counts her change for a drink. I move in like a fog.
She says I'm strange, says she can't put her finger
on it, so I tell her: Listen, the smoke that the poet
lived in was transparent but real, was rising, was
able to suck itself back in the cavern of its womb,
like a tamerlane clitoris no one would touch, to put
one's finger on the mystery of the poet, the wound
of luck, to touch the poet, the rose wilting in the ass
hole, is to touch your own child, is the touch of death,
and to go at the stone, the poet's body, the soul,
to excavate, to polish it soft, is to lead the dance
of death again, and this will only lead to gashes,
crumbling dust, another kind of ill-omened, foreboding
smoke, a fog too dense to see yourself in, a pond
without a cock, another drink, the mirror softer
than a shark, and the breath for to shed blood, listen.

The Earth in You

Pablo Neruda

Small
Rose
Part of a rose
Petal and thorn
Smaller at times
Like a root
And then like a bush
One of my hands
Can hold you
But it takes both my lips
I could never tear you
Away from dirt your den
I could never wear you
On my dress like a brooch
At night
After the rest have left
And they call for the last dance
Your feet touch mine
You're clumsy
You droop
Then morning plows its damp field
You've grown
Like a friend from the past
Your chest rises like a mountain in the distance
Your hair is wet with fog
I can barely put my arms around your strong waist
I feel like moonlight
Abiding a dark lake
You're soft as deep water

Everywhere like the stars
When I lean down
Kiss you
I bloody my lips
With the good dirt of the earth

Swimming towards Women
from **Naegling**

Sergei Yesenin

So long blood
brother until then
when we meet again
why are you so black
friend is it the moon
that makes you sing your prayers to the dead
it's a long swim back to our boat
so we better be going
all I have of myself
out of the water
are my head and arms
and a bird is fighting the flies
for that
like a river comes to love its journey
I came to love you in dreams
the water is so silent
wake up man look on the shore
two women waiting for us
I'll take the one dark as dusk
tomorrow we'll both be dead drunk
for they're dancing
the dance of death

White Rose

César Vallejo

I feel well. Now
a stoical ice
glows within me.
This vermilion cord
unraveling in my flesh
makes me laugh.

Cord without end,
like a gyre
descending
from
evil...
bloody, awkward cord
weaved by
a thousand stilettos.

That it may go like this, plaiting
its wreath of mourning crepe,
and that it may bind the tremulous cat
of fear to the frozen nest, to the final conflagration.

Now I am tranquil
with light.
And in my pacific
a forgotten coffin whines.

Fox

Jean Follain

Sometimes a fox
roams
through our nights
seeking out danger
in the grazing of sweet weeds
and from the long dreams of water
and of youth and shame
filled with the mystery of cornbread
and the fire in the shack
we wake up thirsty

the jungle

the glove in the field

I wondered whose hand

pl———6
got drunk————6

MAD DOGS

And yet I confess a secret loyalty to the memory of my great heroes: Chaplin, W.C. Fields, Harpo Marx, and many others whose names I have forgotten.

THOMAS MERTON

Crest

I   OR YOUR WOMAN

The night was a bad one.
I only saw one other person out:
A big black man on muleback
Riding along the levee, marking the water.

There was a lantern in his hand
And what you could call a grim smile on the lips.
I shifted down gears,
Rolled down the window, turned the radio low.

And said, "Say there, man, how goes it?"
But he couldn't hear me for the rain
And the song on his transistor radio.
"I don't know," he said, "but it's raining,

Raining to beat hell."
Said I, "Do you think it's going to quit?"
"Friend, I couldn't tell you."
When big water will, you call everyman friend . . .

We said our goodnights,
Went on, by mule and flatbed truck, wearing black
Rubber, cold to the bone,
Like divers from different ships meeting below.

All you can do is nod, some of the times.
At least, we spoke, knowing that living
Anywhere near the river
You speak when you can; the only thing you try

To hold is your liquor,
And we had none, that bad night on the levee.
Always down the road, I looked up
In the mirror. And I'm sure he'd a done the same.

II   MIDNIGHT

I always slid off, once
Imagining this cloud was a pall
And the moon was a body.
I don't know who put coins over her eyes.

When I got to Rampion's Ferry,
I thought I was the only one there.
I mean it was quiet,
Except for the current, the cables, and the rain.

I got a piece of rope
Out of the back of my truck, and wound it
Around the generator
Engine; it kicked right off the first pull.

The yellow bug lights came on,
And I saw a body move under a purple blanket.
He cussed me out
For waking him up, pulling his old self up.

There was some kind of fish
In the weave of his poncho; other figures
Of snakes and birds, too.
I didn't mean to wake the awnry fellow up,

I wonder if I did.
A strange odor came from underneath him

When he dragged out his towsack.
It didn't smell of something burning, but of

Something that was singed.
Like the rain, it didn't let up.
"Are we going crosst it, or not."
He told me in a voice, half-blooded song.

III   SOME PAST TWELVE

Someone with a light
Rode up before I could see what all
He was pulling from the burlap:
Blue calling chalk you find in pool halls, ivory

Tusks, a stringer with rotten heads
The good book and another I couldn't pronounce—
Just as worn,
And one of those paperweight crystals that snows.

He had strummed the mandolin twice,
A couple of sounds blue as a fox in trouble
In a snowdrift on a ridge, like weeds
Burning underwater, a few licks of silent fire.

When I recognized the lookout
The ferry wasn't more than a few feet off the bank,
So the mule made it aboard, easy;
Its hooves on the planks like a mad, rough carpenter

Nailing driftwood together.
Oh, we made it across. We didn't exactly
Hit the dock on the head,
But we floated on down to Vahalia's Landing.

We had a good time.
The foreigner played the mandolin, the river
Reached its crest,
And the man on the mule and I drank way into the morning.

They heard us, the ones on land.
"We're a floating whorehouse, without no women."
And in the dead of night,
Rain and all, we motioned them on.

Porch Chair

About seventeen years ago we went to New Orleans
Looking for him. Or was it? "Man, he's been gone,"
A beautiful lady told my father. She had one of her legs
On the bedstead, rolling up her black stocking.

Seventeen years ago and the river is a dream, no forks
Set at death's supper tent. It thinks it is a root, dragonfly,
Rough carpenter. The chauffeur, my father, and I take a night
Train to Atlanta. They're eating sardines when we get there.

He's not there either. So I took off my shoes.
Brand-new shoes, and nowhere to go
But a mud island and a woman washing her breasts
With a blue bandanna.

The radio is a land with no shadows,
The middle of the day and the sheet
Metal rattling like rainwater. It was
Hot, the peaches rotten, so we go home.

Drink soda and eat divinity. We get on a boat. No, we got on a boat.
Don't remember: if it was the sea or the river. It was water.
There were people with fever. Saw a man drop, his mule
Went on, pulling the plow without him.

In no time at all we were in Memphis, or was it? All the sinners
They had to run. In the hotel my father changes his shirts seven times.
Drunk from sickness and dreams, with his islands around him,
His deathward dirt, he plays his poker.

He lost all his bulldozers. Sweat makes the shirts look like maps.
But there are no legends. Long ago, in the South, Charlie B. Lemon,

Tangle Eye, and I scaled fish in the fountain in the lobby of the Pea
Body Hotel. Stranger in the garden I thought you should know.

Killing everything wild, he sits up in bed. "Death I'm gone coldcock you,"
Says he with every bar pit a down payment on a grave.
They put a bucket over my head, then they hang it around my neck,
Fill it with oats like I was a foal.

Where'd he go to, the long-line skinner with the brass-knob hand?
Sent him up for checks and he couldn't write his name.
Strangers in the field, smoothing your clothes, don't put much truck
In the Cemetery of Then, have no luck with your regrets.

Little girl walking up the road, asking someone to braid her hair,
Asking me if the blood in a tick is still blue...
It is summer. The spots on the dog grow into berries, the men are loading
Sacks of shit one minute, unloading ice the next.

What Claude Wanted to Tell Her

Down at the docks the big boats come in
With trunks
Big as bales, and it's still night and the piano
They carry down the catwalk
Winds up mourner's dice.

And the saxophone travels alone in the woods
Like a jeep in low gear,
No one in it, going from tree to tree at the turn
Of the century like an owl. Woo, bruised fingers, too.
The deaf fish without luck all day, without bait.
Down a street they've stolen dark, run it off
Like a mad dog. They told you
Pick lice off the moon, and you grew your fingernails long.
Your love's with the weevil.
You write off to the back of an ad
Hunting a cheap cremation. Drop me a line.

Your children form a suicide club, and the unborn
Intend cancer. Dreams we try not to have,
Leading us into a shotgun church, blindfolded.

It's awful hot and wasps go past our eyelids,
A midget is aiming a slingshot at us, and the saxophone
Is hiding near a cypress, crouched down on all threes.
Panting like a bull frog.

You pick a tick off your thigh. A rocket lands on Venus.
I heard it on the radio.

Woman, I went in on shares and I haven't
Got enough to flag a ride.
I'm asking you now, how come a mule wanders in, drops

Dead in somebody's carport,
And the county won't come get him?

Who knows a judge?

How come you beg dimes for calls you never make?
How come friends you thought the earth of
Die alone
While you're gone after a sack of pork rinds.

Who buries the elephant?
Last Requests, they mean nothing, like wages.
Two bits an hour for the body I spent summers with.
Death in his Coupe de Ville,
Putting up such a holler, making a big stink.

The afternoons of the gar, the nights making soap,
The nights of the oarless boats, I'm guilty your honor.
I haven't forgotten you, God, but where are the dead?
At they hard chore
Changing your tune so the song will sound the same,
Hauling away shit from the chickenhouse of love.

Anchoress

to C.

*This being the true account of a printer who, having been
released from prison on his 100th birthday, rides back to his
homestead, and recalls what was and what never was.*

Deep in the hills there is a cold shack
Where nipples leave their rouge on the mirror

And you pass yourself on the road   riding another way

A night to remember
Night you saw the anchoress
Night you saw big lips in the moon
Blowing its black and bad   sax

Cling peaches and dark bread and roasted bream
Blood tide and stockings used to dip minnows
Honey dew melons as tender as goats and hiccups
Like an imaginary foetus   A crate of bananas
Rotting at the Landing   with no mention of religion
Quail eggs and buttermilk and at the time
Of the year   a woman who will not return
Walking through the snow
With a dead rabbit   If you could only sleep
Inside her
Barn full of birds like a basilica

She wears a dirty white gown sometimes
A sanbenito sewn from split flour sacks

For a long time you've been dreaming of being me
Your heart leans into those dangerous places
Like the wheels on a road grader

The barechested milkmaid
Hauling hay for the outlaw's last supper
She marks her books with leaves
And scrapes hair
From her legs with a butcher knife   once in spring
Once in fall
The deer come down to drink her blood

You can yell in the gully near her place
Like some hunter who broke his own leg
And you hear   yourself   echo
Across the undersides of the   flat
Stones she's marked on
You pass out   under a tree

And when you come to   the moon
Is up   and a bird   goes by   singing its own
Shadow   She flinches on her bluetick mattress
Like foxfire   when it sleets   Bloodknots coming
Undone   Toadstools crumbling from the kiss
Of death   The wind that idiot prince and the hound
Her knight lift their noses from her feet
To the storm
Several hundred miles away   but coming
Every once and a while you dream
A mad woman   way into the night   at her loom
Of lava and snapbeans   always hearing
Things in the stillness around her shack
A stillness like an intruder   an unsteady light

You can call her what you want to   She won't
answer anymore

And you know why the mothers get so sullen
It dawns on you
Her many rooms   with bundles of cured plants
And dried herbs hanging on the walls
Sprays of mandrake seem to just be there
Suspended from the perfect rafters hewned out light
Where you hear yourself   walking   back   and
Forth   not even being there
Where you listen for that stringless
Kite or Lady Jane's Guitar
Making its dive in the hideout on the hill

A submarine of tea and seeds docked in the forest

Of course her lingerie hiding her Will

At the secret wedding of the bear and the trout
You think   The first stone you see   you'll hit yourself
With it
And a peahen comes out of nowhere
Stares at you from the top of the ridge   gypsy walking
And you take a long swallow when she calls
Her Maker

Looking for roots at midnight she holds
The wind for the trees

The pocketwatches she carries in her hat

She passes water in the creek bed
And the sphere of copperheads
Sleeping under the earth
Revolve like the planets

She has a nightmare a posse of vigilantes
Surrounding her with lariats

She spills the cordials in her navel

Let's see   The horse in the meadow
Who can only weep from one of its eyes

The many theories of time

Chokeberries put up with a candle all flame

Spectacles she can take off to look up at the clouds

Then the clouds then my years then
Drag through her hair like a plow
Traveling in dark soil

A garden

The lovers   going through their way in rags
The mooncalf and the urchin
Her diary kept in the white and laid by
Places of the seed catalog
Now on the floor and forgotten but holding the table steady

As she goes to the coop with corn and fish hooks in her apron
She drinks a little homemade wine from a jar

She sits down near an unfinished shed
Drinks more alone
She looks at the old pegs in the foundation
The corners still true

Half naked   she goes about her chores

Drawing water she hears a new tune
On the radio in a pickup that doesn't run
She tries to turn the radio off but she can't
She hits the dash with a hoe

And the milksnake wanders through the loft like a monk
In the bushes   in the bucket   in the swing
Reading the lips of the thawed out lady bugs

The radio in the truck dies like a panama hat

True love can truly be spoken in boots
And jeans and a skirt over that
The words can pass
Into the mouth of a Mason jar
And stay there forever like a message at sea
Like a magician with a magnet
On the end of his wand

Her place now in the pasture like a star
Or a musk come in to graze
Her place now
Not mine and might as well never was

How is it
Some trouser legs tied off
A weary fin you cannot follow being so dog tired
Something now and not was
Returned from so many journeys

And I have not set my foot down
In this nest
To break the young or to be bitten
This is where I wanted to be
Struck and born

This is where I wanted to smell the nice sweat
Of my children dancing in the fields
And where I wanted love
To fill up naturally in the horn like common spit
The teller and the listener

Moon blow your light my way
But don't cut my time

Let the ceremony end slow and in time

Yes the cold forest and the sea
Where you ride shotgun with two trembling fingers

Yes the ice pick
A tree has grown around or a latch
All she needs is a little
Spit and stone for what is rusty

The first loves are not spoken
They are not protected from the weather
They go mad to be spoken and die
Wet and with their eyes clear and open

The stories of the other loves
Are told right good

Because deep in the cities and towns
The photographs all signed love are slipping out
Of the mirrors

Let the record read I'll be damned if I don't
And let the moon hide in my boot

She was
A debutante of solitudes and lowriding
She twirled a narwhal baton
She ate the bones with the fish
She wore cockleburs for sequins
My land under shadow like a majorette in the rain

I watch you work and the wind goes through the ring
In my ear
I can't focus the crosshairs of my sights
The fog follows you through the spyglass
Like a frozen squid

I want to breathe in your room
Touch your ragtime piano
Your long black gloves
For the bees

Here I am the sour old pillow
Waiting for its case
Shanghaied   in the mountains
A long ways from loving

Slow-slung and sixty thousand miles of arteries
Full of your silt and witness

It was a hell of a long time ago   it seems   I wrote
Two X's in her oval looking glass
Just like I was cutting over fang marks
Drawing poison

I could smell her
she tossed me the melon and said I know you but you don't know me uh
I reached down in my other pocket I wasn't that way anymore cause I wasn't
looking at her so much she was still laughing
I didn't know what to swap
I found that black patch and I give it to her
she said whata I need this for thata man gotta one leg not one eye
you never can tell I said your husband might can use it for shade
she tried to tie the black patch on herself she said thata my poppa boy
the man was still cussing his mule with a whip now I could hear him outside
in the light I was sweating like her
she was holding the black patch in place still trying to tie the knot
it wouldn't stay on her head she had too much black hair
hey bambino tie this on for me hey she said
I went over behind her and made a bow
I was breathing like I had been swimming
I remembered Sylvester wanted some ice
there was a picture of a clown spinning the moon on the end of his finger
I told the girl where the wheel was I kissed her on the cheek
I reached in the cooler and grabbed a chunk of ice
I jumped out the wagon and ran all the way to the liquor store
my hand was burning cause I had got dry ice
when I had leaned over my belly touched her on the back
she reached around with her hand and rubbed my side like I was a pony
I didn't have no shirt on either
it wasn't dirty I don't have to ask forgiveness no I don't
maybe the spelling was bad on what it said in the picture I don't know
she rubbed me like I rubbed the trees at night like a flank
I set the melon on the bench
cut it you son-of-a-bitch I said
I looked out in the field I was breathing the dago was rolling his wheel
I don't have to ask to be forgiven

it was like the moon said I love you
boy how come you left out of here without getting the change
never mind I said just cut it
he opened the knife up the sun was at his back
free at last I thought ain't gonna be studying bout sin no more
no more no more
I sang
I went down to the corner get a pack of cigarettes
police drove up said boy you under arrest
hey I like that Sylvester said
he sang
look at them handcuffs look at that bat
whoa back boys I'm coming back
slice it I said
he got out of the hammock and cut the melon in half
he scooped out the seeds from one half with his big black hand
he chunked the handful in the dust
I reached in the other half and got the insides
I threw them up in the shade tree
now he sliced it into quarters
he cut the rinds off and threw them to the chickens
the dog got his tongue hung up on the dry ice
two fuh you and two fuh me he said
man that cantaloupe was good

My father and I lie down together.
He is dead.

We look up at the stars, the steady sound
of the wind turning the night like a ceiling fan.
This is our home.

He asks me to ~~to remember~~ did I remember
~~the sick~~ ~~built~~ the map that will tell us
where we are sleeping.

He asks did I remember his drinking

He asks ~~me~~ if he ever hit me.
Ran I remember his hands.
~~I imagine them under his gloves~~

Now he gets up, and I dream,—
He looks down at me and watches me die.

$8,736.00

52
400   48
                52
5200 $5200

$168.00

THE LAST PANTHER IN THE OZARKS

for Willie Reynolds

To Find Directions

Go to the graveyard.

Crossing the Fork on a One-Lane Bridge with No Lights

The river is up and the deaf and dumb typesetter
Can't make it to work
To lay out the dead.

Snakes are getting what they want on the trestle
And a bullfrog sits on a crosstie
Looking out over the fog
Like a foreigner on a pier.

A white stud horse gallops through the meadow,
The fireflies are all swelling out and green.

The hounds are rattling their teeth against the hog wire
Like men beating spoons in the pen.

The panther is down from the cliffs
Crazy drunk on the young blood in the valley.

Riverlight

My father and I lie down together.
He is dead.

We look up at the stars, the steady sound
Of the wind turning the night like a ceiling fan.
This is our home.

I remember the work in him
Like bitterness in persimmons before a frost.
And I imagine the way he had fear,
The ground turning dark in a rain.

Now he gets up.

And I dream he looks down in my eyes
And watches me die.

[untitled]

Away from our homes
and on roads we thought we knew
holding a light for a stranger.

[untitled]

I see a woman wading the river
there is no river.

[untitled]

Someone turns a light on
in a house down the road
it must be a man
going over all the words
he ever spoke
all the fields he ever left
on his way to open a door.

[untitled]

I listened to the iron cock
washing his silver in the wind
and wondered who would climb the roof
and take him, or would he roost
with strangers sleeping in the house.

No one would sit in the black chair.
It was a bear
that would wake up anytime.

She died in the middle of the night.

The doctor said her heart
blew open like a jar of preserves.

The women made the coffee,
the men went out in the shed
to look over the tools.

The chickenwater froze over
and nails popped out of the roof
it was so cold.

Before dawn I laid my head
in the fur of the couch
and heard her
coming down the stairs
with her cane and her teeth in a jar
on the way to the outhouse,
saying, "Who took my flashlight?"

Pits

We go on and we tremble.
God says we can screw now.
God says to give up all your lovers,
Time to die.

When I was younger I drove a Lincoln.
God said to trade it in.
A tad lovely, then, and terrible,
And sick of my own kind,
I wanted to become a woman.
I wanted to wash the feet of other women
In public, I wanted his eyes
On me, olives on the ground.

I gave you my hand,
Now I go around with my sleeve
Tucked in my coat.

I climb no trees, touch
One breast at a time,
Hold no hands myself.

I go on and I tremble
With your back in my blood,
The clap my mother left me.

With me no more, and now,
And forever, and even always
The dust of my feet
In the desert
I give you stranger my sign,
My peace,
But God you remember
You fucked me out of my hand.

Fine Horses Put Down at Morning

It seems like dusk.

Know that some stayed warm in the truck,
Flies on the hood before morning.

A night
Breaks its own laces once more
Shedding its soles
Like mud on the steps.

Everyone thought of barns floating down the river,
One man French inhaled.
Love and Death, lips on the face,
And tar seeping through the roads in summer.

We run with crooks
All our lives
A shipwrecked honeymoon,
The slime on the stars,
The wind and the other dusks
In the eyes of those
Who came long ago.

Someone's Mother Sweeping All Night

In old homes in the country
A black snake often holes up
On a shelf with the cornmeal
Under the ladies calendar
And waits for power women
To come in early from the churning
And stroke its back with fresh butter.

Wrong Side of the Moon

Men about to commit a crime
Drink another cup
And look at their watch
The face everyone remembers
For its twitch and drooping eye
Always running always losing
A second a day sometimes an hour
A year on the wrist of the dead.

Beautiful Moves

Suddenly a young lady crosses her legs
Behind a window of the movie house of your love,
Smacks her gum and says promise not to leave,
Always come back, even if I sell you the same ticket a thousand times.

Friend of the Enemy

The yolk went down my leg
Like a beautiful snail without a shell,
Went down the hill
To the skillet of water, to the nymphflies,
Into the lips of the pond minnows,
Down the long belly of the gar—the hellbenders
Having dived and lost, then into
The paw of the lame panther
Who loped back to her lair with it.

As for the white, it stayed with me,
Mark of the beast, birth, and trade.

The Justices

Some dead children from other countries
Wake me up with lamps.

They are like miners, their little white shirts
Are dirty with dark marks.

Their bodies are sore, they touch themselves.
One begins to beat a drum

Telling me the names of justices,
Lives I have to take.

I see another face looking in my window.
They tell me she is still dead.

She will come back
But she will never be beautiful.

She will live when no man
Can make a law against another.

In the morning a bird breaks the glass
And dies on the floor.

The Love

A child is walking down the road
In a pair of white shorts.

An old woman passes by
With a beautiful umbrella
And a shepherd on a leash.

The child wants to touch the animal.
The dog bites the child on the thigh.

In a while everyone is looking
For the only thing she loves.

Find the dog and save the child some pain.
You find a way to tell her when they take it away.

The Love

a child in walking down the road
In a pain of white streets.

an old woman passing by with an doubtful umbrella
and a slope on a level.

The child which took the animal.
The dog bites on the thigh

Is unable the unthikn at looking
For the alley thing the there.

Find the dog and say   ild some pain
Find a way to tell   you gun held away

I   her dog and danger
It would some the vected care play.

The woman wrap her hand, she hasn't understood.
The animal in mad, yet she don't unched

like broken wind on his lips I'm gone do what the boy in the temple said to do
(you already missed the punch line there is no sockdologer for the gospel truth)
I have known the evil procreated in the offspring of the bad ones in bad times
I would like to say something good but the way I figure it if you can't say
something good about nobody then don't say nothing atol that's a white washed
lie right there some of my own kin folks tell me you ought not to say that
spitting in the face of God and the white race they're not all bad if well if I
say I could find all these white folks I know so good was good where I wouldn't
have to all time be telling them then maybe they might be right but ain't so
if you take them all as a whole then they is evil quality and quantity
I ought to know I'm white but now just as if I was some writer or something
I'm going to enter these minds this mind that mind of these characters men
I didn't like all my life but later if I'm dead tomorrow that is after living
and breathing with them for so long these whites I got the right to speak
          my mind
you can't help but say yes some of them are evil but you still have some feeling
for them not cause you got the same skin that's like the same name a coincidence
a rebus as if they were something out of the past but they are present he is
          right here
but it is like that part of the past where values are without value
where you no longer distinguish between fear pleasure it is just the past
which is the present it is like a dream a memory of winning or losing
it is all things that have already happened and so they will happen again
and even after they have happened again you still say do you remember
and just like Dark has said to me Dark the only negro I know
who has killed more than one white man and can tell about it
boy there ain't no such word as if he says so they hung Sylvester what of it
I kilt me a whole sty of white mens kilt them in the war and kilt them
at home kilt um up north and kilt them down here boy don't talk to me like
you doing you can't say if only this or that they hung him and that's it
all you can say is it happened and that's it when you think of him you got
to think of him ventually getting hung cause that's the way it was

you can't think back on something that didn't happen because if it was
it is now but it ain't so when you think about it you can't change it you
got to think on the whole thing the whole truth and nothing but the truth
shoot I wish I's young as you was again I'd go through it all gain just to
be your age but I'd still do it I go through all that hell again just to do
it no I don't wish none of it happen different that's like wishing I was white
like thinking some of that going be white when I get to heaven that's woman
talk that ain't nothing but bullshit all my young days I wished everything
was different but I wished myself I didn't never wish I was no white boy
but I still wished myself out so now I know you better quit it sure as
you better tag the man out if you drop the ball when he strikes out
and so now I don't even think about tomorrow I don't even think about what's
up this road I ought to know it's a baseball game you say but I ain't even
knowing that no suh cause that be like saying we play with a baseball and we
don't it gone take you a long time to learn that about us but you will you'll
get up one morning and you'll say I know that and I'll tell that don't be
saying you know how to play without the ball already hell you know how to
fish too but you ain't got to keep nobody alive you might have a pretty good
way with the water but you ain't got to keep from drowning sure as shooting
I'm telling you the gospel ship is coming in one these days it's on the way
now but I ain't thinking about it I'm just my sassing back self ain't even
a christian I'll talk back to yo daddy anytime I ain't scared nuthing
it's coming fah my people let them take the long walk up the catwalk
but I ain't going somebody got to shove the boat back out in the water
I got plenty chilluns on board maybe when you get old they'll be chilluns
of yours on board white chillun maybe everybody gone be in the same boat then
putting out to some different place it gone be the same country but
I don't know how to say it just a different place you might have to stay
behind and get it too would you do it I think you would things is changing
just not like they use to be they might quit that scuffling I don't know
gonna have to learn one way the other though there was a time and maybe still

FLOUR THE DEAD MAN BRINGS
TO THE WEDDING

Over the door of Hell is written: "Therefore!"

THOMAS MERTON

Dusk

You walk across the room in your panties
with a glass of orange juice
and turn off the air conditioner.

Betrayal

The undertaker waiting on the headlights
turning up the drive, a drink in his hands.

1949

A whore blowing smoke in the dark.

The Actresses of Night

black night the plank I am
forced to walk night
the girl undressing I see my chance
by the window I am falling
and it is like being played with
by older girls it is
the black stockings
the young widow takes off
in front of you night
takes off her panties in the dark
and they smell like old coves

The Biscuits

no one was in the room
in the screendoor there was a straw
from a broom
where the woman had shooed the cat
the click beetle was sawing his dust
between the walls
if he clicked eleven times
it meant whoever was
eleven years on this earth would die
he was clicking long numbers
he was making a pile
eight-seven before the hoarfrost
it was Big Emma's time
no one was in the room
death came by and chewed the straw
he doesn't like anybody
rocking in his chair

Willet

It was cold as a dead flashlight.
I put on my boots and gloves,
Set the water on the stove,
And went out to split kindling.
The ax handle was slick with frost.
I breathed on the wood—
I've seen tools go sailing
Into friend, kin, and self—so,
Careful, but mostly because
I had no children or whiskey left,
I caught the moon
Flinching behind the trees.
It was a white flower
Afraid to be cut down from its dark stalk.
In the summer things like the moon
Grow outside my window.
Before light, when my voice
Is a trout under the rocks,
I look at them. The window
Changes at night, becomes a blue mirror
Where the deer run
Through my face, a lair
For all the light in our eyes.
The moths come and die gently.
They are like my friends who never work.
In the hills we are all strangers
With our animals
Drinking in the ponds where we looked
At our young cocks. I wait
For the seasons to throw out their lovers,
I wait for the spring, a gash across my leg.

The dream of bleeding in my sleep, of never
Finding a trace of a wound come morning.

Distant Cousins

My uncle would give me two bits an hour
To look after the moon, the old cow
That chewed its way out
Of the darkness in our fields.
It was good money for then.
He didn't like me asking questions
How he ran his whiskey.
I didn't work much, kept track
Of the change and the busted bottles.
Mostly, I listened to the help—
They rode shotgun on the trucks.
He got his men elected,
Paid to bury the others.
I got wise to lies, men who run at the mouth.
Keep your ears, he'd say,
On what the river brings down
And they'll never send you up to it.
But he towed the line, smiled on the street
And dressed right, like a delta Jew.
I learned a few things—how to collect
From killers, not to slow down at a crossing,
The way to drink coffee with widows.
Children always brought him japonicas.
He gave them silver dollars.
He had bad luck the first twenty years of his life,
Good luck the next twenty-seven. One day, the last day,
He didn't have any luck at all.
He was walking down Buck Island Road in a white suit,
An unlit cigar in his mouth,
Pulling a stringer of crappie through the dust.
Lewis J., the number one driver,

Was walking ahead, looking for the game warden.
They'd heard his truck, and they were
Way over the limit, due for a fine.
He never could tell the Fish & Game what to do.
I wanted to be close to my uncle,
Alive, like the smoke
He dragged through his lungs.
He wouldn't let me.
It was some men from Prentiss County.
The fish were bloody around the mouth
And covered with dust, too.
They were breathing.
Lewis J. ran off, stole a rifle
Out of the game warden's truck,
Dropped everyone of them, drinking soda,
In front of Tyler's store.
Lewis has got six Laundromats in Little Rock,
His son's in law school in Philadelphia.
I run the business now, it's all legit.
And if my boy doesn't fuck up,
He'll be the next governor of this state.

There is nowhere in you a paradise that is no place and there you do not enter without a story

One day when it rained and no one was for working
all the new men came to town to drink.
They left their five-hundred-dollar dogs and shotguns
locked in their trucks.

The man who'd lived in those parts the longest
was not with them.
His truck was across the road at the store.
He'd come to town expecting a letter.
He'd never tied his dog or locked his cab.
The hound was a cur and the level wasn't true.

It was too bad the new men do not take the time
to ask about the ways of the other one.
It would have saved them a lot of sleep.

The rain slacked off. The men came out of the tavern to see.
They saw the dog in the unlocked truck.
They came closer and laughed at the dog.
One man said he'd better lock it,
he'd hate to see such a animal stolen in plain daylight.

The dog jumped out of the truck and bit the man on the heel.
The man kicked the dog unconscious.
He tied it up in a tree.
He yelled at the rest to come outside.
They let their dogs loose.
They stood in the rain in yellow raincoats
and watched the pack tear the other dog down.

The other man had to borrow a gun to shoot his dog,
but he told everybody there
he'd take care of them with his own.

The new men looked up in the rain and pretended to drink,
but their bottles were dry as their throats.

The other man put his dog in a raincoat and threw it in the cab.
He drove off with the ink running on the letter
in his back pocket.

He cooled down when he got home,
glad he wasn't the kind to set fire to his fields
just to say he was burning sacks.

But some nights when what he'd made
out of the letter nights before just wouldn't come,
he'd have to cut the underbrush out of his memory,
walk over the new men's farms,
lean against a pole under the vapor light
and hold his eyes on an upstairs window
until he was satisfied their wives had seen him.

Death and the Young Man

The birds swirl in the afternoon
Like fixings in the dark pot
My mother stirred.

Now the shadows go out
And are lost in the evening
Like wine and blood and ink.

I would like to sink down
In a basket of folded laundry
But the moon is dirty here at night.

When the sun is remembered like broken eggs
In her coat, I come back over my own scent
The dog who stole them.

Ritual of the Grand Dead

You may steal the old dark bottle
off the porch of your childhood,
take it to the river and blow out
the pine knots of your heart.
You may throw the fishbones in the water.
You may go to the schoolhouse
and cut your lust in the desks.
You may listen to the rain one drop at a time.
You may take the wet animal
back to die where you found it
because you've touched it.

Bitch

I come in from the snow
sit in front of the fire
and want to weep.
The snow in my hair melts
and the blood from the stillbirth
dries between my fingers.
The moon is just another safety light
and the maples are the color of guts.
I could have kept her
from dropping another litter, but why
cut out the good times she was having
with the shepherd in the barn.
I will bury everything tomorrow,
go to town, get drunk with a college girl,
let her take me home and tell me how she wants it.
The next day I'll come back
with some new books
and sit down in front of the fern.
Then I will look upstairs
and memory will try to pull its window up
and the heart will come loose
like a window weight
and lose itself in the wall.

[untitled]

The traveler who has never
broken down on our road before
knocks on the white door
one night when it is cold
and the wind is blowing
the soul out of the moon
the woman you are sleeping with
is warm and wants you all the time
you wake up and walk out of the house
to help the stranger you ask him
where his car is he tells you
keep walking down the road.

Light Blue

The white clothes on the line put the man to sleep.
He was sitting on a soda case
Leaning back on the porch.

He rolled down his sleeves with his eyes shut.
He could feel the sun going into the trees.

He wanted to catch the evening ferry
And meet someone across the river.

He dreamed about her
Putting polish on her nails.
He was in the woods and many women
Were walking around him in a circle.
He thought about crosses in their blood.

As it got to be night he could feel the heat in his face.
He was going to open his eyes.
And look up at the moon.
It was like the light blue handkerchief
She gave him to go with his dark suit.

That's when he felt the hot salt all over him
Like broken glass.
He was afraid to open his eyes.
He wondered if he could use any words on it.
But the big woman in the black dress
Was already in the backseat of the car
Rolling the window up with one hand
And making a sign on him with the other.

She was in the car, too.
He saw her biting her nails when they pulled away.

There was a dead snake on his shoes.
He knew there would be a circle
Of little beating hearts in his bed,
And before he could get home
They would be dry and still.

Man is so afraid.

he look down at cock. long ago many
centuries ships land on the enemy's beach, take down
mast in the dark, climb up cliffs in the fog, ram
enemy's door, do bad things in castle, oh yeah, man
go crazy play in blood like baby with duck in bathtub,
man think about favorite dog, got worms in heart, takes
dog to field trial, dog sniffs out man's lies, point
at fool in frozen water, fool man, dead dog, man look
at leaf frozen in pond, man think about woman in new
cabin beside fire, walls bleeding rosin, man forget about
dog, man want son, boy strong, call boy elephant, man
cannot sleep right, have bad itch in butthole, man think
cancer maybe, man wake up beside woman, moon come
in window, man glad he has no city, city can die for all
he cares, man smells fingers, smell bad, man gets up
to wash fingers, man steps on broken glass, sits down
on commode and sucks his foot, man thinks about God,
man says to God If I eat right will You take away cancer,
God no say, man flush pot, man decides go to India,
study other God, other God take away cancer, bring back
dog, make women go crazy, man go visit little
naked man on mountain, man give him all his money,
little naked man say go back home, stand on head with
fresh egg in asshole three times a day, man does what
he says, oh yeah, man think about troopships, man is so
afraid, man take chill, man get old real quick man nobody,
everything dark, man spit in papersack, man look at medicine
on table beside bed, man look at TV, Tarzan movie already over,
so sad so sad, man call doctor, say to make him young,
doctor look at secretary pulling up panties, say oh yeah,
take man's money, man get young, man decide go to

Africa, man think everything swell when he get back
home, put many heads on wall, many skins, first night
wife run off, fool man, so man read book, man like,
so man read another book, soon man read book all time,
don't care about money, don't care about woman, only
thing man remember is what he read, on weekends
go to old cabin, look at pine knots, think about what he
read, think about history, look down at cock,
man learn, once was another man become king, but king
had no sons, king get old, get sad, king get so afraid, look
at his cock, oh yeah, one night king run everybody out of
castle, have private dinner, just with family, and favorite
dog, tell daughter to hop up on table, king takes pheasant
gravy, pours on daughter, rubs daughter's thighs with
gravy, picks up dog, tells dog lick daughter, king tells daughter
not to be afraid, not be sad, tell daughter be strong, daughter
strong, daughter looks at mother, says watch, daughter
takes dog by the mouth, breaks jaws, king says daughter strong,
man know lot about history, man afraid, man go crazy on
street one day, man go jail, man call lawyer tell lawyer shoot two women
save my life, man give lawyer lot of money, lawyer go out
to eat, talks about man, man get out of jail, oh yeah
man like imagine too, man like to clip cut back of magazine,
man like sendoff, man also like guns,
life strange,

Butcher

after Robert Desnos

If you want to you can sleep in the meat.
Before you lie down
You can comb your hair one hundred times in my knives.
I can keep you warm with fish
That aren't even dead.
They're just too cold to move.
I'll stand by the counter and watch over you.
I'll be the hangman
Who ties black cloth over your eyes
When you wake.

Beautiful Kills

I walked into the room
Where my cousin was sleeping
And bit her on the neck
She opened the covers
And showed me the book of Africa
She was dreaming
She was looking for a jungle
And we unfolded all the maps.

The court-probated version of the manuscript placed "Between Love and Death" (*Crib Death*, p. 282) after "Beautiful Kills." It has been maintained there and not duplicated here. — Ed.

lying in state

a man comes in the store with a whip
and a silver pistol in his belt
and says I'm rounding up all the wild horses
the snow was on the ground
in these parts you can hear a deaf man's hands
and one of his hirelings says if
anybody tries to get in our way
we'll blow a hole through them
a bird hits the window
and a man playing solitaire by the stove
stands up with the king of hearts
in his hand and one eye shut
and says over my dead body

how come you talk that way I said he said some towheads tried to hang me
they didn't even break his neck
those blowflies in that posse they thought they hung this nigger
ha ha no sir this here ain't no shuffling nigger what you see
I was looking him in the eye a rowing that boat
he was drinking wine
I didn't take him to be no tapdancer nohow noway not me no sir he was
what I call one mean you better believe it I wasn't messing
with that man the sweat was working up on me because I figured somebody
was fixing to cut down on us
to change the subject I said what was that one's driving name
that's Fireweed he told me and it weren't even dark yet
he said now you mean to sit there he had him a pistol too and tell me you don't
remember me he pulled down his bottom lip
with his finger I saw the gold tooth with the star of David in it
he spit the tobacco juice out between his teeth he reared back he said woowee
boy and I remembered it was a long time ago I was a baby I was
drifting away in a wash tub tied to the raft the cottonmouths was crawling
up through the willow limbs there was a dark face above and black hands
grabbed a hold of me the negro swam a long way with me in his arms
he always smiled there was the star in his tooth we got to the bank he cut
a X in my foot with his razor he said this hurts me more
than it does you white baby he was biting the bottom of my foot he was
spitting the moccasin juice and the blood on the ground all the while
him swatting at things jumping out on him and the gold tooth
with the star of David in it I was trying to catch a butterfly
then he started cutting on himself he kept a saying woowee
just like mosquitoes he picked me up I sat on his shoulders we ran
through the bogue we ran through timber all the time I'm riding up high
on his shoulders bouncing he wasn't no horse

DURING THE NIGHT OF THE HIGH WATER

POEMS WAITING FOR THE SORGHUM
TO COME OUT OF THE BUCKET

for my own good

the moon came in drunk
and woke up my brother
he was dreaming of this girl we saw in town
she was buying beauty lotion and a cheap dress
my brother said how about us getting together some evening
she wouldn't look him in the eye
but she threw her hair over her shoulder
towards her daddy
and bit the skin on her knuckle
the store smelled like an onion
and perspiration under a lady's arms
my brother reached down in his blue jeans
looking for spare change
he didn't have any so he punched me in the ribs
telling me give me six cents for a pop
I bought three peach sodas and a writing tablet
hers was kind of hot and it spewed
over the front of her blouse
when she took the first sip
my brother said don't just stand there boy
go get a rag or something for her
I gave her my blue bandanna
I forgot it had snot and hair oil all over it
I told my brother I sure do wish you'd quit bossing me around
you are destined for misfortune talking like that he said
he drew back but the girl walked between him and me
no fighting now she said let's just go out on the porch
and look at the sun going down
while she wasn't looking he slapped me on the back of my head
he could get away with anything
he said all life was nothing but a featherbed with no sheets

and a busted pillow
he cleared his nose and half shut his eyes and told her his name was
Rudyard Kipling and she almost believed him

smiles of a summer afternoon

here comes a woman with a baby in her arms
a few years from now
she'll be carrying
flowers to his grave
the guitar she saved to get to him
when he played
in that combo
in his sixteenth year
will go through several generations
of spiders

blood mushrooms

the weeds were like sutures
where are the shiftless drivers I helped
get their trucks full of liquor
out of the mud
will the circle
be unbroken
the man smoking a lucky strike
is humming
the hearse only has one spare
an omen
or an instinct of landscapes and advents
a stroke of good luck
like something falling out of a freight car
the scent of coconut pie at a wake
where are the cobwebs you only see when it rains
I manned the light pole
like a dove
the illegal resident keeps time with his foot
and receives his envelope
another summons
our daily bread

boat boy

I use to run a ferry
over a stretch of dangerous water
I only had one to cross
the moon
and she gave me enough
to live on
for so long
a time I can't remember

a koto I found in the Rosedale whorehouse

there was a time when I traveled
in the dark snow
I listened to my foot
prints before
I made them
if I got hungry enough
and no one
was looking
I might share the teats with a black calf

the echo and the answer

most of my life I've lived
over water
so when I sit down at my desk
in the school room
I look around for a bottle
you ought to
pour something from
or shut your eyes
and sip it
or something like that
it's all going
to cost you
and everybody else
a fortune
I look like I'm dozing off
but I am
not really
I am like a star you think is a planet
you look at it so long
you think it's moving
that's logical thinking
not really
it is moving just the same
like the water
I lived on

nothing belongs

like a lamp of claps of thunder
and obstacles
sitting up in bed
and railroads ashamed of themselves
the notebooks are left
in the shade
on the ridges
where the leaves blow
through fire
and the earthstars
it might
belong to a fox
an outline
of its shadow
like a sinkhole
even when you draw
a breath
I get thirsty
for nothing
belongs there

All quotes are mine. They come from a sheaf of Ms. I found hidden in my old
room in the monastery, where I Used to hide bottles of whiskyy. "the mountain
my monastery" , my clouds the cloisters" your body my abbey" are love-sick

As soon as I've whipped every poet under thirty, then I'm going to turn
professional. I'm going to go to Japan, then I'm going to go New Jersey
(do you remember when Kangfish told the judge, pawn it in and meet
muhahamidd al. He has been to Arkansas twice, and I met him both times,
One of the times--it was at the Holiday Inn or the Hogs gymnasium, I was
with Lady Jane and Neal Spearman
my feet will fit sweet William Faulkner's boots like a glove
I'm going to give my gold medals (they are going to have poetry, and Jude
to tool you the trugth I8d rather   in the olymics
                                                          nnext year.
numbskulled   I'd rather get shot by somebody's husband in , than by
a crays writer in New York.
I'm going to be a half-breed. You've heard how they say

You've heard how
You've read how this neo-fugative school of nouw redneck scalwags
tries

Arthur Finn
I'm going to be Jeane Cocteua and William Faulkner at the same time.
And when I get through with the poets, then I'm Barth, tell Coover roll over
the nows. I'm going to play a guit ar behind my back, pick it with
my teeth   for real for real clairyveyant is what Duck
To tell you the truth, I'm not going to get anybody to write living
to wirte in my book9 (If they are living, it'll be me   Univ. said about me
I'll ghost write my own ciriticism
                                                  when I was nine.

If you knew anything about music and Lawrene,
you'll understand when I say I'll   (That was the age I was able to
yodel from the unconscious   pull away from the musis I always
                                          heard

I use to sit around the campfires in the time of the flood, with negroes,
convicts, and wounded arister young wanted for manslaughter,; them
telling me, all of them, but especially that Welsh midget, always in his
cuffs,

SOME POEMS WHO DREAMED THEY
WERE MANDOLINS AND A DARK BREAD

evening the priest

let three rivers flow
and a woman sing to her child

a gazebo of death and blue rosemary

in spite of the night
something crept
past me like numbers of smoke
something that would
split hairs in a drizzle
over nothing

was

I think the tide comes
in for your pleasure
I suspect you have
the premise of a belly
what am I talking about
there's no damn ocean
around here I know it
blood comes and goes
with the moon like sap
and cowboys use to take out
an obsidian blade from their collars
and plunge it as deep as it
would go into their
blue organdy rodeo shirts
when a little tired from the range
they'd see the angel of doom
sail by aboard the ship of death
and they would croon
and they would wish oh I wish
I never won that hand from the Indian
too late my children ride on drowned calf ropers
I think of the face
of death in the oasis the casket of peaches
sliced like flowers

day after tomorrow

the body
the body of the bride
rose up by itself
and smelled like a harbor
a carnival left town
way away from the trick rider my father
traveling through the courtyards
of mystery and wisteria
saying to himself never
this old moon and this whiskey
and a posse of omens
he said these things he must have
been a gypsy
there are times I think he was
like this

the afternoon of another hunter

you are that
a wedding reception for death
a heart beyond doubt
floats in your neck
like a compass
and the leaves like old boyfriends
holding magnets and the final mist
I conclude the hypothesis
of sundown pardon the ritual

POEMS FLOATING UP EYELESS ON
SUNDAY MORNING

death going on eleven

when I got there with the seacoast in my cuffs
and the boogie woogie under my toes
and the silent harp and the plow and the riddle
under my tongue and the sanctuary of dust
and the terror and the unicorn's bowsprit
and the underwater buckskin and the pillars
of wisteria an aura of filth on its haunches
and my pockets sewn up with guitar strings
and my old jug of blood and a rootatoot
toot floating like a sweet number of songs
that slithered off behind the buildings
when I arrived with moonlight when I was
coming down the road like a sleepwalking lion
my sleeves rolled clear up to the feet
of that acrobat ladyluck
gored to death by the quickmud of the pew
on my shoulders I carried prisms and pairs
of white gloves like a confederate
of pallbearers my lungs on fire from tugging
the night of the blackboard like a sled
of massacred Cherokees on the cornerstones
of the backwoods I put down my load
for a while I wrote mock epics in the bus stations
where I waited for myself to arrive
with the real tragedies I'd already
written and when I finished the hero
drowned I left him there with the others
for the bums to bring back to life
I am that papoose who must crawl
over the body of his father the good bull
with his skinned mother on his back

and there are strata of blood
between the things and over the eyes
the thighs lovely as loons at dusk
and I came of age mashing my teeth
on leather and steel until death do us part
like a plowboy tilling the unknown herds of the soil
and when I got there dead tired and miserable to boot
I knew I had my work cut out for me

the girl

she would go after the fog like a real sport
with a jar full of dead bees
the water flowing under her shack
on the St. Francis River
is an evening of firecrackers and short hair
every night died from its rose
every minnow was terrible
like skin you kiss in the dark
the gill of each dream went bad from cunning
I panted from the danger of moist eyelids
all the way home
dawn I forgot

when I got there

I went walking through the Ozark Mountains
I couldn't believe my ears
smoke was coming from a cabin
a girl at a piano
was playing Für Elise

harp

it use to be that I wore a buckskin coat
I could Indian wrestle my girl
and read a play at the same time
I spun the bottle
and the moons of blood
sunk in my hair every month
she would draw the vein from my arm
she would twing it like a bowstring
I went off in the dark morning
before the schoolbus driver was up
and climbed a tree
waiting for a deer to come lick
I shot them
season after season
not knowing the times we can bat
our eyelids are infinite
I strung them up by the hind legs
cut out their glands
and bled them
my girlfriend
laid her slip
over the chair near the fireplace
in her bedroom
I laced my boots with sinews
and wiped my knife with sand
we ate meat
there were days we waited on the lake
to go down
until there were tubs of berries
to be had
the old father passed on

like the dark mules
they plowed themselves under with
how I lost my cherry
I remember it well
it was hard as a rock
to find
like breaking a stray horse
it was a mirage of sound
late one evening

rag of a man who could remember the sound of his hearing leaving him

I tore off a scab without knowing it
he claimed the tide
came in
an echo too
like her

the swarthy one in the garden holding off the invasions of night

night lord after night I do drink with the water
I leave alone so I can put new dirt on the graves
we are all in love with
horses and roses and fins
are dead everything is asleep and in pain
in love and dreaming
about another life if I can sweat
I say to myself and if it is time
I bullwhip my own lookout
unfaithful sailors know they can't
see a thing but they keep their place
and the prow still leaking
out there in the darkness boats
are colliding oh yes they are
even if I was blind or awake I could
still feel the dark like light
like those levels of cold and heat
underwater you know what I mean
when you're dreaming or in danger
that place where the fish live and sleep
sometimes I think I understand everything
but I know I'm wrong and incredible the first
shadow I see when I'm hung
I want to think of hideouts in the mountains
where a man can die there
I remember the girl
who goes to the window at dawn when it's still dark
in the winter and sees the snow she knows
he won't have long she knows she won't
have to go to school the bus it can't run

she is so happy lifting her skirts
I want to rise up again too in the rain
and the dust and move the empty seed sacks
I want to look at how brown I am
when I put on my sky blue shirt
just a few things you learn coming from a barn
where a silent blacksmith is shoeing guitars
where the Negroes can't go wrong
because they are beautiful and right and a joy forever
in their weeping shoes and swimming knives and hotcakes of desire
I tell you I have watched your shadow
and you have given me mine
like wakes and french harps and the chest
of drawers of a blond schoolgirl
with her hair done up by paths and moss and who knows what all
darkness we can all gather one at a time but not one
soul can make a bouquet from another soul
it is too cold to be dreaming
and there is no place for the saddletramp of the bayous
the lover of ribbons and crawdads
the duelist of black clothes and fairly good looking women
it is winter and the wind is my second having dark hair
and I a tremendous limping colt of a poet unknown
to hold back the elastic of socks and panties like a set of triggers
to breathe in the dead eyes of the schoolgirl near the Negro's tent
and listen to her sing will you

vague sonnet

from time to time
the boy looked
at the stars
he ate spanish peanuts
and stole watermelons with O.Z. and Dark
until bad weather came
bad luck like the southern number thirteen
and he could feel the gondolas
guided by women
like a bad smell that was really very good
wandering up the forked canals
of his pants
and then
he shut his eyes
and stumbled in fins and horseshoes
and his eyelids
became so dark
from the starlight

the other wedding of the luna moth to the juke box

I chose black
to wear
like a knight
who must compose
a song
before day
breaks
into its fever
but I was
chosen
by white
worn
by a lady
who already
had
a king
to defend
and so
it is
told
I forfeited
the woes
the grapes
and the furious
mandolins
of my youth
so
it is told

POEMS WHO LEFT WITHOUT
A WORD OF FAREWELL

strut

I walked into one of those old places the Law closed down
and found the tap of a gandyman's shoe
thin and sharp as a razor blade
like a silver root cutting sprouts
in some dirt with no sun
down on the floorboards of the shotgun shack
I looked for the hair
trigger of those miserable days
fine as afternoons we got off early
when we rolled the good times
ourselves down the catwalks
like bales of dresses for our many lowdown women
when we loaded barrels of sorghum
with crow bars taking dead aim
our sweat it ran off
like those camp dogs we loved to kick
every evening
we showed up drunk

eloping boy

he ran with danger
and the best looking of the other daughters
she was setting her hair one evening
like the night done up pretty
in the hotel
and he
who was nothing more
than a lame brat
went to see if they would sell him a bottle
when he got back she was
a widow
the gypsies say love
is so strange
even the sound of it
is like a wounded animal

here rattler here

I was traveling the dark song of the fang
I got to
keep moving

nine men from the hills tuning the mandolins of silence

a stare will become
a scar
if you don't watch it
like a hawk
or gypsy
who just blew into town
hunting no good
to drift like those
who are there
for good and watching
you like they want
you to break
camp before you've made it
what the hell
you're just passing
through like the moon
you just lite there
for a while anyway
like a dragonfly
with its tail
in its mouth
to sharpen knives
and burn
your initials into the body
of some stringed instrument
with a spyglass
you might lose some time
a life maybe
even your good for nothing life
slipping around like that

in your caravan of shadows
eyeing somebody's wife

nobody is going to touch me

the sycamore of loneliness they call it
daydreams while the ax is still afraid
of being alone
it is like a hive of fear it tastes like honey
you couldn't bear
it wouldn't be the pain it would be the touch
of the swarm around you
driving you into it like a nail

the rings

how do I know
they made a sound at all
a fish kept in the ice
and the harmonica full of ants
it sounded forbidden
like sumac tea
I don't know

some shade

sitting there
with a grasshopper I didn't know
I had murdered
in the secret book of Gorinnosho
among enough cane poles for the state of Minnesota
drinking cool water
a blueberry muffin made this morning
still in my pocket like a watch
my grandfather stays drunk hoping his spectacles
will come in on the locomotive
today we know about all there is
we don't know
tomorrow some dogs are liable to run anything

throat

a splendid rabbit
skin it

POEMS DRUNK FROM A PAPER SACK
LONG BEFORE I CAME OF AGE

**moan until the circle of the moon releases the bad
storm coming**

come on down you green-eyed bitch of an evening
get your long hands in the pants of my raft
so the circuit rider death can hunt foxes and crabs
you river where ashes lose one finger to fame I beg you
and the angel of snuff can work on the carburetor
soda crackers and sardines will do
and I will get up before day
breaks loose the convict that it is
and gallops off to town selling many limits of rough fish

she wept and then she spoke

years ago I began
calling poetry a witch
giving it light
which darkens
dark eyes

destiny of quicksand

a child playing the ace of hearts
on the queen of spades
in a room where there is no one
there is a photograph
of a Negro girl
a very dark prima donna
on the mirror with masking tape
her tutu like a corona
her arm needing a tourniquet
and her father asleep in the desert
with his cello the nomad of sound
the lint in her belly
is the bestiary of snores
it is all in the cards marked by spews and sudden light

quest of chants

I dream and it is
another life

mirage

a minnow bucket leaking air
like a tire
on the coupe
of the undertaker
who's come
to make arrangements
while you've gone
to the black island
to dream the carry of your voice
the score of a bullet hole

the child who enchanted deadly snakes

with a feather I ordered them
to salute the adventures
of their skin
the blue one like a constellation
of women prepared to undress
the yellow one who yodeled
the twig's tornado
the orange one to be done with another poet
the final one hanging
like the noose of midnight
the rainbow of pure reason
the fork in the flooded road
the hypotenuse of the spittoon
and the starfish's talaria
under the bed where we scorch
the edges of the Sumiye's soot
where we dream that chess nobody knows
and daub the blossom of the eye
with the sword gliding like boats of lightning
like that child who draws up
the Shibumi of his ego like a wound
and strokes the hides on the fences laid bare
who wanders solitary when it begins to rain
and dips his thumb into the current of the one
and only chance
in the lifetime of the eel's kabbalah
he lets the wind travel through his hair
and evades the eleventh hour
he picks up where she left off
lining up the syzygy of the outhouse and the warped egg
and we know he is following us with his comb

and a log chain around his waist
holding the pose of the moon my mistress
the nest of the phoenix

apocalypse of the logs

stinkweeds and flowers grow in the firewood
the wind that lame vigilante surrounds the wound with in the fog
and burns down his own cabin of vines
the dreary ladder of rope unravels its knots
like a woman making herself breathe smoke
the splendor of a thorn laid to waste
casting no shadow a branch which dies with its gut
sucked in a stem that has become quiet like a fish bone
like the blood running in the moon
waves soaking in their own pants

leech

darkness seeps through the willows of my raft

SOME POEMS WHO SUFFOCATED LIKE LIGHTNING BUGS IN THE BOOTLEGGER'S JAR

no more legends

a girl too young to be wearing hose
got out of a car in Drift Tennessee
and stomped on a bug
you could tell she was not from around here
I was there

a safari of the spirit by water

there is poetry written by dangerous women
in my saddlebags
I do not drink very much wine
but I've seen how it is made
the african who leaves the ground
with his arms close to his sides
and the porpoise who returns
with the dead cabinboy
will inherit the earth
and the stars we leave
the fields to follow
let me go with these ritual women
let me be here as well as there
in my body and mind
let me go through all kinds of water
I want my spirit to swim under the bulls of the dark
let me become like the salmon that soft worker
who goes from pool to pool
to spawn and to die
I want to be with these women
because they have left
the maps in the rum
these women who drink the dangerous song
that makes you still
and the fish and the seething wisemen
will be the ones the honeybees of the soul
who will make a caravan of sacred elephants
and orbit with thirsty tigers
who can take off their black helmets
and discover their own atmosphere
and breathe

the molested child goes to the dark tower again
140 years to the day

you haven't heard a thing
until you've heard
an infant gurgle like a shoal
in its own blood
often a panther or an angel
takes me by the throat
and drags me into its garden of mystery
and muskmelons
where I have the run of the land
as long as I bleed
and sing while I work

mascara

it rains
and I think of bales
crushing the wind
out of children
riderless ponies with ropes tied to the pommels
eyeshadow and dead weights on the other end
and girls who would like to go on
in this world
raped by their stepmother's scrapbooks
the men and women of learning
have left us so much
I prefer to think of the moon

irons

I thought of the delta
like a capsized yacht
and the screen of the Drive Inn
was a centerboard
a plywood tombstone that would warp
with the years
the country clubs
in the cuts of cotton where no
eye can find a lost ball
in the hunting camps the hunted
hoisting up venison
like sails made from hides
on the fairways the caddies
pulling golf carts like catafalques
the worn out holding clubs like oars
I visited the jails with whiskey
under my coat for my best friends
in the dark age before reason
warmed his thin knife
I took things to heart
and set my watch by the enigmas
whistled very vaguely at sundown
for a long time I wore
a bronze and naked crucifix
where sweet jesus had pulled himself out
pegs and all
now I wear blue suede shoes and live
down the street from Elvis
who has a steel guitar like a submarine
full of Negro deacons
and a pair of hands as fast as an anchor

I show up at the cotillions now and then
in tight breeches and no shirt
dark as the other side of the moon
and my legs quiver like a man
led to the gallows pole
like a drunken sailor
who can't take a command

the shepherdboy and the moon

I was fast asleep in my fields when
I saw the swollen waist of light come down beside me
Christabel of the backcountry
I called her
she was like a ballad with no balladeer
she put me under the evil spell of the months
of her blood and tended my rams
with inescapable weddings tidelike
in nature and ceremony
the creeks froze over with the floating
whiskey bottles of fire and nightletters
and my hickory stick turned into
a beautiful snake
who slithered away into some dark guitar

Isinglass

I would take a common ice pick to the blind statues of water
and cut out beasts that looked back at you
I sang under the ground of Macchu Picchu
where the black roses flew
like the birds I carved out
on the mountainous plains of Peru
I crawled back home on the bottom like a squid
and devoured the hasty robes of fanatical missionaries
I hovered as a barracuda for the pied piper's kids
the truth is too simple to say
I was down at the river one day and drank what I found
in the jars hidden in the trees
I thought it was black sap from the roots
I stabbed holes in the lids at nightfall
capturing everything beautiful and dark that gave off light
I set up transits underway to survey the lunar fish
I measured the shock waves of foetal continents and galaxies
I could hold those jars full of wings and fangs and scales
and the dust of moonlight
up to my ears and listen to the blood of night
throbbing like lovers and all time
like shipwrecks occurring in the years to come
like my bad sign hoisted in the saltwater of the stars
like the somber eyes of the rainbow trout in the drinkable stream
I with my ice pick and musical driftwood on fire
I buried some of those jars in the levees I threw some
back to the water
and will return sounding like comets

Canephorae

when you sing things
like flute of the smoking water
or there is a chinese rooster
dragging his long tail through the burning water
the listeners look down at their feet
and go home afraid
even some of the girls in my grade are going
carrying baskets of dirt and broken glass
where else are they going
who are leaving somewhere
with my liver

POEMS BURIED IN THE
MOON LAKE LEVEE

exile

a parasol a footfall a barking
a screen
door coming open
a wayfarer with no good
intentions in his eyes
the ace of hearts and laments
inlaid in his teeth
a lapse in memory
let bygones be
bygones mister
never

so many things keep moving this instant

forsythia and the bad luck of dark ground
trouble looking for a place to lite
something penetrates something is taken
aback the night swells up like a wound
some secret
a waitress with a beauty mark
on the nape of her neck
a run in her stocking
the gunshot
not tonight the morning
watch aways off
the sheriff takes something out
of his pocket
my brother murders a snail
with salt
and the girl's dress blows
up in the rain
whatever it is that startles
the weeds the holy relics
are clutched the stolen truck
coasts past the cuts
with no headlights
for the moment some doves
separate
the tags are bound
to be illegal
he looks kind
of handsome and sly
stepping back into the cover
of the shadows in the thicket
rolling up his frayed cuffs

over the sweet smelling sleeves
of his long underwear
he remembered to pick up his straw hat
pulled down low
over his dark eyes
and does not return

death of the french kiss and the hall of mirrors

at the Fair I went off my rocker in a gondola
in the tunnel I did fairly well

fade away clear light in the roots of the Chickasaw wilderness

a gar
and the scent of chicory
in the saddlebags of a swayback mule
I knew in the realms
of the quarters with its center moving
nothing but old blood
was leaving to come back
antimacassars drifted down like sails
on a ship of sloe-eyed gin and brandy
and a man came riding with his head hung low
his hair full of chinaberries
and the weather
it was warm
like a farmgirl's mist
the stars the deceived the mad
you who did not look the conquered
the sun was in the clorox jar old evening
polishing its own boots
and the wild strawberries
were eaten by long-lost cousins
drowned in no time

furious ballad of courting at the ice house

I made two bits a day selling crushed ice for a Negro
when he came back at suppertime
with a can of sardines I'd say how'd you do
he'd say I did fine
we'd have cantaloupe fish soda crackers and water
it was too hot to drink sweetmilk
along about seven p.m.
he'd poke fun at us well I wonder what they doing
up there at the ice house
so I'd tap a tune with the tongs
he'd play the picks
when that sun went down the field hands could
take their cool shade
until the spunk in the blood got back
then we'd shoot craps into the doodlesocking night
my honey would ride
by on an eleven speed english bicycle
I said her daddy's rich
she got a fine mamma Sylvester said
look there at the pink balloons she's rumbling
in the rear spokes
and she got red aces and clothespins on the front wheel
she'd blow a lavender bubble
I'd swallow
shoot snake eyes and lose
everything I had

gnats

I would just as soon climb the vine
of lowing sadness
that grazes the armpits of the fortune teller
it makes some kind of noise
like a tractor with red hair
I would climb it alright with two pairs of pliers

the shadow of a character standing behind one of the seven pillars of wisdom

he was not from here
never could have been
I kissed his name and gave it to my Shetland
I wrote a letter to Lowell Thomas
asking him to send me a picture of Lawrence
his voice I imagined was like a soothsaying
the remote sadness of the bastard
who goes through names and poets like socks
a voice crossing itself like a bow in the desert
a holy man slit open by light
fleeing the couch of his mistress
his hair was like an abandoned farm
and his eyes were like tattoos
on the shadow of the man whose name was strange
and long as a gust of wind
I can no longer say it
his name
was like threatening clouds
of dust and discomfort it is written truly
the singer's voice like a cool pillow
for the night truly
moving with the scent of mimosa leaves
like a dark belly in the moonlight
like a spirula and a marked woman's veil

I went to bed and astonished what was sung

I really miss the way that crapshooter dressed
I was just a whippersnapper
attending the services of the willow switch
O I shivered in those lowdown dives
when his hand made the door come open
I know how a funeral begins with wheels
and a bow tie from Mound Bayou
some nets are thrown out
a carnival passes through the hamlet
while the rest of you parakeets sleep
the lures I hung up last spring
in the chassis of a flatbed truck
float up at the foot of the crossroads
of the bed like a bunch of moss roses
and I call out for water like a thief
loaded for a game
we've all forgotten

ONE-FINGER ZEN

Everybody Needs Something from a Stranger

when wearing gloves the hands of death
are cold as a wheelchair
and always pointing to an hour
we can't sleep through
the hands are buried
like fire in the upstairs mirror
and are going through rites
on other islands
the hands are the memory of ancient cities
the clouds that pass over a house
when a woman pees in her bath water
when children are poking the air
out of something dead with a stick
the hands that are clear and impure
when they tear bread nobody wants to eat

When We Are Young the Moon Is like a Pond We All Drown In

when I sleep a wind blows
over the strange grasses
of a prairie I don't know
and I feel like a lamp
someone is holding up
looking for a way
through a dark field
I will go out

Curse

we are not the only ones
who have wanted to walk our boats
up to the beach on a warm black night
while the enemy sleeps
and call out brother
before we cut their throats
we are not the only ones
who have picked up the stones
placed by others in holy places
and beaten out the strange faces
of their children like dirt
by the river we have made their women
wash the blood from us
we are not the only ones
who have stolen the wives of the dead
and left the old and the lame
to burn their men in longships
imagine we are home and not lonely
slaves have not driven our women mad
with their talk of magic and death
imagine our love which once cut
through strange waters
is not slow and heavy from the moss of fear
we are here and we are not here
nights in our land are sad
the risings of the moon are like the sores
we have given our wives
and we cannot sleep for what we dream
the others will do
they fill our children's throats with rocks
and place them somewhere under the moon

we feel the grip of dead men
and when the hands reach into our women
they rise out of this sleep
tell us of fish with odd shapes
murking the bottom of the sea
and men with torches
throwing open the gates of the city

Breaking Through the Skin

we sleep in the dust
near our jugs of water
children draw circles around our bodies
as they leave
they kick over our jugs
and water runs in
the circle of our passion
we wake up and slap the master
he holds up a cat
and says if any of you
can say the right thing
the cat will not be killed
no one says the right thing
so he kills the cat
when I get back all the plums
have fallen to the ground
and everyone is weeping in the mud
and the moon is on its way to Argentina
the lord says what would you have said
I roll up my pants
take off my boots
tie them around my neck
I walk away
the lord says see
and shouts me down
if you had been here
I wouldn't have killed the cat

Despair

a man by himself in a bar
feels a shadow behind him
thinks of his wife eating
bleeding meat
hears the rain by the sea
tries to forget his day laid out like dresses for the dead
he knows his heart is closed up for the night
and the people
who are poor and cannot sleep look through the blinds

Dreams of Women from Other Lands

one night I died but I didn't
tell anyone I didn't want anyone
to know I flew up into a tree
I was dead
a panther tore out my heart
but it was white and silent
like the music of the moon
a man shined a match on me
and took my heart from the panther
with a sharp stick
he took it home
to show it to his daughters
but when he opened the door to their room
pulled back the covers to their bed
they were jonquils buried in the snow
he gave my heart to his wife
and told her to play it he was so sad
but she told him no one can blow a flute with no holes
the man threw the heart in the fire
but it would not burn it flew
without light so it knew no dark
it made no shadow for those
who waited with the white paper
and smoked glass of their desire
it slept alone in the shells
and dreamed the creatures that left them
the heart remembered
the life the dead live
like an organ in an abbey
no one touches it like a stone
sewed to meat someone is needed

to thread the needle for the dead
fixing their shoes
far away from their bodies
like lakes in the distance
the sun burning fog off the surface

Children at the Point of Death

All during his life
he thought about them
when they died
they died
strange
they touch birds
say what they see
walk fence lines
with a fake limp
like they were
in pain
so
some of them are dead
some of them are handsome
and some mysterious
silent
but not for long
they tell you
men scarcely know
how beautiful fire is
they tell you stories
they can't remember
if you can
still look them in the eye

I seemed to hear the hog beater
even before I saw him coming
I followed him
I stepped on the back of his cut down
cowboy boots I followed him so close
he reach around and grab me
and tells me how he stole the hog back
how no one would know
cause the evidence was not
there the marked ears were buried
in a stump and the hog was shot
through the nose with a pistol
so no one could tell
it just dropped dead on his place
by the water and he skinned him
and in court they couldn't put it on him
and lord jesus christ I seen it all
and I'm seeing it all somebody get me off this river there's going to be
a WAR I see it the high temperature bullets is going through me clean
up into the sky like the stars the little nailheads in the coffins it's a place
called VIETNAM goodbye mammy wind blowing through dead american hair
o these cosmologies sadder than the sea
and the long presidential horseshit
and the moon say get up you want some more so I open my eyes think see tell

I wanted to be a family man
but I couldn't keep my heart
~~covered up~~
under a map in a blanket

CHURCH OF MY FATHERS

My eyes went down
Over your body
Like a ship on a reef.

CHORES AND MYSTERIES

Something kept eating the bread

I walked off to the pump
And drew water

Something kept taking the bread

I have a black patch
in the woods I wear a vest
I know the snakes sleep under the boat
the top button of my shirt is done
and the leaves show me how to shoot craps
I am the student of the creeks
and a friend with the wind sitting in the field
my classmates look like bark floating away
there is a bird
who made her nest with water moccasin skins
she worked by night
who taught me all I know
my teacher is called Sleep
he goes by Dreams too
my father moves dirt
and the only building I see is the levee
just like that pocket watch
hanging from a nail on the dock
at Spoon's Landing
I don't keep time
sometimes you can see the sun and the moon
my diploma is a blue suck rock a negro
cut out of the belly of a fourteen point buck
I am the student of night
I belong to my eyes

riderless horse

I wake up and it snows
it is like a dream where you lose one eye
to be alone in Snow Lake
with the window like a grave in my bed
is like a riderless horse
drinking water from a pool
early in the morning
look
there he is
over on Sara Bundy's Island
by himself circling the woods
it was long ago he broke
loose from the hearse and galloped
away from the cortege
he swam the river to be alone
he didn't want to carry dead men

1957

Frank Stanford

led to the gallows pole
like a drunken sailor
who can't take command

UNCOLLECTED POEMS, DRAFTS & FRAGMENTS

Bullshit

when we were in Arkansas and Tennessee
I used to run around with this guy named Willis Sims
when we were in Mississippi
he called himself Arkabutla just like the dam
he liked highlife music
and ladies who would walk in with ice picks
when they found out he was fixing to leave
he was always running out
when they asked him what he did
he said he was a road manager for a famous band
but I never seen nobody beat a drum
he was mostly on the road through
and he did make a living
but he earned it kind of strange
he'd be in a pool hall playing dominoes
and all of a sudden he'd throw all the beer and bones
off the table and say why shit if you want to bet let's
bet something worth a little
he'd stand up and point to me and say
I'll bet that kid over there will cut my leg off
for five hundred dollars
I'd be eating some eggs and saying no no shaking my head
and he'd say come on by god you cheap son-of-a-bitches
put you goddamned money where your mouth is
I'll tell you what by god those bloodthirsty so-and-sos
would have a horse blanket spread out over a pool table
and five hundred dollars and a chain saw sitting there
in fifteen minutes flat and telling me choke it choke it
he'd be lying on the table with a big thick wad of money in his mouth
told them it was on account of the pain
you know we had to clear out fast sometimes

and some characters saying watch out for that felt
it's fourteen dollars a running foot
by god I'd do it
take her off just above the calf
he liked to save the knee joint if he could
it was a ball bearng job off a US Congressman
anyway they'd all yell gyp and want their money back
it was all set up you know he'd put his arm around me
and I'd help him out to the truck and we'd split
but let me tell you ladies I played hell getting those wooden legs

Eleven Nocturnal Koans *
from Selene's Pupil

The clitoris which swarms like honeybees

When you touch it
The clitoris of the jellyfish
With its dose of poison

The clitoris
Who fills up with a kind of water
Like a piccolo

The clitoris in the pool
Where the bravest have drowned

The clitoris like a footprint in the snow
Made by a one-legged hermit in the alps

The clitoris of lemons on ice with shrimp
In a chinaman's market
In Mound Bayou Mississippi

The clitoris with the eye of a lizard

The clitoris of spiced apple yogurt
No one has stirred

The clitoris that swells
Like a wet rope
That won't hold a pony or a rowboat

*Written when the poet was seventeen years old. — Ed.

The clitoris which resonates
Like a moonstone
In Domenico Scarlatti's ring

The clitoris
The light years'
Chaperone

futile negative noninspiration *no.* 91
or   the invisible man

when you paint your walls with nonsense
and the sky outside reflects your feelings
bones are vanishing—sensations becoming tiring
discovering there are only floors and no ceilings
the faceless colored man doesn't want your tips but your hand
he wants to try standing cause he's tired of kneeling

When you insure the beggarman's confidence with a dime
hoping he will ask you to stay a while
then you find out he's not the freak but you are
you have got the mind that's on trial
suddenly the beggarmanjudge he is dying and you didn't have to stop yourself
slowly you take his cup and begin your eternal beg for just one smile

[untitled]

the Pre-Raphaelite's little brother
that youth who cut his heart
on the dark waters
every moment he is awake
Xanadu is in danger
let him lay there

The Cid

the page as white as the moon
it will go away
my lover

Spilled Yolks

Seen after my father died
I was in my boat
Reading about the poets of times past
When a wounded dog
Came down the hill
Yelping to beat hell

The wind was blowing
A stranger appeared
Next to the witness tree
He said nothing
He had a handful of rocks
And a grin on his face

Oxford

One evening when I knew the wind
Was up at the place,
I drove a hundred miles
To unchain the swing on the porch.
The moon slept on its stepladder
And the living room groaned
Like my empty belly.
I saw the owl, I thought,
In Dead Woman's Hair.
I threw a stone and called,
But did not enter—
It took winters to lose those briars.
An old man came out of the thicket,
Blood on his shirt, holding a spade.
"Is that you, Frank?
You know it takes seven lawyers
To bury a goddamn dog these days."

Local Attractions

I got up in the middle of the night,
Told her I was going out
To take the variation.
She knew it was cloudy.
I found the star, took note
Of the wet compass.
Something was pulling the needle off.
Nothing was true.
I checked for fire in my shirt—
It was part wool.
I leaned over, fogged the glass,
Felt the place in my head
Where I took the mine,
Lost my balance, fell
Down in the cold meadow,
And drew up like a dropped calf,
All crazy from you and the stars.

Stars

Slices of cold butter the lovers are spreading
over their toast.

Frank Stanford Calls Back to the Owl Who Lives
a Hundred Years *

I

It is Friday morning, raining too much to work,
and the heirs to the Rush place have called
to say they've talked with the neighbors
and they're satisfied with the corners.
They will be sending me a money order.

II

It is midnight before I set foot
outside the door.
The webworms in the persimmon trees
are bonnets on dead women.

III

Poems by friends
come in the mail.
I think of these people I don't know
sitting in their cars near the city limits
drinking beer with their gloves on.
They are thinking of the schoolgirls
coming home at three,
they are tucking their jeans in their boots now,
walking over the dead leaves.

* This is a variant of "Desire for a Killing Frost" (p. 315) which appears in
 You. — Ed.

And the prostitutes are dressing in the dark,
and the orphan is serving early mass,
and the hoboes are remembered
by the students who didn't pick them up.

IV

My sadness waves back
like the heads of grain in another's fields,
it cannot be combined, and no one is hungry.

Youth

My heart is showing its horses
Again in the night
As a man I ask you
To give me your ribbons no one will see
You catch your breath
Like a latch which opens and closes
Without a gate
Though it is not so
I believe I was thrown
Into a rose
The thoughts of you like riders in pain
You were a girl with dark locks
Who left without writing

Pain

One day I began beating my meat
That night I fell

in love with a butterfly
The next day the jar and the lake

The cliff by the water smelled like mayonnaise and thistles
I saw fish down there

as dark as blood still in you
I hit on an idea

the same way a hull touches the bottom
I tore a wing off

like a page from a book
It was a stamp no one would lick

At daybreak the fish struck it
My girl friend moved to Tennessee

I went over to the schoolhouse
and found her dancing slippers

They smelled like jelly
At night I dreamed

of the wing like a petal
and the fish with the fin in its back

Every morning I reached under the water
and felt the moss

growing on the keel of the boat
I smelled my fingers the summer went by

I mailed her part of the butterfly
I told her it would tickle her belly

The envelope was sharp
I beat my meat

She sent me a snakeskin
and said she cut her foot

If you tell
a lie when it's lighting

You'll spit
blood at midnight

One day a rose

Poem

My face is cold
As a snow that wakes up a statue
I wait with my lute like a suitor
In the brave shadows
Cast in the courtyard of the dead
I've taken away the ladies of all forms
The four of them knew my horses and songs
Alone in the middle of the night
I've turned up in their hands
Like the Ace of sorrows
I bring you tonight
The same black flowers I gave
By darkness they are thrown
By light they are taken
I keep breath in my body
Wearing the tight costume of silence
I give you what I will take from you
Tomorrow night I dream
The intercepted messages
The dust in my boots
And you hide me out in the barn
And tend me till morning
I sleep in the afternoon
Then I travel the low road
Combing the straw out of my hair
Keeping your scent black as caviar

Kata at Dawn on the Cliff by the Lake

East of the hills west of the mountains
My heart was cut out
Of rice paper without a sound
And thrown into a pool of water
By a warrior boy of the soft fist school
A thousand years ago
A few moments before he slit his belly
The blood ran down the stones
Of the garden like a barefoot girl
He was forbidden to marry
And my heart was arranged
By the water
In the shape of a tiger
That dreamed
A mirror where two lovers
Breathed as one

Living with Fishermen

I never had any money
Neither did they
But I spent the best part
Of my life with them

They were the only people I knew
Who ate buzzards
And wept over drowned children
I read great poetry in their quivering houses

But they wouldn't swallow
The sesame seeds I toasted
They looked too much like fleas
For them night was one of those soundless whistles

I ate bread
And went to the bathroom at the same time
What they paid for what they drank
You could sell the bottles for more now

They drank more than their guts could handle
Then they tied string and hooks to these empties
And sang until they heard others
Moan far away in the throat

Whistling with His Teeth in a Jar

I drank the bitter coffee
Out of the old cup
And watched the drowsy rooster
Eat his shadow

I heard sorrow again
Up in my lap
Licking between my fingers
Like a rock in a gizzard

How I Showed the Men No-Man's-Land

The party of lost surveyors
Gathered at my fire
Dead and weary
While I cleaned my fish

"See this creek" the field chief
Told his chainmen
"It doesn't appear on the map"

It was dusk
And my fire was going down
Like the sun on the ridge

They looked in the sky
For a star to follow
The wind blew
But the branches were still

"It's odd here men
There must be something underground
The compass won't work
The needle's still
As a ship in dead calm"

I came out of the dark with my deaf dog
I asked them wouldn't they
Take their rest

They whispered among themselves

I offered them biscuits and liquor

"Stranger all we want to know
Is where we are"
So I drew them a map in the dirt
Quietly with my knife

And when they understood
How deep they'd traversed
They looked one another in the eye
And parted company

That night every man looked for his own stone
To lie down beside and die alone

Regret des yeux de la putain et belle comme une panthère

I like to drink at that joint
Where the password is NO REGRETS
The tapster carries two thirty-twos
And honorary degrees from several radio stations.

I don't go there just to shoot
The bull with him though;
It's the creole whore behind the counter
That's got under my skin.

You know how you're down and out
On the river, three sheets to the wind,
Doing some night casting,
Just a little moonlighting

To pay off the bill at the hardware store,
And you decide, "By God, I'm tired
Of drifting. Believe I'll anchor here."
So you let out the line.

You're dizzy as hell, drinking
Hot beer, eyes shut, letting the rope
Pass through your hands,
Waiting for some slack to come up,

Like that stinking wind;
And a few feet before
The section of stolen rail
Touches bottom, a treble hook snags.

You let out with a yell
That will wake up the long-tailed rooster

In the shade of the bobcat;
And the spawning gars

Move away from their nests
Like hogs in a stable
Of stirred-up ponies.
Pain: prostrate, and children in danger.

Something drifts by the bow, something big:
You don't know if it's growing or swimming.
You miss—like bobbing for apples;
So many things get loose on the water.

Me, I'm living on beer, boiled eggs,
And ruined mascara. Tonight,
I'll make enough to buy a roll of dimes
So she can play the box.

She drops them in the sawdust
On purpose; that way, she can lean
Over, looking for them.
Oh me, Oh my, Oh.

I know I ought to be drinking buttermilk
In a movie house somewhere,
But I'm fishing, measuring it up,
Having a run of good luck.

For a long time
I thought the dive's counter was a boat
Turned upside down.
Like usual, I was wrong.

It was a casket,
Shellacked with dark green paint.

It looks like it's seen its share
Of shallow water and sculls.

If you ask for directions, you better leave
Before they say GO DOWN . . .
It's a thousand miles from nowhere,
And not worth the bad luck and trouble.

[untitled]

Night is nothing
but the small shadow a woman-child's foot casts
when she puts on her boots
when the taichi lesson is over.
The moon only rots
if she has no shoes.

As you can see,
I have the blues.

All the blind pilots are going over the letters
from their wives, who think they are widows.

The young girl can still dream
that the trees are full of princes
waiting for kisses to be blown.

Now we have all seen our children
throw kisses to the fish and giraffes,
even if we've never seen our children.

I believe the farmer who stays awake all night,
sacking his mind like oats
for a name for his farm,
is more of a poet than most.

It's about time the white men
got wise to blue guitars
of the delta.

I'm a two-timer and a drifter
so I won't ask you to stay very long with me.

I don't want anyone else to get
two steps from the blues.

Closer is a word the wise and foolish lovers use.
The incestuous roosters of dawn
are all of the time tracking it down.

The ones who follow wicked routine
are always saying, "Make ends meet."

If we have to meet, then I want to
meet you like smoke. Yes, I'd like
to chop the kindling of my childhood once more,
we're the same there. But those days are gone,
for better or worse. So, if we meet at all,
whoever you are, let us meet like horses
smelling one another out
before they mate.

[untitled]

The night, the child, the moon, the drunken sailor,
the woman who wears through her ring like
a pair of Levis that last and last,
the blind Negro who taught me how to strut
when I was six, the look you gave me
the other day, whoever you are, the brave
and the lonely, the animals that see us,
a long time before we shoot them, the bank robber,
the drifter, all of us drink
from the same pool. So, when we meet,
let's float down together, sane,
stoned, drunk, whatever, like those indigo
dragonflies of spring that will be here
soon.

[untitled]

I drink whiskey all day
Write poems in the night
I drink whiskey all day
Write poems in the night

Life be so beautiful
I don't ever want to retire

Ezekiel 12:2 The Clandestine Musicians

The lovers are very wide awake in their bed
And the katydid croons like a lusty monk
I would say drink up boys
But the local authorities have taken them too
All except the informer
Don't worry I know who he is
This morning there were a good fourteen of us
Every man jack aboard was true as a mooring line
You must cut loose in a hurry
This evening I'm making my way
Out of the shallows alone
I swear by the map the kid gave me
And the blood in my boat
And by the Virgin too
This is one son who will see to it
Everyone gets it
Exactly as they deserve
I smuggle you see I smuggle love
If you want to call it that
Like a bird who weaves the rope of his song
Into a knot
Only a few can recognize
You see them
Step back from the ones who are gathered
Disappear into the other voices
As natural as sound
And I hold the note like the reins
To a getaway horse
They know the noose of the chord
I sing the cryptic refrain
One more time to give them

Enough time
To get to the water's safekeeping
You know those two we strum for
They don't have our blood
On their hands
Or in their bed
This night some good men died good women too
But we knew what we were
Up to from the very beginning
We were balladeers of sap and the full moon
And the wind that traitor
Wore an almuce like ours in the dory
Tonight the lovers can sleep
In peace
The countryside is ours for the strolling
If we can sing low enough

riderless horse

I wake up and it snows
it is like a dream where you lose one eye
to be alone in Snow Lake
with the window like a grave in my bed
is like a riderless horse
drinking water from a pool
early in the morning
look
there he is
over on Sara Bundy's Island
by himself circling the woods
it was long ago he broke
loose from the hearse and galloped
away from the cortege
he swam the river to be alone
he didn't want to carry the dead men

Putting Up Fence

I believe the moon wades a creek
Like an albino with a blade
Fixed to a stick.

It rises, red as a place
Where a chigger's been.

Voyeur in the loft, leaving your gum
Stuck to a fork in the barn,
Like a porter paid to listen
With his head in a portal
Of a ship returning before it's due.

Then I come down the road with ice.

Living with Poets

They try to fuck the eyes out of every living thing
Then repent like saints for not doing it

You can tell from the way I talk
I only lived with them a little while
No hard feelings

My car broke down outside this place on the river
Some nice people came out
Offered to tow me in
But I said it wasn't worth it

The days crept up on me like priests
And I still hadn't left

Well the poets hired a guide
And came up the river looking for me
I was asleep in the graveyard
Underneath a mimosa

My friend told them that
But they took it wrong
And took off their hats
And took out their pencils

I was eating grapes and reading
Soon they went their way

I'm not going to give you any of this shit
How I had a vision and went to plow the snow
Reasons for leaving so I could dream

Friends I just ran out of money and time
That big black spook of my childhood
Told me I love you
Boo and So long
And my heart went lame
Like the cold ground I sleep on

House That Molly Built

The body is a garden
For dreams. The body
Is a harbor of subdued light,
A place for winter
To begin, a place
For getting to know you,
A dock for your beds,
Boats no one will recall.
Pictures of the forest in the lake,
Where you cannot tell the forest
From the lake, evening
Listening with the breadfruit of the night,
And pictures of lists, planning for danger,
The deckled edges of your eyes
Planting by the moon.
Entries and curves,
Attics for the stringless harp,
Three kinds of stone,
The nearest mountain
With water running through its belly,
A sad calamity.
Dogwood blossoms
Falling on the hair of another
Dead woman like snow.

The Double Suicide of the Mirror and the Rose

The night carried you away like a river
I couldn't sing the next day
It wasn't a dream it was a flood
Even the palomino was sad
As I rode along the evening I wanted you
To come out of the dark
Into the dark
Like some thirsty watchboy I kept my eyes
Open for the port of your neck
It was so easy to bruise
I wanted your voice with its wooden vessels
The water broke the earth but not your spell
I seemed to sleep in the saddle
The moon was coming up right over there
They took you away in a hearse
If I could only double-cross myself with the holy water of your eyes
I would just as soon spill my own blood as the milk you bathed in
When no one was looking I had my chance
I left the pony on the levee
The catafalque was black like a dream
There was only time enough
To breathe on the glass
I sounded like you when I touched you
Where you wanted me to
I dreamed a sleep with you like a long swim
You played the guitar
Looking towards me in the bow of my boat
When you sang you drowned in the mirror
I knew you were there with the rose in your mouth
So I stared at the river that rode off with you
The horses reared up and tried to break loose

Flowers and water spilled on your lips
There wasn't time so I wrote
The Double Suicide of the Mirror and the Rose
It was such a strain to reach up for so long
On my toes then
I felt like a dancer
You were the one who told me young
Ballerinas weren't virgins
So no one would know about us
I'll keep our troth as sure as the moon
I cross my heart and hope to die
There wasn't enough pane for the Rose
So I put it below
That's when your folks said who is that gypsy
And the coachman hit me with his whip
I swear I wanted to take you with me like a guitar
You will never get out of this alive I was told
Turning over the years like a canoe
I took to the weeds and sulked
Waking up I remembered dreams where you breathed
On my hands so I could play
I wanted to cut my heart out

[untitled]

some children playing beside a river
making homes out of sand
and each child defending his home
and saying this one is mine
keeping their houses separate
not allowing any mistakes about which
was whose when the homes were all finished
one child kick'ed over someone else's home
completely destroying it and the owner
flew into a rage pulling the other child's hair
striking him with his fist and the others
came to help him beat the child with a stick
and then they stomped him as he lay
on the ground until he was bleeding
through the ears and eyes
and then they went on playing
in the homes they'd made from sand
saying this is mine no one else can have it
keep away from here do not touch me
but evening came and it got dark
and they all thought they ought to be going
home no one caring about the house they'd built
out of sand one child stomped on his
another beat his with a stick
as they turned away going back to their homes

from **Canticles of the Banished**

So it is morning
The monk dies at the loom

Where are we going sister

Back
To the woods

The Sound of Trees

Every holy thing wishing to remain holy surrounds itself with Mystery.

MALLARMÉ

When he plays cards with his Fate, he cheats because he draws upon his childhood. When dealing with Mystery, it is best to keep a close watch on the hands of reality. Old myths can be reborn without their heroes knowing it.*

COCTEAU

This morning I walked
Quite a ways.

I drank from the pond
Before light.

Fog came out of holes
In the earth.

It was like panthers
In their den.

Just the night before,
The timber

Was the ship of the
Enemy.

* It seems that Stanford combined three separate Cocteau quotations in his epigraph. — Ed.

The ax blade sinks in,
Like moonlight

Through a lost hook's eye.
Evening comes.

The wind licks its thumb,
Flipping through

The dirty pages
Of its book.

Before I get home
I can smell

Fire chewing splinters,
My supper.

My wife leaves a lamp
On for me.

My limbs are weary
Like her voice.

She would worry night,
Clear as a bell.

She calls animals,
Ties their rings.

She hauls water, too.
Work is work.

Across my shoulder
I carry

A long, slender stick.
What in hell

Does a deaf man need
With a crutch.

Lost Dog and a Wild Hair

I used to be young like that

Billy Willet, Snake Maynard, and myself
Would go up to the line
And buy whiskey on credit.

Big Time Sonny with his prick
Always like rebar.

We'd play the guitars and french harps
And drink all the way back.

Death doesn't fuck around.

It's alright to lose faith,
But don't let go of the way
You lived.

Stay up all night,
Roaming through pastures
In a cheerleader's jeep.

Remember the moon in the woods   flashing
Like a girl running in her panties.

Survive, call it love, call it
Danger, you can say anything.

Like a boat losing its shadow
To the wind, you can lie
Yourself back into bodies
You never touched.

What love there was
Flashes by like chrome
On a fender skirt.

Lighted Room

I'm going to cut me some ham
And wait for death to lace his boots.

The old bushwhacker has seven wives,
Two trucks with good tires,
One with a flatbed for hauling.

In the morning there were soda crackers
Gone from my cabinets, crumbs
On my table, and mud on the floor.

That pint on my radio
With the painting on the bottle,
He took a deep swig.

My dogs sleep with me in the cold.
They look up in the sky like me.
Like a boat with no eyes for the oars.

It doesn't matter what they say.
If you see one glove on the side of the road
You might as well pick it up.

Nothing is going right these days
Except that lowdown
You know who I mean.
And he's moving right fast.

The Long Dark Night
from **Naegling**

With the same hands
That took the doe in the evening
The farmer comes in
And takes his wife
When the moon is red and almost gone
Before the night is even
Dark the bed begins to moan
Like something
Struggling under water
She smells the scent of smoke
On his hands
His knife laid by
The bread and wine on the table
His bloodstained pants hung over the chair
Beside the fire
The woman sleeps completely
In the bed
The farmer goes out into the dark
And dreams of her black hair
The roses of the stolen dances dead
As summer in the book

Bait
from **Naegling**

The woman swims alone through the dark water
Until she sees a man asleep

She circles him
Slowly he wakes up in a ring of fire

And leaves
He moves through the trees

After her
Silence takes his place

They swim so long they don't know
They are swimming

Moving together
In pursuit of one

Another in the dark
Circle of burning water

They are becoming
Weak

It has been so long without a sound
So long since they began

Their journey it seems
Now they are losing

Each other
For another scent

The water takes the song
The water takes the bird

And loses them both
They are so far apart now

They have given one another up
For lost

They have forsaken the motion of themselves
For the motions of some

Other things make them afraid
Of the sound of their own bodies

They don't want
To feel the music they swim in

To touch the chords they made
In the sleep in the beginning

They dream all that will be
Left of them is a head

Without eyes they dream
Of torn lips

They are dead already
But they don't know it

Each of them kiss
A separate hook

Now the boat of the fisherman is coming
The wind on his hands

The night
His fingers are bleeding

A man swims alone through   the dark
A woman is sleeping

And the movers
Working themselves free

From the water like two fish
Snagged to the same line

you must forgive poor Francis down there by the water
writing his poem because he is so melancholy and afraid
one of his girl friends is pregnant for he knows not what
he does neither did his namesake I let them read the minds
of the earth so that they might know me I used them
I have come here again into this poem as the Lord I have
used these two boys but if you could only know the joy
they have given me no matter their sins I love a sinner
who knows who has sinned that is why I wish every one
could see what little Francis the rich boy has been getting to
what he's been stalking like a wolf I wish it was a moving
picture him on the river and all as he says we could get something
across I am glad I am doing the talking not Francis not my father not
the holy ghost all of their styles must flow into mine they will
bring you pleasure and like lovers you will dissolve in me
this is the voice of the Lord as surely as Matthew is
I am speaking help me Mr. Rufus help through this child who is writing
his little saga on account of his miserable loneliness his love of
his own death like a brother and the bleeding Francis is whispering
poems in his ear while he sleeps he goes on writing his
name in the water his prayers to women and the living
not knowing it will never be read although knowing he can
go in peace because he will always be unknown at least that

Tancredi's Light

The man walked down the deep, light, dusty road to his quarters,

carrying his hoe and the hoe of his wife who had dropped dead

in the soybeans many years ago. So he could go on living in

their place he had to tell the foreman he could do both of their

work, he could do the hoeing of two people. And he did. He

won't work in the part of the field the others are in, he stays

to himself, chopping, and talking out loud to his wife as if

she were still busting rows beside him. I see no harm in all

of this; he's old like me. Or are both old at all? I seem to

have forgotten. It's good to sit here in the shade, drinking

my ice tea, commenting out loud on the burnt string of what

goes on here every night and every day. Who knows what I learned

from sleeping? That the ground under this shack is a ship, that

the good fortunes of others are heaping up like snow on the

slopes. No. Feeling sorry is like dancing on the grave of a

shithook. Dreams are worse than sweatbees, but the sun was

built by a carpenter, and he put sand in his lantern in the desert.

What can they take from me now: my twenty gallons of wild wine

bubbling in the chicken coop, the starter for my sourdough bread,

my porch swing where I can just picture everything? You say

what you see. He's home by now, washing his hands in a white pan.

He didnt bury her with her teeth. There is a velvet
box A wristwatch came in.

UNCOLLECTED PROSE

Observants

The one who passed by

This is what you see: a monk playing checkers with a young girl. They are on the veranda of an old farmhouse, far away in the valley. The girl couldn't be over fourteen. She has curly, honey-colored hair, a little bit lighter than the monk's complexion. No one is speaking, but earlier in the day things were different. The monk borrowed a paisley shirt and a pair of blue jeans from the young man, and they walked the yellow fields together. While the girl washed his soiled habit and hung it up to dry on a rope strung from the persimmon tree. His capuche is so white. You wonder why he doesn't smell it, it is so clean. The others are out there, waiting, watching, and when they raise their heads from their cover to look at them, the clouds go by simply clouds, inaudible, cantata-like. And the crows congregate on Crow Mountain.

At the other end of the porch, sulking and brooding over leaving his family and dubious profession, is the young man. A boy, perhaps, but wise enough to die in this state for what he's done. He is leaning backwards in a ladder-back chair, holding it and himself in place with his bare feet, his heels cupped over the rail. He is reading a book with one eye shut. A strand of spider's web, slack as a ship's rigging in dead calm, has fastened itself in his dark hair. A white horse is looking in through the struts of the railing. The monk's horse. If the stallion's eye were a mirror, the young man wouldn't consider brushing the web away, it wouldn't pass through his mind. There is some sugar in his pocket. So far, it has been an Indian summer, but the rains will begin, they always do.

The way they are, the girl and the monk and the young man, composed, like a small pond, you know they think there is no one within forty miles of them. For some time now the monk and the young girl have been wondering when the others will come after them. Whether you want to know the rest of the story is up to you.

The one who found them out

Not anymore it isn't. I hit that slow-talking farrier in the head, and went down there to take a look myself. He's kind of touched anyway, and one more knot on his brain won't hurt. Yeah, I saw all I need to see. There's hard cash lying on that Gypsy kid's soft neck, and I'm going to get it. By God, I'll tell you what happened.

First off, I wrote my wife a letter, telling her everything. I told her be sure and give it to the girl's father right away. He'll pay plenty to know where I am. The girl ran away from home—with the gypsy boy, and her father's men have been scouring the countryside for her, looking high and low. They'll be coming after her now, and I'll be going after mine.

She ran off with him. He was a trick rider in a two-bit side-show. I don't know how old he is, but he's got a wife and children, living from hand to mouth. His wife, she's the high-wire artist. She's got sort of a limp, but what I wouldn't like to do with her. She's older than him, about my age, and dark as shade. I saw her in the bar one night, when they came through town; she had the little ones with her. This was before the kid and the girl left. He was there too, but he wasn't sitting with them. He was standing at the bar, alone, looking off into nowhere, like he was in church or something. The kids were with her in a booth, crying, asking folks for change. He was darker than her, and his skin was oily. He was always wiping his face on his blue sleeve, wiping his hand on his blue pant leg. He'd been to a nig-ger dentist, too. They had a dime-a-ride pony in the bar, and every once in a while he'd flip his children some loose change. He never spoke English to his wife, he just motioned to her with his hand, and drank. When he said "this" it sounded like "thees." He stroked his nose with his thumb, and hissed. He drank heavy for his age. Oh, he had a fair price on his head. The girl's old man would give it, he'd give anything to get her back.

The one who passed by

When they came to town, I liked to go to the show early, before it started, and listen to them prepare, yelling at one another in their native tongue. Whenever the performance was over, parts of the audience would cry out, "Gyp!" They thought his act was two-bit. She was almost buck naked up there on the wire. The men leaned their heads back and the change fell out of their pockets; her children waited under the grandstands. I guess the girl must have come one evening when he gave her one of his better rides.

They met at the river, swore their allegiance, and went away in a boat together. The fisherman told me this. He lent them his skiff. He said he saw it in their eyes, and he wasn't making bait money anyway. They followed the current for several days; he in the stern with the scull, she in the bow, trailing her hand in the water.

On a Friday they came to Red Wine, an abandoned village by the river. That night, huddled together around their small campfire, they saw a white figure approaching on horseback, carrying a bow and quiver of arrows. They looked one another in the eye; he told her to be silent. The next morning, while they lay there asleep, next to their smoldering fire, the fog over the water, the monk brought them gooseberries and stewed doves. The girl ate like a pig, the boy was suspicious.

I don't recall how much time has passed since their first encounter, but I have not seen a week go by that they didn't share each other's company. That morning the monk told them about the farmhouse in the valley far away, as if knowing he, and only he, would be their frequent guest.

Let me tell you about the monk. They say he was driven from the monastery when he was a young brother, and this couldn't have been so many years ago, unless he is one who doesn't show his age. It seems that on the eve of his consecration as a priest, the nuns brought a young orphan girl to the abbot. She tended the bees for the Church, and was known far and wide to be very devout, having a special devotion to Saint Lucy. She was much darker than the young brother, but of mixed blood like him. The abbot asked the nuns to step outside his chapel. He asked the young girl to step inside. She made her confession; and the abbot absolved her, giving her enough stipend to provide for the child.

That evening, at the Chapter of Faults, the young brother fell down on his face and made his transgression known to all the community. The brothers in the monastery, young and old, were all very kind to him. The next morning, during the Angelus, he rode off on a white horse, with absolutely no possessions, under the dark sky. The other young novices and fraters managed to leave the inner court and give him the kiss of peace for his journey. Although there was a rule that they shouldn't, the old novice master did not keep them from it. In fact, he gave him the blessing as he left. In one year's time, the brother could return during Lent, spend one night, and he would receive a bow and arrows to hunt with. A year later, he could spend two nights and a loom would be given him. The next year, he would be consecrated a priest, but he would remain a hermit the rest of his life. And every year after that, he would return with the liturgical garments he had woven for the monks. On one of those visits, the abbot, who was a fair man, presented him with an english horn, the instrument he had missed and longed to play during his years alone. All of the monastery rejoiced and looked forward to seeing the beautiful designs he had woven on the chasubles.

He is a good shot with his bow, I have seen him in the woods. And he can play the horn fairly well. No one but me has ever entered his cave. How he found it is beyond me. No one else knows. It is one of those Civil War caves where the soldiers held up. There is a legend, which I cannot verify.

As the two lost and unknown companies approached one another in the wilderness, a battle was inevitable. And it was so obscure, so insignificant, that it went unrecorded. The old ones say what they saw happen is true, and not a story.

A wounded and dying Confederate captain, knowing morale and food and ammunition were low, sent out three of his men to reconnoiter for these and a place to hide. The officer in charge was a brilliant young man he'd known since he was a boy. If anybody could accomplish the mission, he could.

In a meadow, the three of them saw a farmgirl walking with a pail, holding her skirts high. They rose up out of the high grasses. The young officer took off his hat, asking for her father's lead and the use of their barn; but the other two asked for her. She pleaded with them not to harm her, telling them she could take them to a place where there were plenty of bullets, things to eat, and a place to hide, a place full of cool shade with clear water to drink. One of the foot soldiers was not persuaded, he moved towards the girl, putting his hand on her hair. His own officer, offended by such dishonorable behavior, shot the soldier in the heart with his last bullet. He apologized for the action he had to take in front of her, once more requesting help on the word of his captain.

Seeing he was indeed a fair gentleman, the girl took them to the cave in Zero Mountain as she'd promised. The opening to the cave was large enough for men to ride through on horseback, one at a time. A gust of cold air hit them as they forked off to the left inside the cavern, which opened up wide as a clearing in the forest. The officer was astonished. He made it plain that a small band of brave men could hold off and detain a whole army from such a fortress. It was a perfect place to stand and do battle, the enemy having no access but to charge up the steep mountain to the mouth of the cave.

Already the gallant and immortal battles of the past, waged by the few against the many, were passing through his thoughts. Already, he could see himself reading about this battle to a class of cadets he would teach in his old age, an encounter he devised and was victorious in. He would, after all, go down in history as he'd dreamed. The repose, the ambush, the skirmish, the retreat, the battle, and the victory and the surrender of the defeated.

The lieutenant lowered his head and walked through the cave, the plume in his hat trailing through the webs. The farther back they went the colder it got; and for some strange reason, the lighter it became. Where is the lead and the food, the other soldier questioned the girl, as the two of them, still on horseback, followed her lantern.

The cavern lit up with the sparkle of quartz and ice and some other phosphorescence, as if filled with moonlight. The soldiers were shivering, their breath turning to crystals on their beards. She told them she wasn't misleading; there was meat, berries, produce, fruit, hides, and whatever they wanted preserved in the cave. The other soldier, a country boy, said he saw why they called it Zero Mountain. The officer said they were in need of ammunition, that all the food in the world couldn't kill a yankee. She smiled, poured the berries from her bucket into a tub, then put on a bearskin coat that was hanging on the antlers of one of the deer strung from the cross-rafters above them. It took away the corporal's breath when he looked up and saw carcass after carcass of good, wild meat; he thought he was dreaming. The coiling was a good fifty feet high, and there were layers and levels of the preserved game. There was enough meat to last them, the whole company, the entire duration. She led them farther back, past the provisions of food. She held her lantern close to the walls and the two men had their eyes wide on what she showed them. They gasped when they recognized the veins of silver. It was brighter than a mirror. They had to brush the ice from their whiskers and brows, their breathing was quick. The girl, who was my grandmother, told me the officer told her then that he had never had the pleasure of shooting a man with a silver bullet, but the yankees ought to salute him before they fell for doing so. They laughed, she said. The other soldier, who was neither a farmer nor a gentlemen, fell to the ground, imitating a mortally wounded enemy, and laughed himself sick and hoarse. The idea of killing people with silver bullets. He could see the yellowbellies, he told her, just digging hot metal out of trees in the midst of heavy fire, digging bullets out with their bayonets and knives and fingernails, going after shot which had just missed taking their lives. What a sight to see he told her. If they don't die, the more we shoot the richer they'll be, he told his lieutenant.

Wait. Here come some of her daddy's men. That darn Carl Squint, the one who hit me on the head, must have told them where they were. I thought I had them steered the other way, that darn Carl Squint. A few days ago, some of Riggs' men—that's her name— worked me over good, but I didn't tell them anything. I'll give them plenty to chase this time. I'll pretend I want in and send them to the other side of the county. I'll put their nose to a red fish that will stink to high heaven.

What my grandmother said about the cave was all true. There's a book somewhere in the capital that tells of a strange battle on Spadra Creek—that's right off the river. Union physicians claimed to have taken silver shot out of infantrymen. And there's an old map a surveyor made, showing a branch by the name of Spadra. I stepped it off once, and only found a dry branch, but it was there.

When the young lieutenant charged back into camp with his one outrider, the sentry hadn't time to tell him of his commanding officer's death. They buried the captain near a large witness tree, and a private from Tennessee sang Greensleeves as the captain had requested. His two slaves, personal valets, the only other men in the camp besides the captain and the lieutenant who still dressed in good grays and gold, were given their freedom in writing. One was presented a sword and the other a watch in the will. The two men went into the bushes, took off their uniforms, and lit out in a northeasterly direction. A sentry found the trousers and the jackets neatly folded. They traded the watch for a mule and a jug of whiskey, and they broke the sword for a mule and a jug of whiskey, and they broke the sword in two with a wooden handle, so making two knives. It is said that these two former slaves became famous in history. For what, I don't know.

Although my grandmother never admitted it, she must have seen the officer many times. He was handsome, she said; she must have been in love. She could remember everything about him.

After the burial of the captain, the lieutenant, now the commanding officer, addressed his men: "Gentlemen, it is our unique privilege to engage the enemy in a battle which will, I assure you, be recorded in history, and I will personally see to it that each and every one of you are remembered by name and deed. Not since the Peloponnesian War has a small band of men such as ours been afforded these circumstances, the strategic position to fight against overwhelming odds. Tonight, and every night from now on, each and every one of you will receive three squares a day—with a double portion of meat for supper." There was a loud hurrah. "Furthermore, we found a source of ammunition. Mind you, not the usual source, lead, but silver. Yes, a silver mine, a cold cave atop a mountain, a place with food, a fort where we can make a mighty stand." The men looked at one another as if their commander had gone mad, but the corporal shook his head and spit, affirming everything he'd said.

"Sergeant, give the orders to march." The lieutenant had a sure-fire battleplan. Most of the men would reach the cave, have a good meal and rest, then dig and mold bullets in the smelter. At the same time, a small patrol, commanded by the lieutenant, would encounter fire and evade it. They would skirmish and retreat, hitting here and there on the enemy's flanks, drawing the Union company towards them. The lieutenant would give the impressions of a large camp in the making, and the Union troops, seeing the chance for an ambush, would send out for reinforcements. The plan was to slowly pull back towards the mountain, where the two, mismatched forces would fight. All of this took a few days, and it worked. My grandmother led the other soldiers to the cave, and they set up their camp there. She returned to her farm; and I believe it was in between the lieutenant's daring raids, at night, that they saw one another, and she drew close to him.

A few silver bullets were fired at the enemy, shots fired by the small patrol in light skirmishes. The rest of the company found everything they needed in the cave, including my great-grandfather's kegs of black powder. They also found his kegs of brew. Mostly, the Confederate troops fired the silver bullets into one another, squabbling in the cave. The same men who had given the lieutenant the heartwarming hurrah, who had boasted of shooting yankees in between the eyes, in between bites of roast venison, had fired in greed on their own men. Of course, all this took place in the lieutenant's absence, as he was drawing the enemy towards Zero Mountain.

When he and the others rode into the cave, they found not soldiers ready to fight but quarreling philistines, who had broken off into factions, brothers and friends against the same.

"I know I should have shot you," the lieutenant told the corporal who had seen the cave with him. "I should have shot you like that scum friend of yours when he looked at . . ."

"There they are, Sir, the yankees, at the foot of the mountain," one of his loyal men cried out.

The corporal was sitting down behind a table stacked with newly mined silver, and under the protection of several men, armed and drunk. "Look at you, fighting among yourselves!"

"Look, Lieutenant, there might be a little squabbling over who has how much, but one thing's for sure, we all come to one conclusion, and that's we'd rather have a little less each, all of us, than taking a chance on getting killed and some of us coming out on top. Ain't that right, boys? Tell 'em, Lieutenant, ain't there more than a company at the foot of the hill, ain't they got some good artillery down there?"

The young officer paid no attention to the corporal's questions, instead he answered him with one of his own, "Sergeant, where is the ammunition I ordered?"

"In them boys' bellies on the floor, Suh."

The lieutenant saw the young private from Tennessee who had played and sung Greensleeves at the captain's funeral. The corporal said, "One of the boys thought that harmonica was a chunk of silver he was biting off," laughing.

The last soldier in the patrol rode into the mouth of the cave, "Sir, the yanks are on my tail, coming up the mountain, let's give them hell!" but one of his own men shot him in the back and he dropped off his horse onto the floor of the cave. It was cool enough in the cavern to see steam rising off a wound, my grandmother said; she'd seen it seep out of the dead animals before. The sergeant said, "Now don't none of you worry about the yanks, we can settle all this; one will get you three that if I send the lieutenant down there with a white flag and tell them about this silver, there won't be no fight. We'll all get drunk and start prospecting. Once this war's over, we'll have enough money to move in."

The corporal broke in, "With all due respects, one of you gentlemen please escort our commanding officer to the rear with the powder and berries," he mocked him, bowing at the lieutenant. "I'll just see if me and the sarge can't work out a deal with these yanks."

The loyal followers of the lieutenant charged out of the cave and down the mountainside on horseback. My grandmother heard their yells. They were met by volley after volley, and they rolled down the slope like loose stones, horses and all. They were even taking shots from the rear, from the others in the cave. But one of them managed to ride to the foot of the hill. He looked like a british redcoat by the time he made it to the lines; one bullet would half knock him off his horse, and another would put him on again. The Union troops, a good bunch of lads from Ohio, took off their hats and cheered him on, letting him pass through their lines. They knew a brave man when they saw one, they knew a man who could ride, even if he was dead. They knew he was done for, and they waved him through, and he charged on, out into a field, a meadow where my grandmother was. She saw him. She was picking berries in the meadow, and she saw the wounded rider approaching. At first, she thought it was her lieutenant leaning over that beautiful, black horse. The beast was wounded, too. It had just enough life left in it to take its rider over the fence, but the creature was dead before its hooves hit the sod on the other side. My grandmother ran towards them, tearing herself on the berry briars. The young soldier, no more than a boy, had just enough time to tell her what had happened, just before he died in her arms. He did manage one question, which my grandmother never forgot. He asked her, "What state is this, Ma'am?" She told him. He smiled at her. "I never did want to die in the state I's born in," were his last words. She heard a tremendous explosion, the ground quaked under her. And then she knew. Her lieutenant, refusing to bring down such disgrace on his honor and command, set off the barrels of black powder near the rear of the cave. It sounded like the whole mountain came down on top of the soldiers, like they had sunk into the earth, but nothing could change the cave in Zero.

The explosion had sealed off the entrance to the cave, imprisoning the men in its cold belly. The yankees, thinking they had run into heavy artillery, retreated. When they charged, the next morning, they found no trace of the enemy.

My grandmother never went back there. Like I said, the monk lives there now. He found the place, and he opened the entrance back up. I don't guess a soul, not nobody, has gone up there. What's that?

Only a bucksnort; it sounded like his bowstring. Now I wonder, I wonder what that Carl Squint is up to?

The one who found them out

The last time we hung a Gyp, I tried to pull his boots off to see if he was hiding any coins and jewelry. He wasn't kicking, he was dead. I got his boots off and a turd dropped out of his pants leg and hit me on the head. Those damn Gyps. We got enough rope to hang a caravan with. Besides, we got Riggs behind us, and that means we got the law and the town. I asked one of Riggs' men, "How much you think I'll get out of it if we find her where I told you?"

"Plenty, Squint," he told me.

"What do you say we all get in her pants, kill her, then say the Gyp done it, what you think boys?" I asked them. They were sitting around the fire, drinking coffee. I could tell in their eyes they didn't like me, they didn't like it I was going to get a cut of the blood money. I could tell. That Riggs is filthy rich. His help was loyal, they didn't like me intruding. I could tell. Some of them thought her daddy would give them more if they brought her back alive. She was a looker. That damn horse doctor might of put us on the wrong trail, I told them. I said you better watch him. Nobody lies to Carl Squint. I've killed two men with my bare fists. I'm big. I. One of Riggs' men kicked me, so I went over and poured him some more coffee. I asked the foreman, "Let me cut his oysters out. I want to cut 'em out and feed them to the pigs. Let me do it. You just wait. Y'all laugh at Carl Squint, but I'll tell you. I'll find out where they are, for sure this time. It'll be my day." One of them told me to shut up and go to sleep.

The one who passed by

I miss the dry bed of earth on the knob near the old farmhouse. I miss watching the three of them, lying in the grass, hidden, watching and listening. I would like to be with them. They seem so perfect. But I can't. Their fate is only temporary. Just about the time I become close, they won't even be there anymore. I'm going to stay away from them, watch them, do what I can for them, but I won't believe they'll ever be anything more than strangers, three people I'll never meet.

I miss that little strip of earth. It has rained for a week. The monk only goes out of his cave to gather his food. He is busy at his loom, then he plays the english horn. He prays, I think.

When the fields are dry, still with green, the grass flickers at the slightest wind; it rolls like the aurora borealis. I saw them once, long ago, aboard ship. I saw those northern lights, green. I thought how like the fields they were, the fields of wild grasses and some flowers, and milo and lespedeza. On the ship, I thought the night sky was a dark wind.

When the rain quits, the monk will come out of his cave, hunt with his bow, and ride to see them. The girl doesn't know it, but he is weaving them a blanket for their bed. She cooks for him, huckleberry cobbler and fried fish and cornbread, and brings him glass after glass of fresh buttermilk. He loves to eat and laugh with the girl, and he drinks wine with the boy. They talk about different things. They play checkers and music. The Gypsy likes to be alone most of the time. He can only take so much company. I wouldn't think he's tried to put himself in the monk's boots. I imagine he worries about the girl, about his wife and children. But you can tell they love one another, you can tell by watching them. I only wish I knew what was in that book the boy holds in his lap. Maybe he's trying to learn English. He has a bad accent.

The monk is a deadly shot with his bow. He reminds me of one of those outlaws who lived off the forest in the olden times. I read about them when I was young. Last night, sleeping in someone's barn, as the rain beat down on the tin roof, I had a dream.

A long wound opened up in the moon. I followed the drop of blood, running, like a shooting star. I thought of a buckthorn floating out of a horse's white eye in a tear. The shadows of the monk as he worked at his loom in the early hours before light were coming from the mouth of the cave. His lantern flickered. It began to snow. The rain turning to ice. He quit his work for a while, did nothing, observing through stillness and silence what he could not see. The shoeless horse walked out of the cave, down the mountain towards the farmhouse. I followed the monk's horse. The house was abandoned. The checkerboard was frozen. I heard laughing, the only sign of life. It came from out back near the stable. Two white-headed Negro gentlemen were shooting dice. The horse galloped away, and the two men looked at one another, tilting their heads. Unawares of me, as if recognizing the sound of a horse departing as that of a rider approaching.

I went after the horse with a rope. It led me to the abbey wall. I saw the lieutenant and some of his men strolling through the inner court, walking in black uniforms. In the early fall, before the fireflies go to their graves, the monk, after he drank several glasses of the dandelion wine the girl made, rode across the countryside surrounding the old, hidden farmhouse, he galloped through the ginseng, dock, pennyroyal, gill-over-the-ground, and wormwood, shouting out whatever came to his head. Then he would ride back, out of breath and thirsty, and tie his horse to the railing of the porch. He liked to laugh, and talk slowly in his deep voice, as if he was wading through his words.

The monk's head would glow in the dark. The fireflies would catch in his short, kinky hair. When they went walking, the foreigner liked to walk up ahead of them, speaking to himself in his own tongue. The girl and the monk followed him.

That one evening she persuaded him to stay the night. The young man and the monk were both filthy from working around the place. She sat them down on the porch and washed the bugs out of their hair. The monk's was close-cropped. The Gyp's was long and curly. They sat there, drinking wine, with white suds on their heads, and she laughed at them. Then they went and bathed, and the girl sat on the steps and killed mosquitoes, thinking about what her father would do.

All of them were pretty well lit. The girl and the boy helped the monk into the room next to theirs, put him in a linwood bed, and she covered him with an eiderdown. The wine had gone to his head, so that he felt like he was moving even though he was lying still; I know. He heard them, undressing, laughing, getting into bed. He listened to the Gypsy and the girl make love. The mirror quivered on his wall, like a gust of wind had come in through the window.

Their bedroom is shadow gray. The trim is deep red. That was all the paint they had, what he stole from the circus. I thought of leaving a gallon or two of white near the porch, but I could see that soon he wouldn't be thinking much of spending the time painting a place neither of them would be in long.

He sounds like a stallion. Both of them sound like horses. Later, he listens to the wind, fingers a golden chain around his neck, a medal. He wraps himself up in a white sheet and paces the hardwood floors. I can hear the floors creak from outside. She pulls the spread close to her chin, over her neck, and sleeps well. One night, he takes the monk's horse out in the meadow. There is a full moon. I was up in a tree with a possum and its young. He did some of that trick riding.

If you want to know something hard to believe, listen to this. All three of them were fishing on the creek. She'd spread out quite a lunch. I even thought of slipping over and taking a few deviled eggs while no one was looking. The monk and the young man caught lots of small ones. They put them in a bucket. She'd reach into it and play with them until they finned her. "What lovely fish," she said, watching the bluegills gasp and turn belly-up to the top. She held them in her palm. She made too much noise for the boy, who claimed he needed silence to fish. He walked down the bank until he disappeared.

"He misses his children," the monk told her.

"I don't miss my family," she said, coming back at him.

"It's different, when you have children."

"I don't see why. I'm still a child, according to my folks."

"You are a woman," he said.

"I know."

"Why haven't you told him?" he asked her.

"It will just make things worse."

The cable to the old ferry stretched out across the creek. The Gypsy looked at it; he was talking that foreign language to himself. Over in the weeds, with its tires partly in the water, was a white convertible car. He looked around to see who might have left it. The water was rising, about an inch a day. There was no one there, the car looked abandoned. The top was down and cobwebs were spun all over the upholstery. It was in good condition, though. He opened the door and looked under the seat for a key. He found it, sure enough, just as if he knew who it belonged to. Anybody could have shown him how to hotwire it. It was slow to turn over, but after a few licks it hit right off. He backed it out of the bottom of the creek-bed, and steered back over the trail along the water's edge. He was laughing to beat hell.

They heard a car coming. The monk took hold of the girl and threw her in the water. He cut off a piece of cane and gave it to her.

"Quiet, and breathe through this," he told her. The monk took up a position behind a tree, strung his bow, and waited.

The boy goosed the gas pedal and the car lurched forward towards them in low gear. He turned the radio on, and the monk stepped out from behind the tree and smiled. He waded out in the creek and fetched the girl. They all got in the car and drove back towards the farmhouse. The monk played the horn, and the boy had a strange look on his face; he wanted to meet someone on the road to show off the car, but if they saw a soul, that was all she wrote.

"If only I had a piano here. I have one at home," Madelene sighed as she walked into the front door of the farmhouse, getting ready to prepare the meal.

The monk whispered something in the Gypsy's ear. "After supper, later tonight," he told him, and they began their walk.

She cleared away the checkerboard from the porch and brought out the food. She knew the monk liked ears of roasting corn. It being a wet fall, the flies were bad, and she stood guard over the meal with her small, quick hands. When Brother Tobias and Domingo returned, one gave the blessing, and the other helped Madelene to her seat. But she was not hungry, only the men were. She asked Domingo to fill her glass with wine more than once. She was afraid there might not be enough food. "If we had gutted those fish instead of taking a joyride in the white car..." The boy gave a quick flick with his head, meaning everything was all right, now be silent. As they ate, she gave them butter and watched the fields. Once, I thought she spotted me. She leaned against the railing of the porch, watching the flies settle on the warm hood of the white car, the sun go down, and the men speaking with greasy lips.

She looked out at the cane poles they'd cut, the ends coming out the back window. "You know what we looked like coming down the back road, we looked like... I'm sorry, Brother Tobias."

The monk and the boy did paper, knife, stone to see who got the last piece of cornbread. They split it.

She seemed dizzy, half sick; as if she were leaning over the side of a ship, the first voyage, and not a porch. Domingo wanted her to go to bed, explaining that they planned to be gone that evening. They were going frog gigging. She pleaded to go along, letting them know who was frightened of staying there alone at night. The monk told her not to worry, that she'd had enough excitement for one day. She gave in. Domingo grabbed two forks from the table and walked towards the car.

"Where are you going with my silverware, I brought those from home. For us there were only a few things I could bring."

"I file these down. Tie them on poles. Make gigs. Brother Toby and me, we get big frogs," Domingo said.

The car started fine. As they drove off, she brought the checkerboard back out to the porch. It was too dark, even to see her own moves; the moon wasn't up. The white horse walked near the porch. She led him out into the meadow. All the day had ended and the fog came in, riding shotgun for the night.

She needn't be afraid. There was no need for her to look over her shoulder, unless she was looking for the moon; there was no need, although I could not tell her so. My pistols were loaded, and so were my rifles. I was ready as ever. I had a sawed-off double-barrel stuck in my belt. If any of them rode that night, I could have picked them off like flies. And there was no need to worry anymore about Squint, the good Lord had taken care of him. You won't be hearing from him.

He and some of the others, her father's men, had decided to pass the time of one evening in a tavern, a place far away from those parts where Riggs has the run of the roost. It was too cold and wet a night for a search party. I wasn't there, but this is what I hear:

A redhaired woman named Faye directed them to a hot game, you needed an introduction to get in. But first they watched, had a few, talked it up; at least Squint did. Then they took their bottles over to the corner, near a wicker cage full of songbirds. Four men were sitting around an oak table; it had lion claw legs. There was a sign, hand-painted, which read Knights Of The Nights Of The Round Table. Riggs' boys and Squint couldn't see the face of the man whose back was towards them.

Squint said, nudging one of those with him, the foreman, "If you'd advance me some, I reckon you and I could clean these river rats out."

The men playing were a queer crew, I'm told. There was the big one, who bragged and talked lickety-split. There was the pudgy one, who wore tight-fitting black T-shirts, and picked the bumps on his face and back. There was a fool who was known for his petty thievery; he liked to shut his eyes and hum country music, tunes older than the hills. They were all odd, but deadly cardplayers. They stuck together like pages in a cheap book. The fourth man, whose face the others couldn't see, was Faye's boyfriend, a blind french harp player. And I'd heard of him before, way before any run-in with Squint. His name was Sweet Frankie DuVall. But let me tell you, he was about as sweet as a lemon. Let me tell you, one time the Governor came up here to campaign for reelection. Sweet Frankie didn't like him at all. He and Horse Fly, that's the one with the bumps, were sitting outside on the bench in front of the saloon. Both of them knew the Governor started shaking hands, and he finally got around to DuVall and Horse Fly. DuVall said to Horse Fly, "Give the Governor some of your tobacco." Horse Fly took a pouch out of his trousers and gave the Governor a whiff. "Mighty fine," the Governor said. That proved to DuVall he was a liar. DuVall had Horse Fly fill the Governor's pipe up with it. The Governor lit it up and said as he left, "I'm counting on y'all." Horse Fly slapped his knee, and DuVall looked around, laughing. What was in that pouch was what he sent Horse Fly after in the Stinky Pete out by the hogpen. Dead flies. Riggs and the Governor are thick. I guess DuVall didn't like it what the Governor did when he vetoed that pension bill for the blind.

Faye—she ran the place—gave him the name Sweet. That's because the cardplayers would say when he dealt, "Be sweet to me, Frankie." He was mean alright, mean as hell for a blind man. "Goddamn, we can take a blind man, no matter who his partner is," Squint said to the foreman, watching DuVall and the tall man beat Horse Fly and the fool. "I say he's cheating. Can't a blind man play a fair hand and win against a man with eyes. Something's wrong, here," Carl Squint whispered to his partner.

"Squint, you ever think he might have the touch?" the foreman answered.

Squint addressed the four men something like this, "Y'all mind if me and one of Mr. Riggs' men sit down here?" DuVall cocked his head. The tall man took a short, emphysemic breath. DuVall cleaned the grease off his ugly nose with his thumb and rubbed it on the scuffed toe of his shoe. This was the signal for "take them on." The tall one did all the talking. "Sit down, strangers, name your game."

"Mexican sweat," Carl Squint said.

Faye and Sweet Frankie smiled. He only smiled twice that evening. The night wore on, with DuVall and his sidekick calling most of the shots. The foreman and Squint were losing everything but their rear ends. Finally, Squint couldn't take it anymore. He got bitter over DuVall beating him again and again at the old Civil War game of Boo Ray. Squint made a wisecrack about Miss Faye's songbirds.

He tried to take everyone's mind off the game, but it didn't work. "Can you take him, now?" the tall one asked DuVall. The man smiled, the second time, nodded, took off his shoe and sock, and asked Faye to bring him some mineral oil. Squint and the foreman won the hand.

DuVall asked Faye to bring him some rum to put in his oil. Everybody was wide-eyed when he reached under the table with his bare foot and took a dishonest ace from Squint's trouser cuff with his toes, then laid it on the table. "How about that," some of Riggs' men grumbled.

"Hold on, now," Squint tried to explain. "That card slipped. It slipped down my leg, didn't it, boys. Ask any of Riggs' boys do I cheat. No sir, I knocked that ace off the table. Just hold your horses. I'll see to it that everybody gets..."

"Buster, I ought to dunk your head in Miss Faye's birdcage and let those birds peck your eyes out!" the tall one said.

"Look!" Squint tried to say.

"Let him go," DuVall said.

"So you'd cheat on a blind man, wouldn't you, Squint," his partner the foreman said without asking. He was so humiliated and angry that he couldn't finish what he was saying. "Squint, you just won't ever learn," he told him, taking hold of a shock of Squint's hair with one hand and opening up his throat from ear to ear with a knife he held in his other. Everyone gasped, including Squint.

He was still alive, sitting there, holding five cards, looking the foreman in the eye, then looking at the blind man listening to what they were saying. The foreman apologized to DuVall and his partner. "He was only on one job with us. Just hired 'cause he had a loose mouth. I don't like blood. I'm sorry, Ma'am. Mr. Riggs don't like blood. We going to leave, and I'm saying I'm sorry, and we asking for no trouble. He came in here with us, and he'll go away with us. I'm obliged for the cardgame and for the good liquor, and I hope y'all won't hold this critter here against me or the boys. Miss Faye, if you'll be kind enough to throw me a few dirty rags, I'll clean up after Squint." The tall one told Horse Fly and the fool to help the foreman sop up the blood. The other boys got down on their knees and wiped and the tall one wiped the table and Horse Fly cleaned some yellow mess off the playing cards and the fool whistled. They all kept their eyes on Squint as they worked, quietly and intently, and Squint watched them, unable to believe that in a few moments he would have to bleed to death. It only lasted a few seconds, but it seemed a forever, Faye said. Maybe he didn't slice into Squint's windpipe. They backed away from the table with their heavy towels and left him there with DuVall. The fool tied a white silk handkerchief around Squint's neck, like a napkin, then he began to whistle again. The foreman got his boys together and they paid up. What goes through a coward's mind like Carl Squint's, as he's dying, with only a blind man to look at, I cannot tell you. I can tell you that Sweet Frankie felt sorry for him and held out his hand and took Squint's and held it; the blind man took a bird out of the cage with his other hand, and let it sing on his finger while Squint slumped over and died. He was looking at the bird when he gave up the ghost. The others drug him outside, tied him down, and the search party rode on.

You might get the idea that a man like Carl Squint was all bad, a full-blooded lickspit, but that isn't the truth. No, it's told, good word has it that he'd been seeing a lot of Domingo's wife, and he was helping out with feeding the kids. How about it? Miss Faye said there was a note in his pocket, saying in effect: "If anything should happen to me while I'm after this Gypsy, I'd like to act in kind by giving one half of my share of the loot to his wife and children. They can say what they like about Carl Squint, he said a lot of low-down things, but by God in heaven he didn't live that low. Give my wife the other half. So long." And it was signed, "C. Squint." What a world.

Drawing blood is like drinking. It takes a good man who can quit with just one sip. If they'd pull a knife on their own, they'd sure out the Gypsy. They could turn mean overnight like leaves turn brown. It didn't take long. They wouldn't touch the girl, they wouldn't lay a hand on her. Riggs would kill them without thinking twice. It's a Gyp they'll take it out on. Now I'm not saying they won't think about her, won't dream about her. Maybe the one who holds her and ties her and rides with her and stays up all night watching her through the fire, he might want her, but he won't touch her. She's a Riggs. But when it comes to being mean, they are top dogs.

That popping noise, it sounded like a gun. It was only the monk's cassock, drying on the line, flapping in the wind.

The car that drove off didn't sound like the one driving up when the lights revolved around the bedroom; she reached under the pillow for the pistol, jumped out of bed, and ran barefoot over the unswept floor to the closet. She crouched down beneath a suit of clothes she brought but he'd never worn, she heard some goings on in the yard. The motor was turned off.

She heard the grunts and struggling, not knowing who was overpowering who. Then there was a familiar curse. She flung open the door and ran out of the bedroom onto the porch. The headlights were shining directly on her. Two figures and something huge were silhouetted; Domingo and the monk were moving a piano towards her. She flopped down in the rocker, laughing out loud, with a few tears, as they made their way up the steps. "Jesus," she said.

"This was the idea of the good Brother Tobias. I ask you, Madelene, is he crazy?" he said, hissing his *s*'s like *z*'s, and out of breath and under stress of the heavy load.

"We are moving a piano into your grotto, Madelene," Brother Tobias said.

"I love you," she said.

"I think one of the brothers woke up and saw us, but he probably thought he was dreaming. I knew him, and he won't eat turnips for a month; he'll ask Saint Monica to help him abstain. They don't need it anyway. When I was there, the last time I counted, they had twelve pianos and four organs; they can't use them all." He'd just finished speaking when he noticed her bosom, partly exposed from the low-cut gown. She was so happy she wasn't aware of herself. She gave them directions on how to get through the door. The monk looked back at her, amongst the heaving and shoving he and Domingo were doing, and he saw her arch back with her hands in her hands, he saw her standing in the light, and then out of the light, her body the fast shadow he thought his imagination had forgotten how to cast. She covered herself, drew her gown around her, stepping into the darkness altogether, knocking over the checkerboard and spilling the pieces. She did all this gracefully; but the piano wouldn't go through the doorway.

I climbed out of the tree while the three of them slept. The horse was used to my coming up to him by now. A cassock, some of the boy's bright shirts, and a few of her underthings were hanging out on the line, filling out in the breeze. They were still damp. I touched each piece of cloth as I moved towards the porch. The piano was missing a leg and the keyboard was covered with dust. I brushed the brass cords with my cuff. There was something growing inside the piano, something killing the sound. It was a fern. How had it gotten there, I thought. Was it natural, or had some old monk planted it. The monk and Domingo hadn't seen it. Whoever put it there, if anyone did, knew it needed a damp, dark home. The moon was like my spotlight. I felt around in the piano. I came up with the carcass of a vinegaroon.

Morning came, and I found myself still on the porch, my head against one of the two legs of the piano. There are times I think the monk knew I was watching the three of them; sometimes I had the feeling they were watching me. In ways I felt close to them, but they didn't know me from Adam. Even that very night, in a dream, I thought myself their protector, their keeper, hovering over them like a guardian angel. Maybe I should say: I was in a tent. Something was glowing outside in the ditch, like a hubcap. It was a rhinestone slipper, a woman's shoe. I tore the shoe apart, and strung them on the horse's white mane. My tent was near the water, because I heard a voice carrying, Madelene's voice, "Do—ming—go, Do—ming—go." The horse galloped along the bank. It was lame. There was fresh blood on its leg. My satchel was full of liniments. I held its leg, stroking it. Madelene came down the creek in a small boat. She was holding a candelabra out over the water, calling the names of Domingo and Brother Tobias. I wanted her to call my name.

I slipped back into the barn, hoping no one saw me. It was Sunday morning. The monk came out, changed into his clean habit, and waited on Domingo and Madelene so he could hear their confessions before Mass. Even though their friendship was good and lovely, he told them, they still had obligations. Hiding was not wrong, he explained. "If you do not hide, you will not live. It is right that you stay here, together, away from others. Otherwise...," he cut it short, holding out his hands and shaking his head. "There is no need of a sermon yet. But your days, they are numbered. You are living in bliss, and you are also living in sin. I say to you, live as you do, live as you want, but confess what you do."

Domingo motioned with his head for the monk to follow him around to the side of the barn. The wind blew dust in their eyes, the hay dust.

Then the girl and the monk walked out into the meadow.

I could have heard if I wanted. I could have heard what each of them told Brother Tobias, but I didn't.

That was a lie. I did too. I listened in. I heard from the barn, then I ran out by the back and down into the low place in the field so neither of them could see me.

The monk made ready the Mass. They knelt on the ground near the steps where he had placed the chalice. The cruets of wine were Mason jars, preserving jars the monk had cleaned all the jam from. The flies were bad for so early a morning. The wind picked up, and when he lifted the Host during the consecration, it blew free of his large, dark hands. Brother Tobias gasped. Domingo and Madelene looked puzzled. They got up off their knees and ran after the Host, as if it were a mad butterfly. The monk sailed after it, his long strides overtaking them.

It appeared as if it would lite on the edge of the well. It flew through the barn, sailed over the porch, and went out of vision for a while. The girl had a towsack and Domingo was waiting for it with a minnow net. They held their hands over their eyes looking for it. They were yelling at one another, asking where it was. I couldn't help myself. Amongst all the goings-on, I crawled towards the porchsteps where the chalice had been left. I ran back when I touched it and hid under the house. Then I came out and drank down a few gulps from it like a dog. I expected it to taste like blood. My grandmother had told me about them, the people who drink the blood. But it was homemade wine. Blackberry. Everyone had quenched his thirst on that.

I poured some of it out on the ground to see if it would smoke. I poured some of it in my hands and washed the sleep out of my eyes and the dirt off my ugly face. I set the cup back down on the step nearest the ground. The step was heelgnawed and smelled of what is cleaned from the bottom of people's boots.

They couldn't find it. Then, I didn't know what it was. They couldn't see it out in the field because it was near the porch, under the white horse in a pile of manure. Some pretty dragonflies soared around it. It was fresh manure. I picked it up and climbed to the roof of the barn with it, near the windcock, and tried to throw it away, towards them, but it blew into the backseat of the white car. Then it swirled out of there before I could get to it. A crow made a pass at it, but the Host was sucked in the draft of the silo and out again. The three of them started running my way, so I hid again. It flew over the wildflowers in the field and landed in the branches of a willow tree near the stock pond. The monk told them to be still, like it was a bird. They waited, motionless, as he ran towards the farmhouse to fetch the white horse. But that isn't all he picked up. He got his bow and his arrows. He jumped on the horse and took out across the meadow towards the pond. He strained to cock the bow, stringing it. "Steady," he told the horse. He lined up the arrow and drew the bow, then started talking in a foreign language like Domingo, except it was Latin. I don't know what he said. Madelene closed her eyes. He let go of the arrow. It shot through the very center of the Host, passing in and out—feathers and all, and landed somewhere in one of the trees in the woods on the other side. The tiny, wounded moon-like thing fell into the pond, and, in no time at all, it was swallowed by a fish.

*

The colder it got, the larger the girl's belly got. Domingo was very angry. The monk was his friend and he thought he should have told him. He gave him a dirty look, speaking his Gypsy tongue. "She tell you first. Why? Why she didn't tell me. I the father. So, you tell me: Why you didn't let me know. We like this!" he said, spitting, and crossing his wrists together.

"You know I was not at liberty to. Some things, I can't tell you, when I find them out a certain way. I took a vow."

He lifted up his hand, tilting back his curly head. "Everyone takes vow. I promise my father. He was on deathbed. I swear I become the best, like him, in dressage. What I do? I become trick rider, circus clown. And I promise my mother I would be good boy. Look. You see. You see wife, you see children? No. Rich man's daughter, I love. They coming to cut me here, they want to cut it deep. These vows! Ahh! They are like wine we keep below in the dark. You tell me, Brother, if anyone puts the bottle there without ever a thought of drinking it. Ahh!"

"Domingo," the monk said, "there are those who never touch wine."

"Oh yes, I know these people very well, the ones who don't taste the wine. They drink water, they drink whiskey, instead. Ahh!"

"I am sorry."

"No, you are good, you are good man, Brother. I always glad I meet you."

The boy walked off, mumbling to himself, and then he looked up. Out in the distance, there must have been some other music no one else heard. They say foreigners hear it all the time, the sounds of their home country. They say Gypsies listen for anything. There was something about him, alright. I'll never forget. Once, I saw him asleep on the porch. His feet were hanging over the railing, the chair was tilted back against the wall. He had that book in his lap. His lips were always dark and thick, like the monk's, but they were darker with the drinking he'd been doing in the middle of the day. The monk was gone. And the girl, who had been writing something on a slip of paper—perhaps a list of things to be gotten before the child came—was inside the farmhouse kneading the dough. The piece of paper was on the checkerboard. I guess he was dreaming he was something besides a clumsy rider, a man with a price on his head. A fly was walking in the corner of his lips. What made him do it, I didn't know, but he did. A gust of wind picked up the sliver of paper, rocking it several times before it fell, back and forth, fitting perfectly in place beneath the leg of the piano. To the naked eye, there wasn't enough space between the floor and the piano leg. But he knew. What made him open his eye, I'll never know. There was something about him. And it's beyond me. He waited for the paper to hit the ground. Then he closed his eye and went back to sleep.

Many days followed, and I never stopped watching them, protecting them. I loved the afternoons when Madelene played the piano and Tobias played the english horn. Domingo practiced stunts on the monk's horse, or he tinkered with the white car. I will tell you about that day now: Madelene told them she wanted a candy bar.

"I want a Zero," she said.

Brother Tobias blew the spit out of his horn, looked up at Domingo.

"What will it hurt?" Domingo asked.

"You mean we are going to town?"

"We are going to a town, young mother," the monk said.

It was the kind of bright, crisp day that made you sorry. The clouds were like a few geese. They were sending the new catalogues out.

"Where will we go?" the girl wanted to know.

"We'll go to Ozark and buy a cast-iron stove," Domingo said, "they won't remember me there."

"But isn't it a little late for us to be getting…"

"We get a potbelly stove to keep the chill out of the rooms, for you and that one," Domingo said, pointing to her.

"And a candy bar," she said, putting her arms around him, making him smile, which he never did.

"And some chewing gum," the monk added.

"And a fifth of sourmash whiskey," the boy laughed.

"And some fishhooks."

"And oil for the lamps."

"And a few yards of material, and some white blankets, and some medicine."

"We only got money for few things," Domingo said.

"Don't worry about the garments and the bedclothes, I have plenty of that in my cave. I can make anything," the monk said.

"This is going to be wonderful. I'm going to wash my hair. Let me finish painting the rocker."

"And one more song before we go," the monk asked.

"And some cotton swabs."

"And a headlight."

"And some spyglasses to keep the watch."

"And a tractor to farm this place."

"A peacock."

It was the happiest I'd ever seen them. I wanted to say, "And a spare tire, just in case one goes flat on the road." But the boy said, "And some bullets."

Nobody said anything for a while. Their smiles disappeared. She put the last coat of blue on the chair, so quiet things were you could hear her strokes.

"A song, though, for real," the monk asked.

She put the brush in a jar of linseed oil, got up, and sat down at the leaning piano. If I knew anything about music, I might be able to tell you what they played. But I don't know anything about that. There were her blue fingerprints on the keys. Strands of her hair were the same color. Brother Tobias played, and she sang and played.

"Go like you are," Domingo said.

I knew, then, it was dangerous, what they were going to do, driving into a town like that, but they needed things, they needed to see. I don't think the boy should have called attention to things like he did, I think it was terrible, but maybe they were daydreaming too much. Maybe he was trying to look out for them all.

While the monk was feeding his horse, and the girl was looking in the mirror, the boy got the brush and can of blue paint and slipped out to the car ahead of them. On the left-side front door, he wrote: THE MOON. Then he wrote it on the right-side front door, all the while singing to himself in his own language. The rear of the car was towards them, facing the porch, and he had both doors open, so the other two weren't able to see what he'd done. Why'd he do it?

The girl sat in the front seat with him, and the monk sat in the back. Domingo started the engine, saying, "Let's leave the top down," turning back to look at Brother Tobias. Now, I had to follow them in my truck, and I couldn't see and hear everything, but I could sure put two and two together.

Through all the back roads to town they traveled that day. Out in the fields stood the old implements: the rakes, discs, combines, and here and there an abandoned grain elevator. I've read about outer space, what the astronomers think they are going to see when they get to wherever it is they want to go. You can get books in the drugstore with pictures. That day the broken-down implements looked like spacecraft, ships from the beyond, and the silos were observatories without telescopes. The loose chaff blowing across the state highway in the late afternoon can't be far from the particles of energy and light they see. I followed them and the folks looked at the loud, white car with the top down and THE MOON painted on both doors. That day it was like I drank too much coffee early in the morning. It was like some days when you don't know where you are, who you are with, what you are doing. It's like I'm out there in an outer space where there is no darkness, only light all the time. Some days I don't know where I am. Then I see a lean, squint-eyed boy eating an ear of corn on the heelgnawed steps of an old front porch, a tarantula crossing the road, a pickup running over a hawk's wing, then I know and I squeal like a hog. I root into whatever I see at the moment because I know all those things I have ever seen will do me no good, all that sad blood and passion have fallen into a heap of dust, and I can never turn up another thing in it again. Oh, I know a good thing when I see it.

They were heading over the bottoms, near the river, towards the small town of Ozark. It was Saturday, the worst day they could have picked to go on any kind of a drive. Ozark is named for the mountains around it. It's not real near where the girl comes from, but it's near enough for them to have heard. When the frenchmen came and not the Indians, they said "at the bows" in their tongue, and so the people got around to calling the mountains the Ozarks. It is where the Quapaws looked for the wood for their bows. The bow woods and the bow trees, I know where they grow still, my grandmother showed me. The monk's bow came from there.

"I bet you could pull over and I could take a catalogue out of a mailbox and nobody on earth would see me," Madelene said.

The boy looked up into the rearview mirror and could see the monk looking at him.

They pulled into town and parked in front of the shoe store. Some people walking out, trying out their new shoes like they were just learning to step, were the first ones to read what was written on the side of the car, only I don't think they could read it because one man said, "What's he running for?"

A girl with freckles had a new pair of cowboy boots on. She was walking up and down the courthouse steps. She recognized Domingo. The three of them were worried. "Mr. Gyp, you couldn't ride and suck ice at the same time. I want my money back," she said.

The three of them walked into a hardware store and came right back out again. "I stole a package of iceberg lettuce," Madelene said.

"They didn't have a stove we could buy," Domingo said.

"We better get in the car," Brother Tobias said, looking around.

"Why not let the car stay in one place and only use one penny?" Madelene wanted to know, but Domingo opened the door for her, letting the monk climb in the back first. Everytime they went anywhere new they drove. The car didn't have any tags and the pipes were loud, but Domingo had his reasons. They looked like they came out of a circus somewhere, and I guess that's what he wanted them to think.

After all the appointed rounds were made and after the black stove was in the backseat with the monk, he leaned over the seat and whispered to Domingo, "When do we stop at the liquor store? I'll treat."

"We're going there as soon as we stop and get some ice cream," she said.

"Like hell, you got candy bar, we going to get whiskey."

They pulled up in front of the liquor store and the monk gave the boy enough money to buy what they needed, but the man in the store wouldn't sell it to him, he said he was too young. So the monk bought it. Some customers came out before the monk did, shaking their heads at what they'd seen.

This is the way it was: They were a ways out of town driving not over forty miles an hour, the radio turned up, the top down, all of them bundled up, the girl eating a Zero candy bar, the monk composed in the backseat, his cowl up to protect him from the wind, and a fifth resting between his knees, and the boy, driving like he owned the road, had another bottle in his lap.

"They sure do have some nice things in the Spring and Summer catalogue," she said.

The boy looked up in the mirror at the monk, "You want some gum?"

Then no one spoke for a while as they drove towards home, until Brother Tobias touched him on the shoulder, asking if he would take another road so they could drive past the monastery. I believe he was a little drunk.

They pulled up in the driveway of the large stone abbey. The monks going to their evening office did not notice them. Domingo turned off the car. All you could hear were the bells, wind, and Brother Tobias chewing gum.

The monk took the cork out of the bourbon bottle with his teeth, and took a swallow. Domingo lit up one of the small, dark, fancy cigarillos he picked up in town. "Let's go," Brother Tobias said.

*

They passed many people on the roads that day, and many people saw them, so there is no way of telling who it was, but it was someone. Someone gave them away. And that night two men died. But not the monk, not the young man. Two men took clean, silent shots through the heart with the brother's arrows. The riders managed to break in their bedroom, throw a rope over Domingo's neck, and drag him out past the barn, but that is far as they got. They rode away, leaving Domingo and two of their own behind. The arrows seemed to come from nowhere.

"They know where we are, they're going to kill you now—they'll be back," Madelene said, crying in Domingo's arms.

"It's true," Brother Tobias called out from the haybarn, then he leapt into the wagon below. He brushed the dust and straw off himself. It was a close call. He almost saw me.

"Madelene, I heard something in town. I didn't want to tell you. I'm afraid your life isn't worth the crumbs on this tablecloth. Your father knows you are with child. I heard a man say, 'Ain't old Riggs disgusted with himself. He must feel awful humiliated and all. His own flesh and blood knocked-up and shacked-up with a Gypsy and a crazy nigger priest. I heard he disowned her.' So they know, Madelene. They can make it look however your father wishes."

"He wouldn't touch me, he wouldn't have them lay a hand on me," she screamed.

"It is what you are carrying. He would lift his hand to that," the monk said.

"You say hand? They lift more than that. What they have those knives and rifles for? They didn't bring the rope so she could hang out the clothes. No, they lift more than hand. Next time it will be different. Brother Tobias won't always be here. And they've seen her. If they didn't know before, they know now. I tell you that. I think they knew about the child, but the men, they are all fathers, they were afraid to touch her. But Riggs will put up an award. Then it will be everyone. The lead will fly, yes? And if they kill me first, what are they going to do to you, Madelene?" He pulled up her torn night-dress, in plain view of the monk, and touched her belly. "They want this, they want to get the heels of their boots in this, this!"

The monk got his horn and walked out into the fields, past the bodies of the two men he'd killed. He played until they went to sleep. He drew out a shearing knife from under his soiled, white robe, walked here and there, cutting certain weeds and plants, the names of which my grandmother once told me, but I have forgot-ten. He gathered the stalks, then he skinned the bark from a certain kind of tree, picking up some of the dead leaves and a few of the first new shoots. He made an apron with the pouch out of his robe, and walked back to the farmhouse with them. Madelene and Domingo were still awake.

He paused in front of their bedroom. "Let me start the bread tonight. I'll bake it in the morning, before you are up. And then we'll leave here. Sleep tonight."

"But it is almost light now, Brother," Madelene said.

"No, there are still a few hours of darkness left."

They left early the next morning, leaving behind the piano, the checkerboard, the clean sheets on the line, and the cast-iron stove. Even if I had not known who they were, if I were nothing but a lone-some traveler, I could have followed them to where they were going by the aroma of the warm bread.

But I knew where they were going. I thought of what it must

be like to live like a bloodhound, to be in the presence of a beautiful lady. I couldn't bear to think of them using their boots on the Gypsy and the girl, the light of the next day rising, a circle of men mounting up, wiping the wet dung and mud and blood on the flanks of their horses. Or maybe they would wipe their feet on the porchsteps.

There were pairs of doves all along the side of the road, but I don't think the monk regretted not having his bow. His horn was strapped on the riderless horse, following the car, moving slowly over the ruts and washouts. The pungent bread, wrapped in one of Madelene's clean nightgowns, was sitting on the armrest next to the monk in the backseat of the car. Now and then he glanced at it. Madelene turned on the radio once, but they couldn't bring in any stations. It was past dawn, and the ones who broadcast all night had gone off the air.

At the foot of Zero Mountain, they stopped the car and got out. Domingo didn't even take the keys out of the ignition. They put Madelene on the horse, sidesaddle, and led her up the steep hill to the mouth of the monk's cave.

By and by, there was a confession and Mass. This time I didn't hear, I didn't try to listen. I couldn't see them. I waited for them to come out. It rained. It really set in. I put the top up and got in their car. I watched and I waited. The cave was a good place to hide. They could stay there forever. The rain let up. They didn't come out that night or the next day either. It was cold and clear for a while, not too cold. The moon was on my left in the black gums, and the sun, over in the east, was rising in the evergreens. The next few days it rained so hard, I couldn't see to tell.

I built a fire and got drunk. I really tied one on. It was another couple of days before I really knew where I was. The empty package of iceberg lettuce was over a twig stuck in the ground, and it was already sprouting, even with the rain and the bad soil. That son-of-a-bitch Squint, who hit me in the head, came back to life in my dreams. I was nailing some shoes on the beautiful white horse, and he and the foreman came to question me. I wouldn't tell them a thing, I told them that whatever came across my eyes I was keeping to myself. The girl's father came up to me with a bullwhip. He cracked the whip around my face. There was a white swan in the pond by Riggs' gazebo. He said, "That bird I gave to my daughter when she was a child." Then he popped the whip and tore off one of the great white wings. I had to tell them don't you see, where I saw the four of them. But it was only the old, bald tire on the car blowing out. I got up, rubbed my eyes. A flock of geese flew over.

The farther back I walked into the cave, the colder it got. And darker. I held up a lamp on the monk. He was asleep, next to the loom. I didn't know what kind of beautiful garment he was weaving. A goat was tied to his stool, and next to him, near the fire, slept a newborn child. This room led to yet another, larger one. My breath rose like milk poured out. The walls began to glow with clear, brilliant ice.

All around me, like figures of cold wax, stood the dead soldiers, as if they were waiting for a warm order of breath. I could tell who they were, even their rank. Some had red whiskers, some had sacks of silver on the ground beside them. I blew into their faces, looked into their eyes when I could see that far through the ice. And there were deer with antlers that glowed like Saint Elmo's fire on masts of ships at sea. I think I made out the lieutenant, holding his side, standing upright, insouciant, posed only for life, not eternity.

I walked on. It was getting almost impossible to see because of my own breathing. Leaning against the veins of silver in the walls was the white horse, the ice on its frozen mane like rhinestones. Its eyes belonged somewhere else, underwater, but not to the living, not even to be seen by the living. God it was cold. There were baskets of nuts and berries. And there was such a gaze on their faces. Madelene and Domingo lay on a beautiful, woven blanket, looking towards one another.

The Watchboy's Tale

It was the hooks in her breast. The wound was deep and dark as a creek in the spring. She was only a girl. As long as she was out, he could do it, he could dig them out. If she came to, he wouldn't have the guts or the stomach. A trickle of watered-down blood was coming down her chest onto her belly and into her navel. The little ridge of fat had the blood forking into different tributaries, like lines in a palm, one of which flowed around behind her, and the other finding its way to the inside of her thigh. The wounded girl.

He had taken the aqua-lung off carefully, cutting it loose with his knife, then peeling the black skin of her diver's suit off quickly, so as not to disturb her from that painless unconsciousness he was so thankful for. The waves broke over the gunwales of his small boat and he tried to keep the oars floating, keep the bore headed into the wind. He untied the halter top of her bathing suit. It was thick nylon, like a parachute, and he had to cut the material away from the hooks. He was breathing like a bilge pump. The red water in the bottom of the boat was ankle deep. The minnows swam around her insteps. The more water they took in, the pinker it became, the shade of a dead fish's gills. He imagined her nipples, and he opened his eyes and saw them. He tried to tend the wound, probing into it. Her eyes broke the silence, and then her lips, like a woman pretending to be asleep in a strange room with a new man. He grazed her nipple with the back of his hand. Thunder rumbled. He reached under the boat, feeling for the keel, pulling off a handful of the dark mess that grew there, underwater. He put it on the wound.

He felt himself getting sick. He breathed deep to steady his hand, his eyes. He had to stop every now and then to oar the boat, to keep it on some kind of course. The barbs of the treble hook, two of them, were embedded under her breast. The other barb was broken off in her. She wasn't coming to. It was now or never. He thought of music, drinking wine with a friend on a hot day under a ceiling fan, a room full of plants. He thought of his own dream of snagging, where he caught himself in the throat. The hook lodged in his palate. It was sturdy, bearing the whole weight of his body, although smaller than a fish heart. It was like she and he were the only ones on the schoolbus. There was no driver. There was no other to handle the warning sign. He looked back and saw her, half naked, drinking a Dr Pepper. Her books and an empty paper sack were on the floor beside her seat. The bus made a full stop by itself at the crossroads. Her taut thighs and calves were cool and dark. He couldn't hold on to the pliers.

Both hooks were driven in deep. He bore down on the hog-nosed grips, snipping both barbs in two. She didn't flinch, only her belly caved in and out, and a sweat broke on her brow. The sun came out and the wind died down. The shanks came out easily. He tore the cleanest piece of his T-shirt, soaked it with vodka, and applied it to the wound. He felt her forehead. The cuts and bruises on the rest of her would heal. Her face wasn't nearly as bad as he expected it to be. In the breast, under it, was the deepest wound.

He kept the boat on a course in the fog until he could see. Then he knew he was nowhere. He smelled the blood under his finger-nails, her blood. She was wrapped in everything he could spare to give her. He had his underwear on, that was all. The harder he pulled the oars the more of the cold he could keep off himself.

The next morning his stroke was still the same, always the back of his head pointed in the direction he was going. The molecules of blood sailing through his eyes were forming their own kind of constellations.

Her hair was drying out, becoming not the dark and wet matted shock he'd known, but light and frizzy, the color of parched driftwood. She looked uncomfortably controlled, her body like a figurehead that had fallen from the prow of a ship, always in the same still position. He was beginning to know where they were. He looked over his shoulder more. But a yell would only bring an echo from the high cliffs. There was a secure mooring somewhere near, he knew that. There was a drop of vodka left and half a lemon. He did not drink it. He poured the alcohol on the cut and sucked the lemon. He tried to make her as comfortable as he knew how.

The water in the bottom of the boat was filling up faster than he could keep it bailed-out and row, too. It was much too cold for her. If she woke up, what would he do, he thought. What would he do if she opened her eyes and saw the pink water and the dead minnows? And what would she do if she looked at her body, looked in the water at her face? How would a young girl like her take it. She'll mend back like a beautiful brush after a hard winter, he thought. She moaned. He brought her close to him, as if he were teaching her how to row, and he kept his back into it, heading the boat towards where he thought a mooring was. The skies looked as if it might rain again. The clouds were dark as woods.

They were coming around a little strand. He could see the boathouse he'd remembered, but none of the docks around it. They belonged on the other side of the island, he thought, where the homes of those who only come in summer are. Another storm was making. Her eyes were still closed. Her breath was sweet and bitter. She put her arms around him, burying her head into his chest. Now he wasn't so cold.

He made it around the point, rowing from instinct and the memory of some bearing. The long rope came into his view, without him ever turning his head. He rowed towards the boathouse. He never thought the rope was being dragged through the water, attached to something floating. Their craft hit the other object with a thud, and her head was buried in his chest. It was a houseboat which had broken free in the storm the night before.*

*One version of the manuscript ends the story at this point. An alternate, archival version includes two additional paragraphs, appended on page 718. — Ed.

The drizzle had turned into rain.

The drizzle turned into rain. He tied his own lines to the cleats of the houseboat. His boat might have swamped in another hour. He took her in his arms, balanced the both of them on one steady leg, and shifted their weight to the other part of the other leg up on the wood of the other vessel. It was a floating rectangle, very simple in design. Some of the barrels used for floating under the structure, shifted around as he walked around the corners. He looked down through a crack in the planks and saw a snake glide off a 55-gallon drum into the water. The door had a good lock. He didn't want to break any windows. He looked through one of them and saw in the middle of the room a trapdoor they used to fish through. There was a latch, but no lock on it. It was shaped like a beehive with the top off. He put her down in a canvas lounging chair bolted to the deck. He could hear the rotted cloth tear. He wanted to find a towel or something to put over her. He took off his tennis shoes and pants, and dove into the water. In one breath, he swam under the long dock-like boat, coming up for air in the space of the trapdoor. He didn't know what to expect to find there, so he held his hands up in the compartment first. He made a fist, and jarred the door loose. In no time at all he was in the room smelling the stale not-air, shivering in his wet underwear. The cold and fatigue had given him an erection.

Cold Trains

His hair was white but his beard was black. He was wearing a woman's coat—ermine, probably stolen. I met him on a freight train in Bergman, Arkansas. It was winter. There was a dead Mexican under the hay in the boxcar. He didn't seem to mind the dead man; perhaps he was his friend. I didn't ask. God, it was cold. His gloves were a pair of socks. They belonged to some athletic department. They said so. His eyes were like clods of dried mud. What a liar he was. He and his years aboard ship, him and his women, him and his fights. He told me a different story every night.

Neither of us had eaten for a week. I mean a week. He said, "Whatever your name is, listen: I'm not going to freeze to death, you hear? I only break the law when I have to. I'm not going to starve." His name was Brendan. I never told him mine. I was afraid to.

In the middle of the night, just enough moonlight coming in the old Rock Island boxcar, he would roll up his sleeves and draw on himself. "It won't last long," he told me. He called it the Skin of Dreams. What a leaker. He said he could never be evil, could never be a fool, because he had the gift of good humor. He never smiled.

We threw the Mexican off as we crossed a bridge. I wanted to know what river it was we were crossing, but he wouldn't tell me. I wasn't from around there. He smelled like a depot. He talked to me in made-up accents. He asked me questions but he wouldn't answer mine. Like a child, he was able to turn himself into whatever he wanted. During those days I came to adore this—but to adore childhood is to commit heresy. That night, not knowing what river it was that we'd crossed, not knowing what state we were in, he reached down in my pants. He had his hand over my throat. I don't think he ever intended doing anything else. I really don't think he knew if I was a young man, a young woman. He put his hand over his lips. The bits of tobacco hung there like fleas on a dog's ass. It was like dice that set their eyes in the air. "Want a smoke?" he asked me. "No," I told him.

He brought something out of his coat. It flashed. I moved back, afraid. It was a Life Saver. He'd taken the piece of candy wrapped in foil off the Mexican. I put it under my tongue and shut my eyes. He struck a match and held it over my hair. There were ice crystals. A draft put it out. "I found them in the cuff of some old trousers," he told me, pointing to something he'd found under the hay. He wrapped them around my neck like a scarf. My feet were cold. I seemed to be losing my equilibrium. I took off my boots and shoved my feet into his pockets. There was something cold and hard under his coat. A saxophone. It was like ice to touch it. He brought it out and breathed on it. In this train we were dying, I thought—though it was far from so. I was feeling sorry for myself. I made him play it, expecting a kind of jazz. The music he played wasn't like that, not at all. It was Bach—at least that is what he said. I wouldn't know. Saint Matthew Passion, he said. He played the parts for voice and not for voice. He explained. Maybe he wasn't as stupid as I thought he was?

We were found out and put off in Memphis. There were more trains than I had seen. I'd never been there before. Neither of us had money. They didn't like the idea of a girl with an old bum—he wasn't that old. We took off before they had a chance to ask many questions. In an alley we found an empty refrigerator carton. We holed up there, next to a hotel. There was a can of oysters and red snappers and fish heads which made it smell like the sea. We ate the oysters. One night something was crawling. I thought it was a rat. It was a lobster they hadn't boiled to death.

Each day we thought was our last. We found out the sanitary engineers were on strike. The weather got worse. You could only smell yourself. I told him I was going out to look for something to turn. He hit me in the mouth. It didn't knock me out but sent me into a long, painful kind of sleep. He was gone. He didn't come back for hours. I was ready to leave. Then I saw him running down the alley, a toaster and three loaves of stale bread under his arms. He'd stolen some electrical wire, too. He said he'd be back in a minute, climbing a fire escape. He found a hidden outlet and ran the extension down into our carton. We toasted the bread. We went through the loaves. "This is the best part," he told me, stuffing tinfoil down the toaster. He made a heater.

It was the worst snow in this country in a hundred years, as far back as anyone could remember. In the paper it said some people were wondering if the government hadn't accidentally caused it. Some special, secret satellite had been launched. People were committing suicide. They say the snow is conducive to it. At night Brendan played the music I'd never heard of. Since then, I've heard it in ships, in great halls, in my home.

Interview with Frank Stanford by Irving Broughton

Irving Broughton, publisher and friend, is widely credited with having discovered Frank Stanford. In recent years, he has written a play, Still Being Frank, *a novel,* The Levees That Break in the Heart, *and is completing work on a screenplay, all based in some way on Frank Stanford and his life. Originally published in* The Writer's Mind, *the published version of the interview is distilled from a much longer interview/ correspondence, currently housed at Yale University's Beinecke Rare Book and Manuscript Library.*

It is near light. There is fog on the river. Frank Stanford and I have stayed up all night, drinking wine, looking at films of Jean Cocteau, discussing poets and cinema, and reading Burns and Coleridge. The portable recorder is set up on the porch. In the background, we hear the sounds of crows, coyotes, hawks, and fish.

IRVING BROUGHTON: What does the river mean to you?

FRANK STANFORD: The river is like a traveling friend who keeps going. You remember them and you forget them, but they just keep passing on. They are always strangers and always friends, and that's the way the river is.

IB: What's your favorite river?

FS: I don't think I have a favorite river. I think I might have favorite small creeks or small bodies of water.

IB: Can you stand to be away from water?

FS: Oh, I can stand to be away from the river, but it's pretty hard to be apart from water. I like to be around water.

IB: Why?

FS: Because Lao-tzu said water was the most powerful thing and it was the most passive thing—you could pass your hand through it with force, yet it can destroy cities and towns with its force.

IB: Have you ever felt the power of it?

FS: Yes. The power of it is like there is an eyeball you can't see and the waves come and loosen it out of a head—it's as if a horse kicked another horse's eye and it's just waiting to pop out.

IB: What is strange to you?

FS: A lot of people come up with some neat aphorisms and platitudes about reality and commonplace and inimitable and ineffable ways of living. But I think New York is strange; I think Cape Cod is strange, that Maine is strange. I don't think you should try to say the more experience someone has had, the more varied experience, that therefore he is going to open himself up to strangers.

IB: When did you realize this strangeness?

FS: It took me a long time to realize anything about my past or experiences or that the way I wrote was strange. I thought it was just my way of doing something, and I didn't think it was stranger than what I was reading.

IB: When did you begin to realize this?

FS: Other poets, teachers, and editors pointed it out—people who read my things.

IB: Such as?

FS: Well, the person who thinks I'm the strangest would be Alan Dugan. A letter I received once from John Berryman—he thought my poetry was pretty strange. When editors reject or accept your poems they seem to put on mine—they say they like the music, the architecture, and the originality. But then, a lot of them put that it's no good at all. They don't like it at all.

IB: Do you think they understand it?

FS: No, and I don't think a lot of them want to understand it.

IB: What would it take besides the desire to understand it?

FS: If you had a stack of poems that you had been reading all night, I think you might as well reject mine, too. If a person is quiet enough inside he might be able to catch on to what I'm trying to do in my poetry.

IB: What are you trying to do?

FS: Although I don't want people at the end of it to say that this was obviously a poem, I want it to have the traits of a poem— as a symphony has the traits of a symphony. What I want to do is use movement and rhythm on different levels. I want it to be like the reader was going into reading the poem as they were going for a boat ride in some swift water, and each layer of the poem was a different thing you had to do. One was the river and one was his use of the paddle. Many of the poems around are too simple. They take us for granted. Our sensibilities have been taken for granted too long. I don't think that much of it is really poetry. It's just a coalition of things that might take ten minutes or ten months to write. However, I do believe that maybe it's just that I don't keep up with what's going on, but there are a hell of a lot of good young writers. I don't want to say any names because I would be afraid of leaving some out or maybe not even remembering some of their names.

IB: Do you think you can really capture the strangeness of your work? Or the environment?

FS: I don't go out and say, "I'm going to hunt down what is strange, then I'm going to put it down on paper." You can't do that, and to do it would be like killing and mounting it, and there is enough of that being done. I want to just let it exist in the flux of things. It is the poetry of being awake and asleep at the same time. It's not just night or day, it's both.

IB: I think James Dickey points out that a line of poetry can be too good. Would you say that an experience could perhaps be too good—too strange?

FS: Yeah. I hardly ever use a direct experience. For one, I don't like to do that. For another thing, a lot of people probably think that what a person writes he has done. Such things are too strange, and it would require too much time, and I'm just not interested in doing that. There are things that have taken place that I couldn't touch with a ten-foot pole as far as using them.

IB: George Garrett said of Southern writers that they are a "race of storytellers."

FS: I know there are storytellers, liars, whatever you want to say. It's easy to be in a situation in a room—you're not getting out of trouble or you're not doing it to just promote yourself and company—but it's just as easy to offhand come up with a story. To this little tension of trying to keep the attention of someone else, I would say that he's probably right with those people who identify themselves as a group or race of people. It's still hard for me to think of myself as a writer or a kind of writer—poet is about all. I don't mean to sound self-effacing or naive, and a lot of people agree with this. But I do think of myself as a poet.

IB: How many drafts do you do of a poem?

FS: It depends. I might do a hundred. I might do one. On shorter poems—single poems that aren't in a series—I probably revise over and over and over; whereas the narrative poems under three hundred or four hundred lines, possibly forty or fifty revisions. But poems that are a cycle—I tend to revise the cycle rather than the poem. In the case of a very long poem, say over ten thousand lines, there will be passages which will be very much revised.

IB: Do you have a short attention span?

FS: No, to the contrary, one of my problems is I can sustain my attention too long, thereby being spellbound or overwhelmed by a particular genre or a particular piece, which sometimes makes for neglect as far as other genres are concerned. I've done a little painting recently—just enough to speak of. No music, no filming.

IB: You do sumiye painting. What is sumiye painting?

FS: It's just a form of Japanese painting, and it's done very quickly. The staff is like a pen or a sword. You just sit there, and you may stare at a blank piece of paper for hours and hours, and suddenly you unsheathe it and execute your strokes. There's no revision. I don't say this is analogous to my poetry, but I enjoy that painting.

IB: Who is your favorite violent person?

FS: Carl Orff, the composer, and Muhammad Ali are probably two of my favorites. I would rather have been Muhammad Ali than T.S. Eliot. Or I'd rather have been Brando than Eliot.

IB: Dickey feels Faulkner strains too hard to be literary.

FS: Dickey might have the same problem as his crew of people and the people he was influenced by. They tried just as hard to strive to be nonliterary. It's the same way Lawrence hated himself as an intellectual and he was always trying to deny this. His language is adverbs and adjectives and convoluted sentences that the reader would like. Both sensibilities can be accommodated.

IB: What about Dickey's characters in *Deliverance*? What did you think about the mountain people?

FS: I've seen this phenomenon take place. Take an old, fast, fairly unknown river—except that people lived around it—and turn it into a big reservoir. They have them all over the South now, mainly because Arkansas is one of the first places they started doing it—and Tennessee. I assume you're dwelling on Dickey because he is a very popular poet and writer and a personality in the screenplay, and I would hope it has nothing to do with me. There is a similarity in some of our work—people have pointed that out. I think some of his poems are among the best written, especially the one called "[The] Shark's Parlor." After all, we poets have to realize that, except for Agee and Faulkner—if you can call Faulkner poetry—that only a few of us have broken into the motion-picture industry. We have to do that. We just can't let these second-rate novelists and playwrights keep jumping the gun on us. Just think of this: if Galway Kinnell or William Stafford or Daniel Hoffman or some of these men could have a chance, maybe they wouldn't even want to do it.

IB: Getting back to the *Deliverance* characters. What about the mountain people?

FS: I've come across people that are ornery, and these people do exist. I don't think he intended to stereotype all mountain people like that. It reminds me of the *Easy Rider* film where the hippies got shot. All these things take place. It's not strange, I don't think what happened in the story was strange to Dickey. I think it's easy to indict a screenwriter or a poet for stereotyping, and it's easy to indict some kinds of novelists. But I give the author the benefit of the doubt that he's just not interested in the empty form where he can pull off something that he is interested in—the other man's character.

IB: What types of the novel would it be a problem with?

FS: We've had a lot of war novels—things have a lot to do with the war. A lot of people label all Southern things as "Southern grotesque." They throw it in like that. I've had some Yankee say, "This is Southern grotesque." And I've seen men actively come out against anything that can be construed as Southern.

IB: What makes a genuine poet?

FS: You know that there are many poets around now. A lot of them seem to be fighting over this or that. I don't really know. I don't even know what makes me a poet. I certainly don't want anybody telling me what does or what doesn't.

ɪʙ: Do you ever concern yourself with the morality of dreams?

ғs: Yes, I do. In reality things happen that we try to understand with our consciousness as judicial, and it's the same way in sleep. You wake up and you dreamed something that might not be any stranger than what happened to you the day before. You want to know why it happened, more than any psychological reason for why did I dream this. I want to know why did the action take place? What happened to this man? What happened to this woman? Is it good or is it bad?

ɪʙ: Does this trouble you sometimes when you don't know?

ғs: Yes, it does.

ɪʙ: Can you trace your dreams to experience—maybe something the day before?

ғs: You can come across things that may be insignificant during the day, or maybe not insignificant, and they turn up in that state. But imagine this: that during the day a man is a cartographer for that geography, that terrain, those rivers and waters, and all this land—topography of what he goes through at night. I don't advocate that we should abolish order and accept the chaos of just sleep unless we just want to sleep all the time. I look to William Blake for instruction in those matters. When I come across a problem I can't solve, generally, I'll read a poem by Blake—a very simple poem from something like *Poetical Sketches,* or maybe one of the longer things. I come to some realization. Then I might read something by Burns to lift me up.

ɪʙ: Who are your two or three favorite poets?

ғs: I would think that most of the Old English and Middle English work. I'm talking about English writers. I like all of the Romantics. I like Dickinson, Whitman, Rossetti. I believe I learned more about form from William Blake than anyone else.

IB: Did you learn this "formally" by scrutinizing the poem, or did you learn just by reading?

FS: Yeah, I examine it. When you read something when you're twelve and when you're eighteen, there is going to be something different that you come up with. For a long time for all my poems I took formally I used Blake's as a model.

IB: How young was that?

FS: I would say that I wrote more when I was between the ages of twelve and eighteen.

IB: I've seen those poems and they are extremely competent.

FS: Well, they're competent.

IB: That might be a mild understatement. Some of them are good.

FS: Let's put it this way, when I was in prep school, when I was in the monastery, the epic form was what I dwelt on. I wrote so many lyrics, and there were even dramatic poems—monologues that I said. I composed some really long—longer than anything [of mine] you've ever seen.

IB: How long?

FS: I would say several thousand pages, so I don't know how many lines that you can write or type on a page. There was no effort to put them together in a manuscript. But then some of us would go together and write on things—mostly me.

IB: Talk about the ideal writing environment.

FS: During my college days, it seems the best circumstances were for me to spend long periods of time in a given place that I felt some affinity for, that I'd gotten used to, like this cabin. This cabin had a lot of magical feeling to it. I could get up any time of the day, any time of the night, and I could write in it. I felt so at home in this place. It was so strange, when I think of it now, getting up in the winter, building a fire at three o'clock in the morning, making coffee, going down there and writing or reading. It's a strange feeling. I really became one with that place. It wasn't a possession. It was just a place you could exist in. It was my place, where I spent all of my time.

IB: Did you feel any kind of rootlessness when you got away from that place?

FS: Yes!

IB: In *Hiroshima mon amour* there's that line about madness seizing you and the effect when it leaves.

FS: When you can comprehend and fathom your own madness, it's a delightful situation. When you have to inflict all these wounds on others as a consequence of that madness, there's nothing pretty about that at all. When you're living at the true pitch which is near madness, you feel all right. You can take the extremes of emotions that go up and down on you. It doesn't affect you that much. But when you're not, I don't know. Like you say, when the madness leaves you, then it's hard to live with [the consequences].

IB: Can you define madness?

FS: Madness and poetry in ancient times were related, but I don't think I could define it. I know of a lot of good poets who aren't mad.

IB: Byron said, "I have just thrown a poem into the fire which has relighted to my great comfort."

FS: The combustion and flame for the poet, I suppose, are two different things. Keats said unless poetry's a burning fire, it's nothing as far as he was concerned. I understand what Byron was saying there, and it works sometimes to do things that way—throw 'em in the fire, temper them.

IB: You did that. Did it make you feel better?

FS: In the long run, I guess it did.

IB: How many pages did you throw in?

FS: I had a file cabinet and a desk full of things, and I burned up virtually everything I had written—what had survived up to then. I'd done it before but not at that scale. About nine-tenths of everything.

IB: What's it like—a housecleaning?

FS: Then it was like a housecleaning when you were just about to be evicted. Over the years the house'll get pretty filthy, I imagine.

IB: Is there a Southern sense of humor?

FS: I suppose people from other parts of the country would like to think there is, but hell, I think of a Northeast sense of humor or a Midwestern sense of humor. I guess you just have to say there is.

IB: You're a great observer—delaying trips at bus stations.

FS: Not so much just to observe. I don't think I'd delay a journey just to observe. I did it so I could meet a person; I wanted to talk. Not just to meet but I wanted there to be words, too.

IB: What did you talk about?

FS: I met this Indian once. He didn't look like an Indian—he had about one-eighth Indian in him, but he'd married an Indian woman when he was fourteen. He talked about his early days in Fort Smith, Arkansas, going off into Indian Territory and fighting his way out of various places. He played the fiddle and had an invention he'd made. It was a ball on a cord up his sleeve. He could throw his hand out of his pocket and this ball would come flying out, hit a man on the head, and knock him out. I never understood the way he rigged it up, but I'm sure it worked. He was a real barroom brawler.

I was reading Eldridge Cleaver, sitting in a bus station—reading that for thirty minutes, and quit after thirty minutes and was reading *The Golden Apples* by Eudora Welty—no, that was just a joke. What was I reading? Chekhov, I think.

IB: Could you be accused of observing to put ideas into your work?

FS: I could. I never put any of those in my work. I'm just interested in the man or the woman. I hardly ever grind it up into literary hamburger meat—I just enjoy it. What's so strange about that? Just talkin' to them. Why shouldn't somebody else do it—just enjoy talkin' to 'em? Why shouldn't somebody take the time to talk to somebody?

IB: And miss their trip?

FS: It depends. If they're going someplace and somebody in the family's dying, they better go. But I wasn't in any hurry. Not really. I'm glad I stayed.

IB: Have you done that much?

FS: Often, often I've done it. I stayed in a lot of people's houses and missed where I should be.

IB: You like people then?

FS: Yeah, I do.

IB: What kind of people do you like?

FS: Any kind, I like any kind. Just like any kind of music. I listen to a certain kind of music most of the time and probably am more solitary most of the time. But I still like them all.

IB: You once described all the strange people at the bus station and how you felt sorry for those people?

FS: Yeah, I did. I sure did.

IB: If I give you another drink of beer, will you describe them?

FS: Who am I thinkin' of who was struck with the sad faces— lookin' around? Maybe Dostoyevsky.

IB: How do the abject people affect you?

FS: I'm sad when I see a really indigent people, people that are down in their heart and soul. I wanted to help them, but I don't know how I can. Then you're uplifted—you meet a lot of people like Zorba the Greek. Just what Kazantzakis was talking about, thinking about.

IB: Have you ever felt that by talking to people you were actually helping them?

FS: If they thought they could truthfully confide in me, if they believed in me, if I took a load off by maybe saying a few kind words, maybe so. But I just don't know. I think under many circumstances—yes. But I just helped because I talked to them. Maybe anybody could have talked to them.

IB: What did you say?

FS: Well, this one ole boy, I was sitting in there readin', and I had my knapsack and things. The only reason I was in there was because it was cold, and I don't think anybody was out on the road.

IB: In the bus station?

FS: Yeah. And he said, "Friend, if yeh put yeh saddlebags in the next seat, I'll sit down and tell you the story of my life." That sounded like a pretty damn good proposition, since he was about seventy-something years old. So he sat down and started talkin'. We were at this bus station and he started going into his life. I liked the way he talked about ridin' a pony over into Oklahoma—killin' a few people, gettin' out of trouble. I think he was about thirteen when he did it. He was real happy that I'd listen to him, and he wasn't bullshitting. You can tell with those old sons-of-bitches, when they say that stuff and they're not tellin' the truth. But this man was tellin' the truth.

FROM *The Battlefield Where the Moon Says I Love You*

all of this
is magic against death
all of this ends
with to be continued
I wave so long with a handkerchief
to the horses on the range of my dreams
every scene is sculptured from wood with splintered fingers

INDEX OF TITLES

LIST OF ILLUSTRATIONS

Images courtesy Beinecke Rare Book and Manuscript Library, unless otherwise noted.

ABOUT FRANK STANFORD

Frank Stanford was born Francis Gildart Smith in 1948, in Richton, Mississippi. He was adopted by a single mother, Dorothy Gilbert Alter, the first female manager of Firestone. In 1952 Dorothy married Albert Franklin Stanford, a levee engineer from Memphis who subsequently adopted Frankie, as he was known, and his younger sister, Ruthie. The family moved to Mallard Point on Lake Norfork near Mountain Home, Arkansas, in 1961, following A.F. Stanford's retirement. After his father's death, Frank was enrolled in Subiaco Academy, a Benedictine monastery and prep school near Paris, Arkansas. In 1966, he graduated from Subiaco and enrolled in the University of Arkansas, where he took graduate-level creative writing workshops. He left the university in 1970, before completing his degree, and started working sporadically as an unlicensed land surveyor in Fayetteville, Arkansas, and married Linda Mencin in 1971. They would divorce after three months.

In 1971, Mill Mountain Press published Stanford's first collection of poetry, *The Singing Knives*. Stanford and Irving Broughton, the editor and publisher of Mill Mountain, spent much of 1972 traveling through the South and New England, interviewing and filming poets and writers, an experience that deepened Stanford's interest in filmmaking. In 1974, Stanford married the painter Ginny Crouch, whose drawings featured in his early books. Returning to Fayetteville, in 1975 he befriended the poet C.D. Wright, with whom he founded Lost Roads Publishers. The midseventies saw the publication of a number of his manuscripts, both poetry and prose, including the 1977 release of his magnum opus: a mostly unpunctuated, 15,000-line poem, *The Battlefield Where the Moon Says I Love You*.

In June 1978, Stanford took his own life in Fayetteville. He is buried at Subiaco.

ABOUT THE EDITOR

Editor, translator and publisher, Michael Wiegers's previous titles include *This Art, The Poet's Child,* and *Reversible Monuments: Contemporary Mexican Poetry* (co-edited with Monica de la Torre). He is poetry editor of *Narrative Magazine,* and serves as Executive Editor at Copper Canyon Press.

Lannan Literary Selections

For two decades Lannan Foundation has supported the publication and distribution of exceptional literary works. Copper Canyon Press gratefully acknowledges their support.

LANNAN LITERARY SELECTIONS 2015

Michael Dickman, *Green Migraine*

Deborah Landau, *The Uses of the Body*

Camille Rankine, *Incorrect Merciful Impulses*

Richard Siken, *War of the Foxes*

Frank Stanford, *What About This: Collected Poems of Frank Stanford*

RECENT LANNAN LITERARY SELECTIONS FROM COPPER CANYON PRESS

James Arthur, *Charms Against Lightning*

Mark Bibbins, *They Don't Kill You Because They're Hungry, They Kill You Because They're Full*

Malachi Black, *Storm Toward Morning*

Marianne Boruch, *Cadaver, Speak*

Jericho Brown, *The New Testament*

Olena Kalytiak Davis, *The Poem She Didn't Write and Other Poems*

Natalie Diaz, *When My Brother Was an Aztec*

Matthew Dickman and Michael Dickman, *50 American Plays*

Kerry James Evans, *Bangalore*

Tung-Hui Hu, *Greenhouses, Lighthouses*

Deborah Landau, *The Last Usable Hour*

Sarah Lindsay, *Debt to the Bone-Eating Snotflower*

Michael McGriff, *Home Burial*

Valzhyna Mort, *Collected Body*

Lisa Olstein, *Little Stranger*

Roger Reeves, *King Me*

Ed Skoog, *Rough Day*

For a complete list of Lannan Literary Selections from Copper Canyon Press, please visit Partners on our website:
www.coppercanyonpress.org

Poetry is vital to language and living. Since 1972, Copper Canyon Press has published extraordinary poetry from around the world to engage the imaginations and intellects of readers, writers, booksellers, librarians, teachers, students, and donors.

WE ARE GRATEFUL FOR THE MAJOR SUPPORT PROVIDED BY:

 THE PAUL G. ALLEN FAMILY FOUNDATION

  amazon.com

 the POINT — WHERE LESS IS MORE

 4 CULTURE

 golden lasso

Lannan

 THE MAURER FAMILY FOUNDATION

 ART WORKS.

National Endowment for the Arts — arts.gov

A& OFFICE OF ARTS & CULTURE SEATTLE

 WASHINGTON STATE ARTS COMMISSION

Anonymous

John Branch

Diana Broze

Beroz Ferrell & The Point, llc

Janet and Les Cox

Mimi Gardner Gates

Linda Gerrard and Walter Parsons

Gull Industries, Inc.
on behalf of William and
Ruth True

Mark Hamilton and Suzie Rapp

Carolyn and Robert Hedin

Steven Myron Holl

Lakeside Industries, Inc.
on behalf of Jeanne Marie Lee

Maureen Lee and Mark Busto

Brice Marden

Ellie Mathews and Carl Youngmann
as The North Press

H. Stewart Parker

Penny and Jerry Peabody

John Phillips and Anne O'Donnell

Joseph C. Roberts

Cynthia Lovelace Sears and
Frank Buxton

The Seattle Foundation

Kim and Jeff Seely

Dan Waggoner

C.D. Wright and Forrest Gander

Charles and Barbara Wright

The dedicated interns and faithful volunteers of Copper Canyon Press

TO LEARN MORE ABOUT UNDERWRITING COPPER CANYON PRESS TITLES,
PLEASE CALL 360-385-4925 EXT. 103

Hidden Water, a companion edition of outtakes, variant editions of poems, and ephemera, edited by Michael Wiegers & Chet Weise, has been simultaneously published by Third Man Books. Contact thirdmanbooks.com for further details.

THIRD MAN BOOKS

The Chinese character for poetry is made up of two parts: "word" and "temple." It also serves as pressmark for Copper Canyon Press.

The poems are set in Minion.
Book design and composition by Phil Kovacevich.